Answer to Jung

Making Sense of the Black Books

Lynn Brunet

Brunet, Lynn, 1953-
Answer to Jung: Making Sense of the Black Books/Lynn Brunet
Includes bibliographic references and index.
1. C. G. Jung, 1875-1961 2. The Black Books 3. criticism and interpretation 4. trauma and dissociation 5. Freemasonry in literature

Permission to use material from *The Black Books, 1913-1932: Notebooks of Transformation, Volumes 1 through 7* by C. G. Jung, edited by Sonu Shamdasani, translated by Martin Liebscher et al, granted by W. W. Norton & Company, September 2024.

Cover image & cover design by Lynn Brunet

First published 2024
by Lynn P. Brunet
https://independent.academia.edu/LynnBrunet1

ISBN: 978-1-7637282-0-2 (pbk)
ISBN: 978-1-7637282-1-9 (ebk)

A catalogue record for this book is available from the National Library of Australia

NATIONAL LIBRARY OF AUSTRALIA

To my daughter, Alice, who has patiently borne with my crusade against one of the worst forms of child abuse and my son, Daniel, whose best defence against these practices has been to create the most loving of environments for his own children.

Contents

Acknowledgements

The American Psychological Association defines *ritual abuse* as:

> organized, repetitive, and highly sadistic abuse of a physical, sexual, or emotional nature, perpetrated principally on children. The abuse is reported as using rituals and symbols from religion (e.g., upside-down crosses), the occult, or secret societies. It may also include the creation of pornography or the selling of sexual access to children. Victims may be forced to engage in heinous acts, such as the killing of animals, as a means of coercing their participation and silence (APA, "Ritual Abuse", 2018).
>
> *APA Dictionary of Psychology*, 2018

This study could not have even been conceptualised without the work already done in this field over the last four decades by survivors, therapists and researchers. Together, they are creating a shift in the collective conscious awareness of these cruel practices. I particularly want to acknowledge those who have personally offered me their support over recent years: James Randall Noblitt, Professor of Clinical Psychology at Alliant International University in Los Angeles, and Pamela Perskin Noblitt, who have drawn together some of the most significant international research into ritual abuse and mind control in several key texts; Ellen Lacter, a clinical psychologist and advocate for survivors of ritual abuse, who tirelessly shares her deep understanding of the mechanisms and effects of these practices with others in her profession; Alison Miller, a clinical psychologist who has treated and learned from survivors of ritual abuse and mind control to develop a protocol for their effective treatment; and Dr Valerie Sinason, a poet, writer, child psychotherapist and adult psychoanalyst, who has brought together others in the field to address society's collective inability to deal with the concept of extreme trauma and abuse. These individuals have been working in this field for decades. Their persistence in pursuing this work, despite the limited acknowledgement of the existence of these practices amongst mainstream elements of their profession, testifies to their ability to truly and deeply listen to their clients and remain unphased in the face of what can only be described as a confrontation with evil.

Special appreciation for their support goes to two fellow survivors of ritual abuse: Wendy Hoffman, therapist, consultant to other therapists and writer who has shared her personal testimony through a series of publications and online presentations over the years; and Neil Brick, therapist and well-known advocate within the survivor community through the S.M.A.R.T newsletter (Stop Mind Control and Ritual Abuse Today) and the Survivorship of Extreme or Ritualistic Abuse organisation, who has given me the opportunity to present my research at his online conferences.

Much appreciation goes to Robert Shatzkin, the Permissions Manager for the publisher W. W. Norton, for copyright permission to use Jung's words, and to Dragana Favre, Marybeth Carter and the committee of the International Association of Jungian Studies for inviting me to present a paper on the *Black Books* at their 2024 conference and a paper on *The Red Book* in 2022. A thankyou is also due to the support staff at Draft2Digital for enabling the publication of this work and providing help where needed for a newcomer to the self-publishing process.

Lastly, I must thank my constant friend and supporter of my work, Julia Young, and my friend, Leonie McNabb, who has courageously shared some of her own story with me. Most importantly, I will forever be indebted to the love and support of my children, Alice and Daniel Brunet.

Abbreviations

AASR	Ancient and Accepted Scottish Rite
BB (1–7)	C. G. Jung, *The Black Books, 1913–1932: Notebooks of Transformation, 1-7*

All biblical quotations refer to the Authorised King James Version of The Holy Bible, containing the Old and New Testaments.

1
Introduction

One of the key questions for researchers and for those with a passion for the work of C. G. Jung is whether his now published *Black Books 1913–1932* might provide us with more insight into the complex and confusing narratives that are contained in *The Red Book*, also known as *Liber Novus*. But if anything, they simply add to the mystery with more confoundingly obscure material and a series of frustrating discussions with his 'soul' that continue for many years. This opaque material involves references to magic and to strange, inexplicable symbols that his soul imparts to him. This study will demonstrate that the journals reveal a great deal more about Jung's disturbing inner journey, but the argument it makes is not a comforting one. It demonstrates that the additional material in the *Black Books* confirms the findings of this author's previous study, *Answer to Jung: Making Sense of The Red Book,* which argues that Jung's active imaginations represent traces of an excruciating initiatory process that he appears to have undergone, seemingly in his childhood and youth (Brunet, 2019). Jung had connections with Freemasonry through his family line and the first study demonstrates that his fantasies in *The Red Book* are not entirely original but closely resemble some of the higher degree rituals of Continental Freemasonry. Combining these ritual elements with an interpretation based on the psychology and physiology of trauma, the overall conclusion of the initial study is that Jung's fantasies appear to be detailed memories of a cruel initiatory process.

Expanding on the trauma reading of the previous study, *Answer to Jung: Making Sense of the Black Books* focusses primarily on the material that was not included in *The Red Book*. Here Jung records extensive discussions with his soul where she offers him advice but often frustrates him with her enigmatic answers. On October 9, 1916 he presses her to at least provide a glimpse into what these fantasies are about and she answers with a series of questions: "Temples in deserts? Secret societies? Ceremonies? Rituals? Colorful robes? Golden images of Gods of terrible aspect?" (*BB 6*, p. 268). His soul follows these questions with the phrase, "none of them", as if taunting him with an answer to his spiritual puzzle and then retracting it. However, it is these themes, the ritual practices of secret societies, which the previous study has identified as the source of his active imaginations. On some level, then, it seems that Jung was aware of this within the first three years of his internal journey. But whether he was ever able to fully connect with his own deep inner knowledge about the source of his fantasies is one of the questions that will emerge in this study.

Answer to Jung: Making Sense of the Black Books demonstrates that not only were Jung's fantasies based on the Masonic rituals, but that much of the material in the later journals, including the philosophical themes and so-called magic rites, appear to have been based on distorted versions of the information provided in a handbook for Scottish Rite Masons, *Morals and Dogma of the Ancient and Accepted Scottish Rite of Freemasonry* (1871), by the American Freemason Albert Pike. It suggests that Jung's initiators were drawing on Pike's lectures about the ancient mystery cults and their gods, but twisting the information in order to confuse him and to create a false sense of profundity, combining this with further arduous trials. We already know that Jung told Freud in 1907 that he was sexually assaulted as a boy (Freud, Jung, McGuire, 1974, pp. 94–95; Bair, 2004, p. 71); these two studies, taken together, demonstrate that he may have also been ritually abused.

The Black Books 1913–1932: Notebooks of Transformation were published in October 2020, eleven years after the publication of *The Red Book,* edited by Sonu Shamdasani and accompanied by Martin Liebscher and John Peck as translators. The journals are elegantly reproduced in a seven-volume boxed set. *Book 1* contains the editor's introductory essay, notes on the translation and reproductions of some of Jung's paintings from *The Red Book*, while *Book 2* to

Book 7 contain facsimiles of Jung's handwritten journal entries in their entirety and their accompanying English translations.

The fantasies in *The Red Book* are drawn from Jung's journal entries from November 12, 1913, when he was 38 years old, until June 6, 1916 and were often accompanied by troubling inner states; but in order to understand these visionary experiences he continued to use these journals into his late fifties. Jung began to record his active imaginations while alone in his study. They were a series of visions or fantasies that he experienced on a regular basis, sometimes nightly or over several nights, accompanied by disturbing or frightening emotions and bizarre and sometimes ridiculous scenarios. Looking back on the writing process in 1925 he said that he felt he was practising a rite and felt compelled to write everything down, recalling the wording of these rites. He says: "Sometimes it was as if I heard with ears. Sometimes I felt it in the mouth, as if my tongue formulated words, and then it came, that I heard myself whisper a word to myself. Under the threshold of consciousness everything was living" (*BB 1*, p. 25). Such a description suggests a bodily memory of words both heard and spoken. But, more often than not, Jung tended to approach these mysterious words from an intellectual perspective, rather than through a fuller engagement with his bodily sensations and their associated emotions. In accordance with his own system of four psychological types - thinking, feeling, intuition and sensation - he classed himself as a thinking person with a correspondingly undeveloped feeling side (Jung, 2009a, p. 295, n. 178; 2009b, p. 338). His chosen method was to turn to the various philosophies and beliefs of the ancient and medieval worlds in search of answers. In a letter to a colleague, he wrote that Gnosticism and neo-Platonism might supply some answers to these baffling narratives, but then added: "what's completely missing, is modern material to compare it with" (*BB 1*, p. 67). As the previous study has demonstrated, the modern material that Jung lacked can be found in the Masonic rituals practised in Switzerland during the years of his childhood and youth.

The fantasies that made their way into *Liber Novus* were drawn from *Book 2* to midway through *Book 6*. There are only minor differences between the original and final versions. These differences include grammar changes or sentence modification and the inclusion of comments of a more personal nature

3

in the journals, including instances of self-criticism and some references to his relationships with women. But as the journals progress there are increasing interactions with his soul as well as dreams that are not mentioned in *Liber Novus*.

Book 2 runs from November 12 to December 29, 1913. It contains the fantasies that were reproduced in *Liber Primus,* the first book of *Liber Novus,* with the last three entries forming the beginning of *Liber Secundus. Book 3* goes from December 30, 1913 to January 14, 1914, which were recorded in *Liber Secundus* to form another 12 chapters. *Book 4* runs from January 14 to March 9, 1914; these were transferred to *Liber Secundus*, taking it to the final chapter "The Magician". But in this journal there is more material, including five complete entries that are not found in *Liber Novus. Book 5* runs from March 13, 1914 to January 30, 1916 and is reproduced in the final part of *Liber Secundus* and then in the third book, *Scrutinies.* In this journal there are eight entire entries and many additional comments that are not present in *Liber Novus.* Furthermore, the language becomes increasingly aggressive as Jung rages against his soul. The gaps between entries are becoming longer and at one point "the voices from the depths" are silent for almost a year.

Book 6 extends from January 30, 1916 to May 21, 1917. The entry dated October 9, 2016 is the last to be directly recorded in *Liber Novus*. From this point onward Jung continues to communicate with his soul via his journal entries in order to try and understand the previous visions and fantasies. He now begins to face more of his emotions and some of the bodily feelings these experiences produce, such as anger, fatigue, weakness, suffering and unbearable heaviness. He records a few dreams in this journal and also engages with the concept of the Mysteries and notions of magic. Sometimes, he gets physically sick during this process and has to cancel his sessions with patients.

Book 7 completes the entry of May 21, 1917 and continues to December 15, 1932. On two occasions these entries are broken into various sub-dates, such as a section on runes under the entry of October 7, 1917, and one containing a series of dreams in August 1919. They become more sparsely separated and sometimes there are years between them. Philemon and the sorcerer Ha reappear in this journal and Jung has a discussion with them, some of which is included in *Liber Novus*. But not included in *The Red Book* is the advice he seeks from Philemon and his soul over his relationships with two women, Maria Moltzer and Toni Wolff. He also records many instances of sleep disturbance and the dreams associated with them until the journal tapers off with entries recording the death of his mother and funerals for friends and colleagues, along with a prophetic dream about his wife's cancer. Jung was 57 years old when he recorded the final entry. In their entirety, the *Black Book* journals were kept for 19 years but by the end he is still struggling to understand the mysteries they contain.

Summary of *Answer to Jung: Making Sense of The Red Book*

As stated above, this study is a continuation of *Answer to Jung: Making Sense of The Red Book* in which the author argues that the fantasies in *Liber Novus* appear to be memories of a series of initiatory dramas based on the distorted use of Masonic rites (Brunet, 2019). *Answer to Jung: Making Sense of the Black Books* represents an opportunity to test this thesis and take a second look at these fantasies along with an investigation of the additional material in the journals. But in order to do so it will be necessary to provide a brief summary of the findings of the first study, which can be passed over by those who have read the first *Answer to Jung*.

The frequent expressions of pain, suffering, confusion and torment in *The Red Book* suggests that it is dealing with trauma of some kind and so this study incorporates elements of the psychology and physiology of trauma. Jung was well acquainted with psychological concepts of dissociation, amnesia and trauma and was, at one point, a student of the pioneering French psychologist Pierre Janet (1859–1947). Janet originally coined the term *dissociation* to refer to the dis-association of the mental processes, the "splitting apart of psychological functions that normally go together" (cited in Healey, 1993, p. 66). Today, one of the leading researchers in this field is the American psychiatrist Bessel van der Kolk, who regards Janet as the real hero in the history of the psychology of trauma. He elaborates on Janet's original definition of dissociation, calling it "a compartmentalisation of experience ...

[in which] traumatic memories are characteristically stored separately from other memories, in discrete personality states" (van der Kolk, 1996, p. 306).

Jung was born in 1875 and his childhood memories are, themselves, an important point of reference for a traumatic reading of *The Red Book*. In his autobiographical account, *Memories, Dreams, Reflections* (1963), he outlines a series of childhood experiences, some of them terrifying and extremely perplexing, and asks questions about their possible sources. His earliest childhood dream of a ritual phallus in an underground chamber, at the age three or four, still perplexed him in his eighties, while his solitary games in later childhood seemed to be pervaded by a profound spiritual quality and intense emotions. This produced a sense of being two personalities: No. 1, the ordinary schoolboy and No. 2, the one who inhabited a private other world. In this account he also mentions that his paternal grandfather, Carl Gustav Jung (1794–1864), was an ardent Freemason and, for a time, Grand Master of the Swiss Masonic Lodge; his grandfather also altered the family's coat-of-arms to include Masonic symbols (Jung, 1963, p. 220).

While recording his nightly fantasies in *Liber Novus* Jung describes a profound sense of fragmentation and the feeling that his soul is multiple, but despite their confusing and often terrifying nature, he begins to realise that the fantasies are, in some way, connected with the tradition of the Mysteries that first appeared in the ancient world. These secret forms of worship or cults involved a series of rites and initiatory ordeals, along with mythological themes and a set of doctrines that conferred a new status on their initiates. One observation he made in 1925, after contemplating the nature of his fantasies for over a decade, was that they reminded him of Mithraism, the mystery cult of the Roman soldiers, and that his fantasies were based on Mithraic symbolism "from beginning to end" (Jung, 2009a, p. 252, n. 211; 2009b, p. 197).

The initial indicators of a family connection to Freemasonry, along with the memories of his early childhood experiences and the sense of a deeply fragmented psyche, raises the question of whether Jung's fantasies could have been memories of a series of terrifying initiatory ordeals undergone in a Masonic context. If so, this would correlate with reports of the ritual abuse of children that first appeared in the early 1980s which were, for a long time, entirely discredited as being fallacious. But a body of research by psychologists, sociologists, social workers, and forensic scientists has steadily examined the evidence since that time to confirm the existence of cruel initiatory practices on the young that have the capacity to systematically shatter the child's psyche into multiple fragments. These practices involve a severe form of physical, sexual, psychological and spiritual abuse enacted repeatedly throughout childhood. They are accompanied by ceremonies and staged events involving symbols, rites, magic and spiritual or ideological beliefs, sometimes coupled with hypnosis, that are used to confuse, indoctrinate and terrorise the children (Sakheim & Devine, 1992; Becker, 2008; Lacter & Lehman, 2008; Noblitt & Perskin Noblitt, 2008, 2014; Epstein, Schwartz & Schwartz, 2011; Miller, 2012). Reports of this type of abuse in Masonic contexts or using Masonic ritual or regalia, accompanied by Gnostic beliefs, have also appeared in the literature of ritual abuse (Katchen, 1992, p. 10; Kent, 1993; Morris, 1997; Scott, 2001, p. 127; Brunet, 2007, pp. 227–269).

In order to determine whether it might be practices of this nature which lie behind Jung's fantasies, the study provides a background into the various Masonic rites practised in Switzerland in the latter part of the nineteenth century, when Jung was a child. These rites include the Rectified Scottish Rite, the Ancient and Accepted Scottish Rite, the Memphis Rite and several others and involve many references to the ancient mystery cults, along with Gnostic themes. Amongst Freemasons and other scholars there is the belief that Masonry has similar rites of initiation to that of Mithraism, and so Jung's recognition of its important role in his fantasies is another indicator that Masonry might be the modern source that was missing from his own investigations (Mackey, 1905, p. 197; Burkert, 1987, p. 41; Hutton, 1999, p. 59). However, it appears that his fantasies are distorted or spurious versions of these Masonic rituals. Freemasons have long acknowledged that their rituals can be manipulated and have created the term Spurious Freemasonry or "irregular practice" to apply to the use of Masonic rites in ways that are not sanctioned by the Grand Lodges (Mackey, n.d., "Spurious Freemasonry"; Buck, 1911/1967, p. 86). Spurious Freemasonry can range from a simple misrepresentation of the wording or actions in the rituals to a gross misapplication of the rites in clandestine and sometimes unethical contexts. The overall argument presented in the first *Answer to Jung* is that Jung's fantasies reveal a great deal of material that suggests the indoctrination of religious, spiritual and ideological beliefs using ritual theatre, physical and psychological abuse and trickery, seemingly undergone in his early years.

The study then proceeds to work through each of the chapters in *The Red Book* chronologically, beginning with the first book, *Liber Primus*, examining both the fantasies and the accompanying paintings alongside the various rituals of Continental Freemasonry. Jung's use of biblical quotes and scenarios of Christ's crucifixion, as well as the sense that he is undertaking a number of journeys into the desert, places some of these fantasies in close alignment with the 18th Degree of the Ancient and Accepted Scottish Rite, also known as Rose Croix. In this degree the Masonic candidate is first required to contemplate Christ's crucifixion and then undertake a symbolic journey into the desert in search of the Lost Word. But whereas the Masonic ritual is meant to be undertaken in great solemnity and dignity, Jung describes an experience of mockery and torment, terror and confusion in both physical and psychological terms. He wonders why he experiences this in palpable terms as if he is wandering through hot sand, suffering dreadful thirst and feeling oppressed by the leaden heat, raising the possibility that he might have been in a hypnotic trance. Hypnosis has been used in the Masonic system since the eighteenth century when Anton Mesmer toured the Continental Lodges, but given that many fraternal practices are bound by oaths of secrecy these practices are rarely discussed publicly. One exception to this are the comments made by the American Masonic author and medical doctor, J. D. Buck (1911/1967, p. 51), who refers to the misuse of initiatory knowledge as black magic and decries the use of hypnosis within the fraternity for the sole purpose of the humiliation and degradation of others.

There are several fantasies in *Liber Primus* which resemble other Masonic rites and at one point in *Liber Primus* Jung seems to recognise that his fantasies might be mystery plays. An early draft of one chapter was entitled "The Mystery Play, First Night", but in the final version he crossed this title out, changing it to "Descent into Hell in the Future", implying that he was unsure about this. Further fantasies in *Liber Primus* involve a similar hypnotic state, including the final chapter "Resolution" in which he undergoes another strange experience. This is where he feels he is on the cross in the role of the Divine

Child, with a white serpent in his right hand and black one in his left, when suddenly the black serpent winds around his body forcing him into the position of the crucified Christ. He then takes on the countenance of a lion and he is told that he is Christ, thrusting him into a state of rapture. The imagery in this scene aligns with the symbolism of Mithraism and in the Sage of Mythras degree in modern Freemasonry the brothers wear a plate attached to a white sash that depicts a serpent coiled around a lion; the lion representing strength and the serpent wisdom (Yarker, 1911). Jung's experience seems to be a hypnotically induced state creating terrifying bodily sensations and the sense that he has become the Christ. In the literature of ritual abuse there are reports of children being hung on crosses to simulate Christ's crucifixion (O'Donovan, 1994; Lacter & Lehman, 2008, p. 90; Miller, 2012, p. 65).

The following chapter in *Answer to Jung* addresses each of the fantasies and paintings in *Liber Secundus*, the second book of *The Red Book*. Here, again, it demonstrates that the plots, characters, settings and philosophical themes of the fantasies are very similar to those found in further degrees of the Ancient and Accepted Scottish Rite (AASR) as well as in other rites, such as the Rectified Scottish Rite, the Memphis Rite and a more unusual rite that originated as an anonymous text in eighteenth century Germany, known as Crata Repoa. Some of the fantasies involve stock characters like the devil and hackneyed plots involving castles, towers and beautiful maidens such as "The Castle in the Forest". These narratives leave Jung feeling embarrassed and disgusted with the banal nature of his own imagination and disappointed that his own experience of the Mysteries is far from the profound mystical experience conveyed in texts he admires, such as Dante's *Inferno*. "I am truly in Hell – the worst awakening after death, to be resurrected in a lending library!" he says (Jung, 2009a, p. 262; 2009b, p. 222). However, the analysis of these plots demonstrates that they are very similar to those used in some of the higher degrees of Freemasonry which the Masonic author, John Yarker, describes as "the effete exoteric puerilities of some of the modern Rites" (1882/2005, p. 112).

While some of the fantasies in *Liber Secundus* are simply baffling for him, others reveal intense states of terror and confusion, especially as the fantasies become more and more disturbing. He describes "The Sacrificial Murder" as "the vision I did not want to see, the horror that I did not want to live" (Jung, 2009a, p. 290; 2009b, p. 320). Here, he comes across a marionette with a broken head, a small apron and then the mutilated body of a small girl, her head decapitated and her skull and brains mashed. A shrouded woman stands next to her and tells her she is the soul of this child; she orders him to take out the liver from the mutilated corpse and eat it. He reluctantly obeys, almost fainting with the disgust and horror of the act. Then removing her veil, the woman reveals that she is *his* soul and that it is the divine child that he has murdered.

This appalling act leads Jung to struggle with what it means, but a note from his journal tells us that it might be a theatrical trick: "The curtain drops. What dreadful game has been played here?" he writes (Jung, 2009a, p. 290, n. 149; 2009b, p. 322). This type of trick is one that has been found consistently to be enacted on ritually abused children. In these abuses the child is made to believe that he is actually handling a corpse. These corpses may or may not be real, and may have been theatrically contrived, but the children are led to believe that they have been responsible for terrible acts themselves (Fraser, 1997, pp. 189, 191; Miller, 2012, pp. 195–197; Noblitt & Noblitt, 2014, p. 156). A series of paintings accompanies this entry and they are examined in terms of the symbolism found in the Kabbalah. These paintings imply the application of a ritual abuse practice known as the Reversed Kabbalah, where terror is used to remake the child's psyche and where demons or 'black angels' are invoked (Katz, 2012, p. 92).

Some chapters in *Liber Secundus* reveal the bodily positions Jung was in during a visionary experience, along with the sense of being drugged. In the chapter "Death", for example, he has a vision of a multitude of the dead flowing to the sea, but he experiences it as if he is suspended by his feet and feels a sting on his heel which takes his breath away and paralyses his muscles. Such a description suggests a drugged state as well as one of the practices used in ritual abuse where the children are hung, sometimes upside-down, during ritual events (O'Donovan, 1994, p. 3; Lacter, 2011, p. 59; Noblitt & Perskin Noblitt, 2014, pp. 62–63). Some of Jung's paintings supply information about the types of drugs that may have been involved. The first painting in *Liber Secundus*, for example, depicts the letter D with an illustration of an eye, the body's heart and circulatory system, as well as the depiction of a vine with a yellow flower. This plant was identified as the Curare vine, used medically since medieval times, where it was known to paralyse the body but leave the patient conscious (Wudka & Leopold, 1954). Curare has reportedly been used in the ritual abuse of children (Katz, 2012, p. 95).

Other paintings reveal information about magic practices. A painting accompanying the chapter "First Day" may be alluding to a practice in Ceremonial Magic known as the Middle Pillar exercise. In this painting Jung depicts a small figure in front of a central pillar; his head has reached the ceiling of the architectural structure while the circular structure above him extends far into space, suggesting an expansion of consciousness. The occultist Israel Regardie (1938/1945, pp. 47–49) likens the Middle Pillar exercise to the Masonic symbol of the three pillars, with the middle pillar representing a state of equilibrium and ultimately a mystical state of astral expansion. But he warns that it can also be used by those wishing to practice witchcraft or demonology in order to create an escape from the body, or in psychological terms, dissociation. Regardie advises that these magic practices should only be used by well-prepared adults and are not to be used by the young. In Jung's painting we appear to be looking at the figure of a youth practising this ritual, implying that he may have been trained in this exercise during an initiatory process in order to produce a state of extreme dissociation.

The chapter "Nox Tertia" appears to be describing a theatrical scenario in which Jung is made to believe that he is in a madhouse, while "Nox Quarta" conveys a biblically-based paedophilic scene with the prophet Elijah who revived the son of a widow by stretching himself upon the boy. This vision takes him into a state of self-loathing and he describes it as "that holy-evil pleasure of which you do not know whether it be virtue or vice, that pleasure which is lusty repulsiveness, lecherous fear, sexual immaturity" (Jung, 2009a, p. 304; 2009b, p. 368). The final chapters of *Liber Secundus* deal with further aspects of magic. In "The Gift of Magic" Jung is offered a magical rod, an instrument of black magic, but he is warned that the acceptance of this rod involves sacrifice. Reluctantly, he accepts the rod but is disturbed by it and wary of its effects on him. This section does not appear to be related to any Masonic rites but suggests some other form of occult ritual. In the final pages of *Liber Secundus* Jung describes the split between his original self and the new "son", his manufactured divine nature. This divine part now ascends in a sea of light in a final act of dissociation, leaving him alone in the night of pain.

The third book of *The Red Book* is entitled *Scrutinies*. It begins with a tirade of self-reproach as Jung identifies that his soul has flown to the heavens after all of these initiatory ordeals, leaving him a bare and empty shell. But while describing these ordeals and admitting that they feel like personal experiences of some kind Jung cannot identify where they come from. At this point the figure of an old magician, Philemon, who first appeared in *Liber Secundus*, comes to him, but Jung is wary of him as he sees him as a practitioner of the black arts and a charlatan. Philemon's first words to him convey a master-slave relationship, leaving Jung dismayed at his confusing and meaningless statements. This book contains further initiatory ordeals and a debate Jung has with his soul over her role in the dissociation process. This then becomes a conversation between Jung, his soul and Philemon that appears to be an attempt by his middle-aged self to revisit the inexplicable memories of a terrifying indoctrination process undergone when he was a minor. At this point Philemon begins "The Seven Sermons to the Dead", outlining the Gnostic concepts behind the initiatory ordeals Jung has undergone. But these sermons leave Jung even more confused and distressed, and the dead, those parts of himself that hold the pain of the ordeals, are left howling with rage at such a corrupt use of Gnostic philosophy.

Answer to Jung: Making Sense of The Red Book concludes by tendering several alternative explanations to the argument that Jung's fantasies appear to be memories of an excruciating initiatory process based on abusive versions of Masonic rites. It asks whether Jung might have actually been insane, as he did describe his experiences at one point as "doing a schizophrenia" (2009a, p. 201; 2009b, p. 28); but it concludes that he was not mad. It then proposes that he might have been an active Freemason consciously veiling his Masonic initiations for some purpose, but there is no evidence that has come to light suggesting that he joined the fraternity. It then asks whether the fantasies might represent some form of "channeling" as he was raised in a family that was involved with spiritualism. But just as the practices of mediums during the turn of the century were proven to be the product of clever tricks and sleight-of-hand, so too, is the ritual abuse of children laden with similar trickery aimed at convincing them into believing a whole raft of extraordinary scenarios. Finally, it asks if Jung's fantasies were all based on his reading, a more convincing argument proposed by Richard Noll (1997, p. 50), who addressed the reports that Jung published in his lifetime about his active imaginations and the role of the ancient mystery cults. As Noll points out, prior to the development of his theory of the Collective Unconscious in 1912 Jung had proposed an earlier theory of Cryptomnesia in which he argued that the experiences of mediums and the creative work of poets and artists were the product of the unconscious processing of previously learned but forgotten information. The argument presented in this study suggests that Jung's earlier theory of Cryptomnesia might be a better explanation for the content in *The Red Book* than the Collective Unconscious, not simply because he had read about initiation practices but because he appears to have undergone them.

The study concludes that Jung's "dark night of the soul" recorded in *Liber Novus* appears to have been a flood of memories associated with the abusive use of occult practices. By examining the plots, characters and symbolism of each of his fantasies and comparing them with a selection of Masonic rituals from Continental Freemasonry, it argues that it appears that Jung was initiated during the years of his childhood and youth. Through the power of dissociation, Jung seems to have repressed the memories of these bizarre and frightening ordeals until his mid-life period when his adult self was better able to confront them.

Albert Pike's *Morals and Dogma*

The author's previous study of *Liber Novus* revealed many similarities between Jung's active imaginations and the various Masonic rites practised in Switzerland when he was a child and it found that the AASR was the most frequently represented rite. This study will demonstrate that a particular text, Albert Pike's *Morals and Dogma of the Ancient and Accepted Scottish Rite of Freemasonry*, a handbook for Scottish Rite members published in 1871, may have also been a source used quite heavily by Jung's initiators. It will demonstrate that the philosophical and magic themes, in particular, that appear throughout the *Black Books* often mirror similar discussions throughout *Morals and Dogma* and that this text can provide explanations for the curious magic symbols and ritualised wording that accompanies them. These themes will be discussed in Chapters Three and Four.

Albert Pike (1809–1891) was an American polymath and larger-than-life character who played a key role in the development of the AASR, both in America and internationally. He is described by members of the Order as "one of the most astonishing men of the nineteenth century" (Guthrie Scottish Rite Masonic Centre, n.d.). Pike was a Confederate army general in the American Civil War, a renowned lawyer who fought for the rites of American Indian groups, a poet, author and linguist, familiar with multiple languages including French, Latin, Greek, Sanskrit, Hebrew and some native American languages, and a slave owner and supporter of slavery. He was initiated into Freemasonry in 1850 and became Sovereign Grand Commander of the Scottish Rite in 1859, holding this role until he died (California Freemason Online, 2002). Within the Scottish Rite he is highly revered and regarded as a mystic. However, his enemies have focused on his creation of an Indian brigade which scalped and tomahawked Union soldiers in the Civil War (Blanchard 1950/2002, Part 2, p. 229). Today, in some non-Masonic circles, he is seen as a divisive figure due to his support of black slavery and the rumour that he was a key figure in the Ku Klux Klan; his statue was torn down during the Black Lives Matter protests in 2020 (Smith, 2020).

Morals and Dogma has had many editions since its original publication and this author is drawing on the first from 1871, readily available online. Interestingly, the preface to this edition very openly acknowledges Pike's tendency to plagiarise. It states:

> In preparing this work, the Grand Commander has been about equally Author and Compiler; since he has extracted quite half its contents from the works of the best writers and most philosophic and eloquent thinkers. Perhaps it would have been better and more acceptable if he had extracted more and written less. Still, perhaps half of it is his own; and, in incorporating here the thoughts and words of others, he has continually changed and added to the language, often intermingling, in the same sentences, his own words with theirs (Pike, 1871, p. 4).

This explanation probably accounts for the rather erratic nature of the writing, as it jumps from one ancient belief to another, often without a clear argument linking them. As a consequence, *Morals and Dogma* comes across as a rather rambling and chaotic text, though one littered with thoughtful insights and wise advice to the author's Scottish Rite brothers. The preface explains that Pike "claims little merit of authorship", but somewhat hypocritically, he clearly points out that the text is copyrighted so that *it* cannot be republished. (1871, p. 4). Discussing this point his brother in Freemasonry and contemporary, Albert Mackey (n.d.), states that *Morals and Dogma* is not really a commentary on the Scottish Rite degrees but meditations on metaphysics, theology and cosmology. He notes that at the end of his life Pike was quite open about the flaws of this text, admitting that it had never been finished. For Mackey, this explained why there were whole pages taken word for word from other writers or re-written in his own words without accreditation.

During this author's analysis of the magic themes and incantations in the *Black Books* the problem of unreliable authorship occurred repeatedly. The magic themes in Pike's work were based on the Kabbalah, for which he drew on Eliphas Lévi's *Dogme et Rituel de la Haute Magie*. Eliphas Lévi was the pen-name for the French occultist and magician, Alphonse Louis Constant (1810–1875) and he, in turn, has been described as a most unreliable source, as were many others who explored the western esoteric tradition (Karr, 2023, pp. 9, 133). Fortunately, this layering of authorship does not directly impact the argument here: that Jung's initiators have drawn quite heavily on Pike's *Morals and Dogma*. As we shall see, rather than being a problem of layered sources, the alteration of Pike's wording in Jung's active imaginations seems to have been a very deliberate strategy, adding to the already confounding nature of the magical elements in his encounters with his soul. So the references to *Morals and Dogma* here are not being used as an authoritative source on the subject matter they contain but to demonstrate how closely some of Jung's active imaginations resemble the wording in this text. But Pike's lectures, I believe, are not espousing evil; he is not, for example, suggesting that these ancient belief systems are to be used to traumatically indoctrinate a child. In fact, at one point, he specifically warns his fellow Masons to refrain from damaging the young, stating: "Break not into the house of innocence, to rifle of its treasure; lest when many years have passed over thee, the moan of its distress may not have died away from thine ear!" (Pike, 1871, p. 159).

The perspective and layout of this study

In 1959, in a conversation he had with Miguel Serrano, Jung summarised his overall attitude towards his work:

> All my work has been directed toward myself; all the books that I have written are but by-products of an intimate process of individuation, even when they are connected by hermetic links to the past and, in all probability, to the future (Serrano, 1997, p. 79).

This concept is expressed even more succinctly by the present-day clinical psychologist and attachment researcher Beatrice Beebe who states, "most research is me-search" (cited in van der Kolk, 2014, p. 109). This approach is true of my own research. I am an artist, art historian and survivor of Masonic ritual abuse and my discovery of Masonic themes and traumatic content in my own artwork led to a PhD examining Masonic themes and trauma in contemporary art (Brunet, 2007). From there, the research has evolved into a series of case studies examining the presence of initiatory themes in the work of a number of artists and writers, both modern and contemporary (Brunet, 2009, 2019). Occasionally, throughout *Answer to Jung: Making Sense of the Black Books*, there will be references to my own initiatory experiences where they are similar to Jung's, as was done in the previous study. Here, I am following Jung's own approach when he stated in a lecture in 1935 that his main contribution to psychology was his own "subjective confession ... [because only when] we admit our personal prejudice [are we] really contributing towards an objective psychology" (cited in Bair, 2004, p. 415). This statement was quoted in relation to *The Red Book* but it seems even more relevant in an examination of the *Black Books,* as this is where we see much more of Jung's private thinking about his fantasies.

In the previous study the analysis of Jung's active imaginations was comprised of a close reading of each of them in the same order as they appeared in the chapters of *Liber Novus* and my first impulse in addressing the *Black Books* was to examine the journal entries in a similar methodical way. However, due to the fact that a great deal of the material from *Book 2* to half-way through *Book 6* is reproduced in *Liber Novus* with only minor variations, a different approach had to be taken. Instead, this study will focus on a collection of themes drawing support for the arguments across the *Black Books* as a whole. For the sake of readers who do not have the time or availability to read through the seven volumes of the *Black Books* it will attempt to include as many examples as possible of material that does not appear in *Liber Novus*. It will hopefully provide clear and descriptive summaries of many of Jung's visions, dreams and discussions with his internal characters and will sometimes focus on the differences between the journal entries and the final versions.

What this study does not do is to follow the cautionary advice offered by the editor Sonu Shamdasani who warns the reader in *Book 1* not to look for a causal and retrospective analysis of the fantasies and who reiterates Jung's own stance in this regard when he states: "at the core of the individual is a mystery of life, which dies when it is 'grasped'" (*BB 1*, p. 45). One of the main tenets of the ancient Mystery tradition was that it was always to be surrounded by secrecy, to be deliberately impenetrable to outsiders and only understood by those who had undergone the trials of initiation. Shamdasani's warning sounds very much like these ancient cautions which emphasise concealment. But as the previous study has argued, what we are looking at in Jung's fantasies is the *misuse* of the Mystery tradition, aimed at imprisoning the psyche of a child or young person and creating a form of spiritual slavery, a serious and urgent human rights issue and one in which ritual trauma plays a role in organised abuse (Salter, 2023). To pull back from looking for a cause would be an act of betrayal of those who have undergone similar ordeals and faced their painful memories. Known today as *ritual abuse*, one definition by the American Psychological Association states that it is:

> organized, repetitive, and highly sadistic abuse of a physical, sexual, or emotional nature, perpetrated principally on children. The abuse is reported as using rituals and symbols from religion (e.g., upside-down crosses), the occult, or secret societies. It may also include the creation of pornography or the selling of sexual access to children. Victims may

be forced to engage in heinous acts, such as the killing of animals, as a means of coercing their participation and silence (APA, "Ritual Abuse", 2018).

An increasing number of therapists encountering such cases, along with the mounting research conducted over the last thirty years or more and the many books, theses, survivor memoirs and survivor groups suggests that ritual abuse is real and a continuing threat to children in the present.

Indeed, to not analyse the *Black Books* would contradict the whole purpose of Jung's project of recording his inner experiences over so many years. In his discussion of the role of dreams he includes all other manifestations of psychic activity as susceptible to systematic analysis. "No psychic fact is accidental", he says, "being always the product of a complicated combination of phenomena; for every existing mental element is the resultant of anterior psychic states and ought in theory to be capable of analysis" (Jung, 1974/2002, p. 4). While Jung may have struggled in his journals to penetrate the mystery of his active imaginations, due to their confusingly unintelligible nature, there has been much research since that has addressed a severe and complicated type of abuse, which can lead to a profoundly altered psyche not unlike the one Jung describes.

Chapter summaries

One of the key features of the diaries is Jung's rich use of language to capture the intensity of the process he is undergoing; often it demonstrates a feisty resistance towards his own soul and other inner parts for participating in these inexplicable mysteries. So, apart from the introductory chapter and the conclusion, Jung's own words will be used for chapter headings and subheadings and will be retained elsewhere where their colourful nature clearly expresses his outrage as to what is happening to him. The layout for the following chapters is as follows:

Chapter Two is entitled "My soul ... You were my error". It is based on a question that his soul asks: "I am not a human being. What am I then?" (*BB 6*,

p. 300). Throughout the *Black Books* Jung has frequent conversations with his soul, whom he generally addresses in the feminine form. In the early entries she appears to be a young girl but then undergoes various shifts, becoming a bird and a serpent, and eventually a dark anima figure with an extraordinary amount to say. The conversations between them often degenerate into bitter exchanges, at times redolent of a never-ending domestic argument. This raises the question: What are these conversations and is it really his soul speaking?

Drawing on neuro-scientific research into the association between memory, imagination and the brain, as well as psychological concepts of introjection and alter formation (van der Kolk, 1996, 2014; Schacter et al, 2012; Miller, 2012; van der Merwe & Sinason, 2016; Davies, 2019; Lacter, 2021) this chapter will to try to answer some of the questions about who or what Jung's soul is and the nature of their relationship. Additionally, it will examine a theme that appears throughout the journals that Jung did not include in *Liber Novus*: his relationships with women. The next part of this chapter will ask how the characterisation of his own soul impacts his relations with actual women, as he describes them throughout the *Black Books*.

Chapter Three is entitled: "In which underworld am I?" (*BB 2*, p. 159). Even from the first month of his journal-keeping Jung became aware that he was being led on an internal journey that was taking him into domains that bore many similarities to the ancient Mysteries, their philosophies and gods. These mystery religions included Mithraism, Orphism and the beliefs of the early Christian Gnostics, but the fantasies contained bizarre and ridiculous elements that did not match these traditions. Jung had been researching these ancient traditions for some time prior to starting the journals, but his interior journey is filled with excruciating emotions such as fear, terror, confusion, and even suicidal ideation suggesting that they are not the product of disinterested scholarship but something else.

By focusing on the versions of Jung's active imaginations in the *Black Books*, and in particular on the material that was not included in *Liber Novus*, this chapter will examine the philosophical themes Jung encountered along the way, the different gods that he confronts and his associated dreams. It will demonstrate that the framing of the philosophical discussions often mirrors similar discussions and sometimes the actual wording used throughout Albert Pike's *Morals and Dogma* (1871), a handbook for members of the Scottish Rite (AASR), which the previous study found to be one of the Masonic rites most frequently associated with Jung's active imaginations. These lectures seem to have been deliberately distorted in Jung's fantasies in order to create confusion. By *Book 6* Jung has begun to relate his experiences to the concept of "post-Christianity", implying that an attempt to replace Christianity with a system based on various forms of the ancient Mysteries lay behind his ordeals. This chapter will explore the ways in which spurious Masonic versions of these ancient traditions were used to contribute to the trauma, pain and confusion of Jung's inner journey.

Chapter Four focuses on the magic themes in the *Black Books* and is entitled "I warned you about magic. Devilish stuff gets into you" (*BB 6*, p. 263). References to magic, both black and white, appear throughout *Liber Novus* and were discussed in the previous study. However, this chapter will examine the material in the *Black Books* that was not included in *Liber Novus*. The entries from June 1916 in *Book 6* until July 1919 in *Book 7* contain lengthy and complex conversations about magic between Jung, his soul, Philemon and other inner characters such as Atmaviktu, Ha and Ka. But despite nearly three years of attempting to understand this dark area Jung has still not reached any real clarity and is just as puzzled by it as ever, at one point describing it as: "Truly a Danaid's barrel of endlessness and meaninglessness" (*BB 7*, p. 180).

This chapter demonstrates that Jung's abusers have again drawn on Pike's Scottish Rite lectures, deliberately muddling the teachings in order to create a false atmosphere of evil magic and nonsensical magic symbols. The use of magic practices, including black magic, is a noted feature of the ritual abuse of children in the present era (Finkelhor et al, 1988; Smith, 1993; Becker, 2008; Miller, 2012; Noblitt & Perskin Noblitt, 2014; Lacter, 2021). As well as demonstrating the similarities with the Masonic teachings, this chapter will point out the parallels between Jung's encounters with magic and present-day reports of its use in cases of ritual abuse.

Chapter Five concerns a series of dreams recorded in *Book 7*, his final journal. It is entitled "What sort of dreams are these that rob me of sleep?" (*BB 7*, p.

206). From August 1919 Jung begins to focus more on his dreams; they are accompanied by further examples of active imaginations and some final discussions with his soul. Some of them are filled with overwhelming fear and interfere with his sleep, while others appear to be directing him back to his original visions and fantasies, as if he must turn to these for answers rather than rely on the confusing, argumentative and sometimes nonsensical conversations between himself and his inner parts. This chapter will trace the themes of these dreams and examine the last conversations he has with his soul, taking us to the final entries in the *Black Books*. It will demonstrate, again, that Pike's *Morals and Dogma* and several other Scottish Rite rituals will provide more answers to the obscure symbolism appearing in these dreams and in his final fantasies.

Chapter Six is entitled: "But what is my calling? The new religion and its proclamation" (*BB 7*, p. 211). A thread that runs through the *Black Books* is Jung's struggle with vanity, ambition and the question of whether he should become a cult leader. While the creation of *The Red Book* was to be a healing process for Jung himself, his soul was also pressuring him to complete the work in order for it to become a "holy book" for a new religion. This chapter asks whether Jung might have been groomed to become a cult leader from an early age, although he ultimately rejected the role, and that the type of pressure being placed on him was not unlike that found in abusive cults.

In 2008 the British psychiatrist Joan Coleman, who worked with a series of clients reporting extreme abuse in organised groups, made the observation that the techniques used on her clients were very similar to those of mind control and programming practiced during the Cold War. This chapter will place Jung's active imaginations and discussions with his soul alongside an example of Cold War research: a detailed study undertaken by the American psychiatrist Robert Jay Lifton (1961/1989) into thought reform practices in Communist China. This chapter will demonstrate the similarity between Jung's experiences and those of the Communist prisoners as well as the techniques used in present-day cults in the West.

Chapter Seven, "Final Thoughts", will address the question of whether Jung was ever able to fully connect with his own deep inner knowledge about the source of his fantasies. Citing several key thinkers of his own time who addressed the initiatory tradition, it briefly examines the various times when Jung records a conscious realisation that he may have been initiated in similar ways to these old traditions. On several occasions he also makes comments that indicate that he suspects their modern source. The chapter then summarises the role that Pike's *Morals and Dogma* played in his fantasies and briefly discusses Jung's theory of the Collective Unconscious in the light of these findings.

2

"My soul ... you were my error." (*BB 6*, p. 300)

On May 21, 1917 Jung recorded the following conversation with his soul:

> J: My soul, I heard of errors. You were my error. Yes, you were my
> participation in the opposites, in good and evil. I did good as good, evil
> as evil ...
> S: So you did. I didn't know it was an error before I sloughed off bird
> and serpent off from me and took the form of a woman ... I am not a
> human being. What am I then? (*BB 6*, p. 300).

Throughout his active imaginations Jung is in frequent contact with his soul
but as the above conversation tells us, his soul takes on different forms
throughout his inner journey. At first Jung embraces his renewed connection
with his soul, after admitting to a long period of searching for himself outside
of himself. As his journey progresses his soul acts as an adviser, imparting
wisdom where needed, but more often than not his soul seems to be deliberately
trying to confuse him. This provokes so much frustration and distrust in Jung
that it emerges as a stream of criticism towards his soul, resulting in frequent
bickering between them and creating an atmosphere redolent of a domestic
argument. "Once I adored you, then I loved you, now you threaten to become
contemptuous to me. You seem to me dull ... you blabber only to yourself, and
go round in circles", he says (*BB 5*, pp. 210–211). At other times his soul has
conversations with his other inner characters and they, too, sometimes argue.
This aspect of Jung's active imaginations, where his inner characters take on
independent personalities and behaviours, will be addressed in this chapter in

an attempt to understand who or what his soul is. Comparing the material in the *Black Books* with their final version in *Liber Novus* and then focusing on the extra information that was not included in *The Red Book* this chapter will ask: what is Jung's soul, what forms does it take and what roles does it play?

In religious contexts, as Jung was well aware himself, it is not uncommon that rituals can be used to cultivate the imagination producing experiences of the gods or other spiritual entities (*BB 1*, p. 25). The previous study has demonstrated that many of Jung's fantasies in *Liber Novus* closely parallel particular Masonic rites from the latter quarter of the 19th century, especially those of the Ancient and Accepted Scottish Rite (AASR) (Brunet, 2019). It argues that they appear to be describing memories of frightening initiations that he has undergone early in life, some of them involving gods or spiritual beings. But by recording these encounters in detail he discovers that he can use his imagination to quell their power, thus helping him to deal with the fear or pain they elicit. For instance, in the fantasy where he meets the fearful giant Izdubar he learns that he can use his imagination to make friends with him, to make him light as air or to shrink him to the size of an egg and put him in his pocket (Jung, 2009a, pp. 281–284; 2009b, pp. 291–298). In 1928 Jung commented on the use of fantasy arguing that it worked to influence the unconscious mind in order to transform a situation of terror to one more acceptable emotionally (2009a, p. 260, n. 15; 2009b. p. 217).

Jung was well aware, even from his earliest study into the trance states of mediums, of the research that was being done in his own time on fantasy, hallucination and imagination (*BB 1*, pp. 25–26). He also knew that there was an underlying relationship between our life-experience and our dreams and waking fantasies, both of which can reveal aspects of deeper psychological significance (Jung, 1974/2002). He talks of life events that evoke strong emotions and have an enduring impact on the psyche and notes that these intense events can form a complex of associations in the psyche that can appear in various forms in key dreams. But the very nature of these complexes is often disguised in the dream in order to protect the dreamer from facing uncomfortable realisations about himself. This understanding of the relationship between a person's life experience and the obscure representation of difficult unconscious material formed the basis of Jung's process of dream analysis with his patients.

In the *Black Books* Jung opens himself up to self-analysis by recording his dreams alongside his fantasies, but chooses only a certain number of these dreams to be recorded in *Liber Novus*. This may be partially associated with his intention to reduce the personal content of *The Red Book* as it was originally intended for a public audience, but it may also be associated with the differences between the dream material and the fantasies produced through the active imagination process. By comparison, the dreams tend to be vague and generalised in tone, whereas the fantasies are far more specific in their details. Much later, after developing his concept of the Collective Unconscious, he writes that the active imagination process can, to some extent, replace dreams and spontaneously amplify the unconscious contents and archetypal material contained within them (Jung, 1947/2001).

Jung's earliest journal entries in *Black Book 2* cite a number of dreams related to the representation of his soul as a child, which will be explored here. But the representation of his soul changes throughout the journals and this chapter will trace these shifts, noting how much Jung understood about their complexity. In the next part of the chapter, it will introduce more recent neuro-scientific research into the association between memory and imagination, and the psychological concepts of introjection, dissociative identity and alter formation (van der Kolk et al, 1996; van der Kolk, 2014; Schacter et al, 2012; Miller, 2012; van der Merwe & Sinason, 2016; Davies, 2019; Lacter, 2021). It will try to answer some of the questions about who or what Jung's soul is and the nature of its relationship to him. Additionally, it will examine a theme that appears throughout the journals that Jung did not include in *Liber Novus*: his relationships with women. It will ask how his characterisation of his own soul impacts his relations with actual women, as he describes them in the journals.

"... and why a girl?" (*BB 2*, p. 153)

In the earliest entries of *Book 2* (November 14 and 15, 1913) Jung is trying to understand why his soul appears as a child, and a girl child at that. Perplexed by this, he even asks if God is a girl child, but dismisses this idea altogether. Casting his mind back to a dream he had in 1899, he describes a vision of a very beautiful ten-year-old girl in a gauze-like garment hovering about one metre above the floor. Then the image changes into an overweight old woman and an older age man standing by a marble statue. Jung states that this vision or dream came back to him after a very long time. The question of why his soul is a girl child becomes the basis for his metaphysical contemplations on the nature of the soul in the chapter "Soul and God" in *Liber Primus*, where he concludes that his soul is a child and that the God in his soul is a child, albeit admitting that this idea is repugnant to him.

If we turn to the time when Jung first had this dream, when he was 24 years old, it might be relevant to ask what was occurring for him then: it was during these years that Emma Rauschenbach had become very important in his life. They were engaged in October 1901 and married in February 1903 (Museum Haus C. G. Jung; Clay, 2016; Bair, 2024, p. 78). It is said that he had known her since she was a child, as their mothers had been friends. At one point he had been a guest of the Rauschenbach family where he had seen a shy young girl at the top of a fine staircase and said he believed he had seen a young princess and had been transfixed by the sight of her, although he only saw her for a moment. At this point he had known, with absolute certainty, that she would become his wife. There are varying accounts as to when this momentous sighting occurred. Years later, Jung, himself, said that this was when she was 14 and he was 21 (Wehr, 1987, pp. 90–91; Dunne, 2000, p. 25). But based on interviews with the family, it was more likely to have occurred in 1899 when Jung was 24 and Emma, 17, a date that would correspond with the time Jung had the dream cited above (Bair, 2004, p. 76).

Regardless of which was the actual time he first saw Emma on the staircase it is possible that his dream of 1899, which depicted a young girl elevated above him, could be read as a metaphorical description of her as his soul-mate, socially and perhaps even spiritually above him. That his dream then portrayed an old man and an old woman together might simply be the prediction of a life-long marriage between them, which actually came to pass. However, the old woman's appearance, suggesting she was fat, may be a dream reminder to not expect the young girl's figure to remain slim and appealing; while the old man next to a marble statue suggests that he will remain firm and erect. His dream self was clearly not without its own gender bias towards ageing in men and women! So, was the young Emma Rauschenbach the initial symbol for his soul that his psyche presented to him in his dream of 1899?

This simple or uncomplicated reading would be appropriate to a young man of 24 in his first serious romantic attachment; but Jung's psyche, as we know, was far from simple, especially at this difficult mid-life moment, and even in these same early journal entries complications appear. He describes deliberately separating himself from his soul, saying that the love of women tore him away (*BB 2*, p. 152), implying that the love of women (plural) is related to his separation from his soul. The problem of the women in his life and their relationship to his soul will be addressed later in this chapter, but given the fact that this theme appears so early in his active imagination process it does beg the question of whether Jung's initial impulse for his journey into his unconscious might have been associated with guilt over the betrayal of his marriage vows. A conclusion similar to this is reached by Maria Guerra, who argues that the break with Freud and the outbreak of the war was not enough to prompt the experiences he recorded in *The Red Book*, but that it was the intensity of guilt, despair, anguish and suffering associated with his romantic relationship with Toni Wolff that catapulted him into his flood of internal experiences (2011, pp. 26, 37). This could certainly be the case but this discussion will demonstrate that the content of his active imaginations appears to be associated with a far more profound underlying disturbance involving initiatory scenarios from a much earlier period in his life.

On November 15 Jung recalls another dream from the previous Christmas period, involving his children and a beautiful white dove in a marvellous colonnaded hall; the dove turned into an eight-year-old girl. Before turning back into the dove, the child says: "Only in the first hour of the night can I become human, while the male dove is busy with the twelve dead" (*BB 2*, p. 156). Now there is a male dove as well, and his underlining of the statement suggests an important arcane meaning to its presence. Upon waking, Jung interprets this dream as helping him to make a personal decision and uses it to confirm that he should now put all his faith in another woman in his life: Toni Wolff. Only much later, in 1925, did he begin probing the symbolism of the twelve dead in this dream, linking it to various traditions including the Zodiac and even Mithraism, which then led to an analysis of his childhood memories (*BB 1*, p. 17, n. 19).

The significance of this dream so early in his internal process cannot be overstated and the inclusion of the marvellous colonnaded hall hints that we could be looking at a Masonic rite. The presence of the boy and girl dove suggests that it may be along the lines of Cagliostro's Egyptian Rite, a spurious Masonic rite established in the 18th century in which children played a role. Count Cagliostro was the pseudonym of an Italian by the name of Joseph Balsamo (1743–1795). He became known in Freemasonry as a charlatan and Masonic imposter for his creation of Egyptian Freemasonry in London in 1777, followed by its successful propagation on the Continent and a surge in Egyptomania in the lodges (Mackey, n.d., "Cagliostro"). In Paris he was associated with Anton Mesmer and applied mesmeric techniques, or "crystal vision" mixed with alchemy, sex and magic during the initiations, which appealed to the Parisian elite (Harrison, 2019, pp. 103–104). Henrik Bogdan classes Cagliostro's Egyptian Rite as "fringe masonry", which he describes as groups that make no pretensions of being masonry but can nevertheless generate a following due to their charismatic leaders' claims to special powers or secret knowledge (2010, p. 233). This secret knowledge included the practice of sexual magic along with Masonic and Hermetic symbolism.

Egyptomania was to continue to infect the high degrees of Masonry into the 19th century (Bogdan, 2007, pp. 97–98). In Switzerland, an Egyptian rite created by Jacques-Etienne Marconis was introduced in 1856 and was adopted by the Order to which Jung's paternal grandfather belonged. This was the Beneficent Knights of the Holy City, the highest grade in the Schottisch Rektifizierten Ritus (Rectified Scottish Rite) (Bair, 2004, p. 12, n. 41). A reference to Cagliostro's Egyptian Rite appears in Albert Pike's lecture for the 30th Degree or Knight Kadosh in *Morals and Dogma* (1871, p. 593) but he does not provide details of the rite. However, a discussion of Cagliostro and his rite by a 33rd Degree Mason, H. R. Evans, includes a description of the rituals and the role children played within them:

> In the admission to the Masters Degree, great pomp and ceremony was involved … In this degree a young girl (sometimes a boy), in a state of innocence, and called a pupil or dove (colombe), was introduced. The Master of the lodge then, with great ceremony, imparted to this child the power he possessed of communicating with pure spirits … The dove (girl child) was clothed in a long white robe … she was enclosed in the tabernacle, which was hung in white (Mackenzie, 1877 cited in Evans, 1919, p. 15).

The tabernacle arrangement of Cagliostro's magic rites is described by Eliphas Lévi, which he interprets allegorically. It was to be built on the summit of a mountain and contain three storeys; the ground floor was to contain the refectory, and the next floor above, a circular chamber containing twelve beds around the walls and one bed in the centre; this is the dormitory for the Twelve Masters in which the candidate must pray and sleep for forty days and nights. There, the candidate is said to receive divine light, his body filled with the purity and innocence of a child as he sleeps, leading him towards immortality. Cagliostro drew the ideas for his rituals from the Egyptian *Book of the Dead* and other ancient documents and also claimed that he could summon the dead, magically evoking phantoms in mirrors or vases of water (Evans, 1919).

It appears, then, that Jung's dream of the girl and boy doves and the twelve dead might be a memory of witnessing or participating in a version of Cagliostro's Egyptian Rite in childhood. The boy child busy with the twelve dead could then refer to part of the ritual involving a temple sleep or hypnotic trance in communication with the Twelve Masters. The concept of a temple sleep as a healing method reached its high point in ancient Greece in the temples of Asklepios where those who entered drank water from the Fountain of Forgetfulness and the Fountain of Memory and slept in the sanctuary where they experienced dreams or apparition of gods, heard voices or underwent terrifying visions before recounting their experiences in the Chair of Memory (Ellenberger, 1970, p. 33). A temple sleep appears in a later fantasy, "Nox Quarta" in *Liber Secundus*, where Jung awakens from a dream within the fantasy to find himself with the librarian's cook in the kitchen. He then returns to the library and asks the librarian if he had ever had a temple sleep in the kitchen. In Freemasonry the word "kitchen" is code for the First Degree (Bogdan, 2007, pp. 76–77).

Both of these dreams, the one of the ten-year-old girl floating and the second where the dove turns into a child and then back again, could also be read as a description of dissociation, a reaction commonly noted amongst survivors of childhood trauma (van der Kolk, 2014). Jung recognised something similar himself and, as his research progressed, he likened the fantasy of the soul flying as a withdrawal into the unconscious or land of the dead (1963, p. 233). In contemporary discussions of trauma, the sensation of floating or flying has been linked to the "fight or flight" response when the individual is confronted with a terrifying or life-threatening situation. Here, the non-linguistic areas of the brain can accommodate the experience leaving the conscious mind amnesic to the original events; in effect, these memories are dead to the traumatised individual (van der Kolk, 1996). Interestingly, van der Kolk describes the function of the thalamus during a terrifying encounter using a similar analogy to that found in Jung's fantasy of the cook in the librarian's kitchen. He states:

> ... the thalamus functions as a 'cook' – a relay station that collects sensations from the ears, eyes and skin and integrates them into the soup that is our autobiographical memory. Breakdown of the thalamus explains why trauma is primarily remembered not as a story, a narrative with a beginning, middle, and end, but as isolated sensory imprints: images, sounds, and physical sensations that are accompanied by intense emotions, usually terror and helplessness (van der Kolk, 2014, p. 70).

In the process of recording his unconscious material Jung has shifted his experience from unnamable sensations, images and feelings into narrative form. So, besides the possibility that he might have been remembering an actual ritual, the two doves in his dream could also represent the part of the psyche that escapes the trauma by dissociating from it (the floating girl) and the part that remains alongside the traumatising memories (the boy enclosed with the other "dead" parts of the psyche). The fact that these themes remind Jung of his own childhood suggests that the dream is prompting him to bring these memories to the surface.

The next appearance of a girl child in his dreams is recorded on November 26, 1913 (*BB 2*) in an entry not appearing in *Liber Novus*. It is a very brief dream where a little blond girl kisses him, producing tears of emotion and a feeling of support for a talk he was to give in London. Here he recognises the return of his soul in its child-like form, both comforting and reassuring. But in the next entry and those of the following month he experiences a series of fantasies that take him into states of terror, doubt, madness and confusion with inexplicable journeys in deserts, underground caves and other arduous trials, accompanied by feelings of scorn. Each of these fantasies is addressed in the previous study, demonstrating that they closely relate to a series of Masonic initiation rites, particularly those of the AASR (Brunet, 2019). By this stage Jung is conversing with his soul, who has now taken on a much harsher disposition.

Jung's entry of December 22, 1913 (*BB 2*) is where his soul is again represented as a girl, now with black hair. It is a fantasy as opposed to a dream, suggesting that it might be a clearer memory of an initiatory scenario. The girl appears amongst a group of religious figures: the mother of God with child, Saint Peter standing next to her, holding the keys and bowing, the Pope in triple crown with a festive audience, a Buddha and the Goddess Kali, along with the biblical figures Elijah and Salome. This scene appears to be some kind of tableau vivant where costumed actors pose against a scenic backdrop and accompanying props. It is recorded in the chapter "Instruction" in *Liber Primus* and in the previous study it is identified as being related to a Masonic ritual, The Scottish Master of St. Andrew in the Rectified Scottish Rite, the Order to which Jung's grandfather belonged (Brunet, 2019, pp. 44–45).

Jung's version appears to be a distorted enactment of the rite and a farcical interpretation of the meaning of the ritual. Two days earlier Jung had recorded a horrifying speech addressed to him regarding the birth of the divine child in the most degrading of terms. It concludes with "you are a veritable God" (*BB 2*, p. 178). The placement of the girl child representing his soul amongst these religious figures raises the question of whether this scene may have been theatrically contrived. Was a young girl participating in the ritual, as in Cagliostro's Egyptian Rite cited above? Or was the boy Jung perhaps dressed as a girl and positioned there to trick him into believing that his soul had been elevated to the highest spiritual realms, that is, in the company of the Gods?

The festive audience (the onlooking Masonic members) would then provide the finishing touch, adding to the ruse.

However, the interesting thing about Jung's version of the fantasy in *Liber Novus* is that he deletes the reference to the girl and as the entry continues, he talks about being a fearful schoolboy stepping into his father's house, and not a girl. So, it seems that by the time he has written the final version of this fantasy Jung is identifying more with his own boyhood. In the final version the deletion of the girl with black hair leads to a completely different meaning. Now, it describes the biblical character of Salome, wringing her hands, and he is told that she is his sister and their mother is Mary, causing him great confusion (Jung, 2009a, pp. 248–251/ 2009b, pp. 184–193). As Jay Sherry notes, Salome had been an icon of the femme fatale in the fin-de-siècle period and during the time when Jung visited the United States in 1909 a "Salome craze" pervaded the dance halls and burlesque houses (2008, p. 44). In Jung's case, as the previous study argues, his disturbing connection with her is not due to a popular culture fad, but rather to the belief, inculcated through the trickery and psychological torture of the initiatory ordeals, that he is as corrupt as the most evil woman in the New Testament. At one point, having pursued a complicated rationalisation of this fantasy, he concludes "Salome is my soul" (Jung, 2009a, p. 250, n. 196; 2009b, p. 190).

Salome reappears much later in his final journal, in July and August 1918, more than two years after the last entries used in *Liber Novus*. Here, Jung describes her as "heinous dancer, you tiger with the bloody claws" (*BB 7*, p. 187) and has long, argumentative discussions with her regarding his relationships with women, her magic power over him and the role of sensation and pleasure. As the argument builds, she becomes vicious, saying: "I will scourge your eyes, stab your heart, tear apart your diaphragm, tangle your intestines" (*BB 7*, p. 188). In these conversations his soul is also present, so Salome is no longer taking this role but has become another internal part. In the final discussion where she appears, on August 26, Jung inserts a new identity into the conversation: the "anima" is now his new name for his soul and Salome is described as a Medea, adept in magic and cooking poisonous potions.

It appears that for some time Jung was shifting these inner parts around in an attempt to try to understand who and what they were. When he begins to use the term "anima" for the soul he regards it as the part that turns inwardly towards the unconscious as opposed to the persona that turns outwardly. Even earlier, in 1913, he records his soul asking him: "Do you actually know who I am? Have you grasped me, defined me, and made me into a dead formula?" (*BB 2*, p. 167). In the chapter "Soul and God" he states this formula in a highlighted section beginning:

> *If you are boys, your God is a woman.*
> *If you are women, your God is a boy.*
> *If you are men, your God is a maiden.* (Jung, 2009a, p. 234).

This formula, as Jung was to admit in 1925, led to an over-emphasis on the role of the anima and into arguments with himself about the problem of God (2009a, p. 234, n. 57; 2009b, p. 135). The identity of these inner parts and their meaning was far more complex than a simple formula would allow.

The early dream split between the girl and boy doves reappears in Jung's later journal entries, though in different forms. On May 21, 1914 (*BB 5*) he contemplates the male aspect, the one that remains with the dead, calling the part that remains below his "brother I" who suffers much and was the one crucified, and the soul, that part that flies away as the one who experiences much happiness, leaving him feeling bitter towards her. But along with his soul's profession of happiness she says that she loves to drink blood, a statement that angers him, while his brother self feels he is loaded with the dead as if he is in a battlefield. In the following entry, two days later, Jung describes how his soul ascended into heaven in his greatest hour of torment, but according to her, this was out of inner necessity as she could not bear the horrors or excrement of the world. She even describes this escape as of the utmost benefit. Such comments from his soul leave him in a state of incomprehensible fear. In "*Scrutinies 2*" in *Liber Novus* he added that he was unable to connect these concepts with his own personal experience and did not understand what he was suffering from, concluding that it must have had something to do with the future outbreak of the war. In February 1916, still unable to fully grasp the meaning of these comments and of the complexity of the characters expounding them, Jung addresses his soul with disdain as "you separated doubleness" (*BB 6*, p. 221).

The splitting of the psyche during traumatic experience, where parts of the personality carry the pain and memory of the trauma, while other parts are freed from the experience, is at the basis of today's understanding of trauma-related disorders and their diagnosis, such as Dissociative Identity Disorder (DID). The history of the concept of trauma-related dissociation shows that by 1908 Jung was very aware of this form of psychological fracture, largely due to his work with Pierre Janet, and observed the splitting of the self in his dementia praecox (schizophrenia) patients (cited in van der Hart, 2016, p. 70). Finding a similar splitting in his own active imaginations was not only terrifying for him but revealed the complexity of this process, leading to his conclusion that he was "doing a schizophrenia" (Jung, 2009a, p. 201; 2009b, p. 28). But his inability to identify their cause demonstrates the power of his internal censor, a term which both he and Freud used to describe the internal resistance to a repressed complex unless it is represented in a disguised form in dreams (Jung, 1974/2002, p. 7). In a discussion of the history of this concept of trauma-induced dissociation James Randall Noblitt, a professor of clinical psychology with a focus on ritual abuse, comments on Jung's confrontation with the unconscious in *The Red Book*, noting the identity fragmentation. In a brief note he asks "was Jung, himself, a ritual abuse survivor?" (Noblitt & Perskin Noblitt, 2014, p. 96, n. 7).

Jung's entry of May 21, 1914 raises another question. Why does his soul, which he has identified as an innocent girl child escaping some sort of horror, a natural dissociative response in relation to traumatic experience, suddenly become a drinker of blood and a compassionless advocate for a human form of survival of the fittest? Jung, himself, seems to be pondering this when he states: "If you were not my soul who rose to the eternal realm, I would call you the most terrible scourge of men" (*BB 5*, p. 227). To understand this shift we need to look back at the fantasy where he eats the liver of the dead child, first recorded in his journals on January 12, 1914 (*BB 3*). Here, to his absolute horror, a shrouded female figure tells him that she is the soul of the dead child and then, after he has committed the foul deed, she asks him if he recognises her. He says she seems strangely familiar and she answers that she is *his* soul and reveals the face of a young maiden with soft blond hair. This is clearly another theatrical trick, which Jung himself recognises, as in the journal he records the curtain dropping and realises that it is a dreadful game (*BB 3*, 136). But he does not include this observation in *Liber Novus*.[1] So it seems that Jung has been tricked into believing that the evil female figure in this fantasy, the drinker of blood, is his soul, just as he was tricked earlier into believing that the evil Salome was his soul. By conflating these evil female characters or false "ritual souls" with the child's natural dissociative response, it causes Jung endless confusion right throughout his journals.

The crucifixion referred to in the dream of May 21, 1914 (*BB 2*) is the scenario he had recorded on Christmas Day the previous year. It was a fantasy rather than a dream and in it he is now a boy. It was transferred to "Resolution", the final chapter in *Liber Primus*. In the fantasy there is no real disguise; it seems to be representing something factual, albeit strange and hardly believable. This is where Jung describes undergoing a crucifixion like Christ or Mithras where he also has the feeling of floating. This fantasy was interpreted in the previous study as the memory of an abusive version of a Masonic initiation rite where he appears to have been under hypnotic suggestion to experience the feeling of being crucified himself and that the trauma of this produced a dissociative response (Brunet, 2019, p. 48). The original version in *Book 2* confirms this reading of hypnosis because directly after he describes himself in the position of the crucified Christ, with arms outstretched and the sensation of his body being squeezed by the serpent, he makes a statement that was not included in *Liber Novus*. It says: "But I am back in front of the crystal, still in the same position" (*BB 2*, p. 196). This was the crystal that he is told to gaze into where he sees the image of Christ on the cross in his last hour of torment. Hypnotic trances based on crystal-gazing were woven into Cagliostro's Egyptian Rite and, as we have seen, Jung could have participated in a version of this rite in his boyhood. The question to be asked here is why did Jung delete the sentence about the crystal in *Liber Novus*? Was he becoming aware that he might have undergone an experience in some sort of trance or under hypnosis based on the practice of crystal-gazing? Did he not want his future readers of *The Red Book* to interpret it this way? It does suggest that Jung was editing his experiences and perhaps his suspicions of how they might have come about.

Jung's concept of his own soul is based both on the dream representations and those of the fantasies. However, in the dreams the childlike versions talk only minimally, if at all, whereas in the fantasies his dark anima or "ritual soul" has an extraordinary amount to say. By examining the nature of the conversations between Jung and his soul we may be able to make sense of what is occurring here.

"Go to hell, you old cocotte." (*BB 6*, p. 277)

Jung's conversations with his soul, still envisaged as a woman, go on much longer after the journal entries that were incorporated into *Liber Novus* and there are countless examples of them. To try to cover them all would be a pointless exercise, so instead, some general observations will be drawn. These conversations often degenerate into bitter disputes with abusive language and harsh criticism hurled between them. This irascible behaviour, on both sides, has been going on throughout the journals and in the later ones he calls her insulting names like "concubine of Heaven", "divine monster", "wicked daimon" and "gruesome devil" (*BB 5*, pp. 262; *BB 6*, pp. 251, 253). These angry outbursts are in response to his soul's ongoing harassment, torment and mockery of him; she becomes his manipulator, providing seemingly wise advice that often contains a hidden barb. By February 1917 his frustration with her has reached a climax as she is resorting to sentimentality and presenting herself as a scorned woman. His reaction is harsh and damning: "Go to hell, you old cocotte," he says (*BB 6*, p. 277). In response, she presents a written statement for him to read, pleading her case as a forlorn and despised woman. But he answers her with harsh sarcasm and after reading it dismisses it, telling her it makes him yawn. So why has his soul become like an opponent in a vicious struggle rather than a soothing imaginary companion or wise inner self helping him to deal with traumatic events? And why are his soul's comments, explanations and arguments so much like those of a completely developed human personality? Is this complex character really his soul or something else?

As we know, Jung was already aware that events involving strong emotions in an individual's personal past could produce complex of associations in the psyche that frequently appear in various forms in their dreams. He used the term "reaction-dream" to describe those dreams that are essentially a reproduction of events in an individual's life that have caused a trauma (Jung, 1974/2002, p. 48). He cites the dreams of individuals who have undergone severe shock, such as the many cases produced during war, and describes them as "a spontaneous self-portrayal, in symbolic form, of the actual situation in the unconscious" (Jung, 1974/2002, p. 51). The record of his active imaginations suggests that these complexes might also be found in the more conscious process of waking fantasies where the imagination plays a key role.

Jung's experiments with his own psyche during this period took place in the context of the development of psychoanalytic theories concerning the unconscious motivations that drive internal attitudes and behaviours. The concept of defence mechanisms such as "projection" and its counterpart, "introjection", had been introduced by both Sigmund Freud and Sándor Ferenczi and have undergone alterations in their definitions since (Truscott, 2012; Vogt, 2018, pp. 23–29). But while Jung discussed projection extensively, both on a collective level and a personal one, for example when discussing dreams, he did not use the term "introjection". Instead, his use of the term "the shadow" or the dark side of the ego expressed a related idea (Vogt, 2018, p. 24). We do know, though, that Toni Wolff later used the term to describe Jung's introjection of her in order to realise his own anima (*BB 1*, p. 95).

The concept of *perpetrator introjects* is a more recent term described by Ralf Vogt and related to "man-made traumatic experiences, which become internalised through dissociative processes ... [and] to be complex psychological models, that we were forced to take in early in life because our boundaries were violated by an aggressor" (2018, p. 3). Alison Miller notes that introjects, or internal copies of abusers, are common in dissociative disorders where a strict father or other family members are involved (2012, pp. 45–46, 51–52). But she notes that in mind-control survivors these introjects are deliberately created by the perpetrators, who put themselves into the personality systems of their victims in order to control their inner world. This is often done during a rape. Ellen Lacter describes these strategies used by perpetrators as "calculated, psychologically-sophisticated, dissociation-savvy abuse" (2021). Given the argument that Jung's fantasies appear to be closely related to abusive versions of Masonic rites, a focus on the internalisation of an actual aggressor, or perpetrator introject, could be useful for an interpretation of Jung's irascible relationship with his female soul.

Brain research conducted in the 21st century may help to understand more about how the introjection of a perpetrator works. In 2007 a discovery that the brain network which underlies memory is also the same one utilised by the imagination was one of the ten top scientific discoveries of the year (Schacter et al, 2012, p. 677). These brain areas came to be abbreviated as the default network and prompted further research.[2] An earlier discovery, in 1994, had already demonstrated that there were specialised cells in the brain's frontal lobes that related to the quality of empathy; they became known as mirror neurons (van der Kolk, 2014, p. 58). These findings may be relevant to Jung's relationship to his soul as they demonstrate that the brain network that functions in the imagination process is also engaged when an individual is taking on the perspective of others (Schacter et al, 2012). In Jung's case it is clear that he has been able to imagine his soul as a complete personality in order to have such detailed discussions and arguments with her as if she is a full, albeit flawed, human being. She even becomes a writer herself.

In a recent overview of the current state of the science of the imagination the cognitive scientist Jim Davies (2019) takes this brain research a step further and proposes a theory that might be of use here. It bears a relationship to the established psychoanalytic notion of introjection, but in the way that it is used in the creative realms. He cites surveys of fiction writers who say that their characters often evolve to have complete personalities and minds of their own, to the extent that the authors can lose control of their characters; sometimes the characters even refuse to act in the way the authors want them to and "misbehave" (Davies, 2019, pp. 199–200). He cites the example of Alice Walker, who wrote *The Color Purple* and who described her own characters developing their own narratives, histories and anecdotes that meant that she sometimes had to kill them off. Davies also notes that some authors feel that they are recording what their characters do and say rather than creating the stories themselves and some have imaginary conversations with their characters. This phenomenon sounds very much like what Jung is doing with the characters from his inner world.

Davies proposes a theory about what is happening here in terms of the brain mechanisms involved. Basing it on the overall concept of the close association between memory and imagination and the scientific data that suggests that imagination draws on memories, he argues that these fleshed out characters appear to have evolved through a process of automatisation (Davies, 2019, p. 202). This process occurs in the attainment of complex skills such as learning to drive, where the once difficult multiple tasks eventually become automatic and unconscious. He suggests that once the author has created a clear mental model of a fictional character, it becomes automatised and the author eventually no longer needs to reason out what this character will say or do, or how they will react; this may feel that their behavior is coming out of nowhere. He argues that the "old brain" plays a role here, its workings largely unconscious, and likens it to the ancient Greek notion of ideas coming from nowhere as those being delivered by the gods or the muses.[3]

The act of remembering is automatically an act of imagination because, as Davies explains, memories are reconstructed every time they are retrieved. But asking how to distinguish between a real memory and make believe he states that real episodic memories tend to be more vivid than make believe (Davies, 2019, p. 44). As van der Kolk observes, this may be due to the amount of adrenaline that is released at the time, especially if the event is a terrifying one (2014, p. 176). In such situations, he says, the more adrenaline that is secreted, the more intense, accurate and precise the memory of the event will be.

In Jung's case, his terrifying experience of believing that he has eaten the liver of a dead child would easily qualify for just such an intense release of hormones at the time of the original experience, leading to a largely accurate memory being recorded. Though seemingly bizarre, it would have been imprinted deeply into his unconscious mind, to be released cathartically when his analytical mind later recognised that it was a theatrically staged event. Davies also describes the difference between hyperphantasics, those whose mental images are extremely detailed, vivid or accurate and aphantasics, those who are unable to imagine (Zeman, 2016, cited in Davies, 2019, p. 15). According to these definitions Jung would be classed as hyperphantasic and his extremely detailed imagery, described both verbally in his journals and visually in his paintings, along with his professional position as a psychiatrist and leading figure in the early psychology movement, suggests that his fantasies need to be taken seriously.

So, based on the above research it could be deduced that the characters that populate Jung's inner world were originally drawn from the initiatory memories that first arose when he began to explore his dreams and fantasies in 1913, many of which involved extreme fear and even terror. Once these characters had made themselves known to him, then, like those of the fiction writers mentioned above, their personalities could take on a life of their own, having become automatised. They can now fill the pages of his journals with their opinions, explanations, criticism and complaints and become completely independent and even out of Jung's conscious control. This means that he could now have discussions with them as if they were real people with all their attendant personality flaws.

It is perhaps interesting that the fiction writers described above note that the shift into autonomous behaviour only occurred amongst the main characters in their novels and that minor characters remained less fleshed-out and stereotypical. Davies also observes that in dreams the characters tend to be stereotyped and without much depth (2019, p. 205). He relates this to the fact that during dreaming the pre-frontal cortex that deals with language is relatively quiet, and suggests that in dreams these characters need not be deep but are there to serve a function.

All of these observations seem particularly relevant to Jung. As we have seen, the dream characters that represent his soul are quite different from those in his fantasies: the girl child and the female dove in his dreams appear briefly, and apart from the one key statement about the twelve dead, say little. Their purpose appears to be to prompt him to remember and to comfort him. Whereas his fantasy soul, represented in female form, is extremely complex, and seems to be based on a blend of the evil character Salome and the shrouded woman who urges him to eat the child's liver, both encounters that have been identified as abusive ritual enactments seemingly employing costumed figures in a theatrical context (Brunet, 2019). This complex and diabolical version of his soul then becomes a main character in his active imaginations. This results in much confusion for Jung as one part of him is perfectly aware that he is actively imagining this demonic soul character in order to try and understand what all these fantasies are about, whereas another part of him suffers deeply from his encounters with her. In terms of the brain, this appears to relate to the fact that Jung's "new brain" knows full well that she is imaginary, but his "old brain" reacts as if she is real and converses with her based on the automatisation of her evil personality.

Throughout the fantasies Jung represents a host of characters, most of them remaining minor and having less to say in his imaginings. Those represented in *Liber Novus*, in order of their appearance, are the spirit of the depths, the hero Siegfried, the prophet Elijah who accompanies Salome, the serpent, Jesus Christ, the Red One/Devil, an old scholar and his beautiful daughter, the tramp, the anchorite Ammonius, Izdubar, Ha the black magician, the librarian and the cook, Ezekiel, characters from the Grail legend, Philemon and Baucis, the dwarfish elemental spirits known as the Cabiri, a hanged man, a raven, a shade who commands him to drink blood from a carcass, the dead who comprise the audience for the Seven Sermons, the old doctor in the turban, and a blue shade identified as Christ. As the previous study demonstrates, each one of these characters relates, in some way, to the Masonic rituals cited. Besides his soul, who takes centre stage, only a few of these – Philemon, Ammonius, Elijah and Salome – develop into more fleshed-out personalities that, through the process of automatisation in his imagination, are able to have in-depth discussions with him as if they are real human beings.

Philemon appears firstly as an old magician alongside his wife Baucis, but then reappears in *Scrutinies* where he delivers "The Seven Sermons to the Dead". At the end of *Scrutinies 3* Jung states that he thinks Philemon has been behind much of the information he has recorded in his active imaginations. On January 10, 1916 (*BB 5*) Jung records a speech that he later recognises as the words of Philemon, spoken in a soft deep voice. They are transcribed, with slight variations, into *Scrutinies 5*. The speech conveys starkly conflicting advice about the divine female presence in his soul: she is a heinous, cunning woman, evil to the core, and is to be removed completely. But then at the same time Jung is told to cling to her, never letting her out of his sight; she is a devilish mystery, a lecherous bitch and a dreadful nightmare that must be captured and locked up by Jung, her prison guard. Given that his dark anima and his master

41

Philemon appear to have originally been characters within the initiatory scenarios and therefore members of the abusive group who seem to have treated him so cruelly, it is clear that Philemon's depiction of Jung's anima as pure evil is intended to manipulate and control him and sow a deep sense of misogyny into the psyche of the young Carl Jung. So how does this characterisation of his own soul in the journals impact his relations with actual women?

"I speak of polygamy ... Women heal the wounds." (*BB 6*, p. 229).

It could be argued that by engaging in these ongoing quarrels with his imagined female soul in his journals Jung was able to spare the women in his life from too many displays of his unresolved anima problems. By being consciously aware of his internal battle with her he could therefore enjoy more civilised and intellectual dialogues with the many intelligent women in his circle. But, of course, this created other problems, not the least of which was the impact on his wife, Emma Jung, who complained to Sigmund Freud of her struggle with holding her own in this situation and telling him that all the women were in love with her husband (Freud/Jung, 1974, p. 467). The conflict over the women in his life is a theme that runs throughout the *Black Books* but was omitted from *Liber Novus*. For our purposes, though, the journals may provide further material to suggest that the foundation of these struggles may also lie in the initiatory ordeals and training.

In the journal entry of November 14, 1913 (*BB 2*) Jung describes deliberately separating himself from his soul and completely losing contact with her when he finds himself drawn to women. On the following day he hears someone crying inside him but ignores this cry. It seems that there is a part of him that he does not want to listen to, something that he is not yet ready to face. But rather than turning to the one crying, his thoughts revolve around a present-day love triangle and he begins describing how he met a woman three years earlier "whose soul seemed to me more valuable than my marital anxiety" (*BB 2*, p. 155). The young woman to whom he was referring was Toni Wolff, a young patient with whom he had a love affair when working as a psychiatrist at the Burghölzli, following another affair he had had with another female patient, Maria Moltzer (*BB 1*, pp. 60–66). Jung describes his decision to give himself to Wolff as a blessing upon himself, his wife and his house. Such a comment implies an inordinate insensitivity to the needs of others, particularly those of his wife, and reveals an attitude that was to remain with him throughout much of his adult life. In an exploration of the emotional impact on Emma Jung of her husband's behaviour, Imelda Gaudissart asks several important questions about Jung's seemingly casual attitude about his affairs: "What price did he pay for his choice to behave in the way he did? What kind of inner torment, what sort of acutely painful split, did his behavior cause him to endure?" she asks (2014, Ch 7, par. 20). It is in the *Black Books* that Jung reveals the full extent of his inner torment over this situation.

An early dream related to this theme, again not recorded in *Liber Novus*, appears in the entry dated December 12, 1913. This dream elicits so much disturbance as to cause him a sleepless night and three days of torment. It likens him, "from start to finish" to the main character in "Der Apotheker von Chamounix", a poem published in 1883 by the Swiss writer, Gottfried Keller (1819–1890) (*BB 2*, pp. 167–168, n. 91). This tale was a satire directed at the German poet, Heinrich Heine (1797–1856), written when Heine was still alive. Helen Walden suggests that Heine would probably have been amused by it rather than offended (1938, p. 21).

The first part of the poem is a blood-curdling tale of the death of Titus, the apothecary of Chamounix. Titus was the ardent lover of Rosalore, but he was not faithful to her and seduced Klara, an innocent mountain-maid whose fingers dripped honey (she kept bees). Rosalore's love for him turned to hatred and she knitted a scarf for him, laced with gun-cotton, an explosive substance of cotton soaked in nitric and sulphuric acids from his own pharmacy. Titus wore this scarf when going out to shoot a wild mountain goat, however Rosalore followed him and he mistakenly shot her; at the same time this ignited the gun-cotton in his scarf and his head was blown off! (Walden, 1938, p. 23). It is not difficult to see why Jung's dream likened him to Titus and this rather amusing, though tragic, love triangle, as we have already seen his thoughts turn to Toni Wolff on November 15. While Jung proceeded with his relationship with Wolff it is clear that a guilty conscience was asserting itself through this dream, and that it was reminding him that he was damaging both his wife and himself in the pursuit of this affair. The fact that the poem dealt with the death of an apothecary might have also resonated with Jung, whose attention turned to the study of alchemy later in life.

The poem was in two parts and the second part, again satirical, deals with the imagined death of Heinrich Heine (Walden, 1938, pp. 23–24). Keller depicts Heine entering the gates of Heaven where he meets with the literary masters Goethe, Schiller and Lessing. With Lessing, he comes to blows and falls into a huge sea of ink in which there are horrible sea monsters: the spirits of untalented scribblers. This scenario is, in fact, a dream and he wakes up, but then dies anyway. Before he can enter Heaven, he must undergo Purgatory and Keller depicts him literally "put on ice": he is placed in an icy cage once inhabited by Klara, the seduced maiden, who has now qualified to go to Heaven.

It is a silly tale, but the fact that Jung related himself to the entire poem reveals the depth of his struggle, not only with his love relationships but also with doubts about his own writing skills in the face of these German literary giants. But at such an early stage in his active imagination process a dream that deals so openly with sexual guilt is not to be brushed off lightly. While it may have been commenting on his present-day marital situation it could also be said that the dream was acting as a catalyst, prompting him to remember other more repressed experiences where guilt played a major role, such as the initiatory ordeals being discussed in these studies.

We may have seen evidence of the source of Jung's attitude towards women in the fantasy where he meets the doctor in *Scrutinies 13* in another heart-breaking scene filled with trickery. This character wears a long coat and a turban and offers healing and joy. In the previous study he was identified in relation to the 32nd Degree or Sublime Prince of the Royal Secret where one of the roles taken by the members is the Grand Hospitaller and Surgeon (Brunet, 2019, p. 158). In Jung's fantasy he offers the blissful love of women as healing for the wounds of the initiation experiences, a source of comfort that the adult Jung appears to have sought in his extra-marital affairs. In the original version, recorded in his journal on February 21, 1916 this character is a Turk professing Islam, announcing Mohammed and promoting the benefits of polygamy. When the doctor says: "Women heal the wounds. They know about medicines … They know how to treat sick children", Jung asks "am I a sick child?" (*BB 6*, pp. 229–230). The fact that he is able to ask if he is a sick child suggests that by 1916 Jung is becoming aware that the roots of his torment may lie somewhere in childhood and that it is his child self that is being drawn to women to be healed. But he chooses not to include his question in *Liber Novus*.

Around this time Jung begins to use the term "maternal soul" in his active imaginations (*BB 6*, pp. 235, 240), displaying a shift in his relationship with his anima and possibly indicating more awareness of his own inner child's perspective. One of the final paintings in *Liber Novus* (Image 155) is a depiction of a great mother figure in a positive light, but this motherly aspect of the soul was previously distasteful to him. Nearly two years earlier, on April 15, 1914 (*BB 5*) in an entry not recorded in *Liber Novus*, he asks his soul what she wants and she gives him a kangaroo with a joey in its pouch. He finds this painfully grotesque and the motherly aspect of it ridiculous, but it is also fraught with meaning and his soul tells him that the kangaroo and the pelican are both symbols of Christ and encourages him to become a child himself. The reference to the pelican as a symbol of Christ is well-known in Christian art but it also appears in Freemasonry. It is a prominent symbol used in the 18th Degree, also called Knight of the Rose Croix, where according to Albert Pike: "The Pelican feeding her young is the symbol of the large and beneficent power of Nature, of the Redeemer of fallen man" (1871, p. 212). It is possible that Jung's episode with the pelican and kangaroo, creatures symbolically associated with the protective maternal instinct, may also be a reference to the 18th Degree, the Masonic rite that played a major role in his earlier fantasies (Brunet, 2019).

So now, in 1916, Jung seems to be looking for a way to connect with the child part of himself, as his soul had previously urged, and it is possible that Jung's soul as evil temptress could now be replaced by a more positive all-embracing madonna symbol, promising a more constructive relationship with her and some answers as to what all of this means. However, Jung does not give a voice to the child part of himself; he does not engage in an imaginary conversation with him, as he has done with the introjected characters. Instead, he continues the irascible exchange with his dark anima figure and the frustration continues. "You subterranean! How long does your rule last?" he writes (*BB 6*, p. 247). It is perhaps relevant that Jung records this tension on the day after his wife Emma presented a paper, "On Guilt", to the Association for Analytical Psychology where she discussed the relationship between sexuality, sensuality and intellectuality (*BB 6*, p. 247, n. 230).

Jung's imagined soul now begins to present herself in conflicting ways. On the one hand she urges him to focus less on others, to rest and focus more on his inner work, but then he complains that she annoys and harasses him, not allowing him to get on with his work. In September 1916 he is still asking his soul who she really is and calls her a "heathen monster" (*BB 6*, p. 256), as her answers are unbearably heavy for him and fill him with disgust. She describes the women in his life as her rivals and her most dangerous opponents and tells him to cease writing moaning letters to the two women, Maria Moltzer and Toni Wolff, urging him to let go of Wolff. But in a contradictory statement on February 20, 1917 (*BB 6*) his soul says she wants to drive him to women! On October 22, 1917 she says "the black one" (Toni Wolff) is now good, and even necessary, for him. There seems to be no pleasing his fickle and jealous half-daimon soul. But in all of these imaginings Jung does not even mention his wife. The fantasies seem to be a way of playing out his inner turmoil without actually admitting to himself that he is feeling guilty. They may even represent an enactment of how he thinks his wife might be feeling, even hoping that she would be as insanely jealous as his imagined soul is. But by all accounts, Emma Jung was handling the situation with a great deal of dignity, preferring to turn inward rather than make her own feelings known.

On February 11, 1918 (*BB 7*) Jung records a couple of dreams that appear to be comments on his affairs. They reveal the depth of hurt he is inflicting on others, as well as on himself, which he cannot fully acknowledge in his waking hours. In the first, a character named the Baptist, a married individual, destroys a lover with venom from a "complicated glass apparatus" turning the lower part of her body to stone, possibly a reference to the destruction of the sexual aspect of the relationship. Then, in the dream, he is destroyed himself, along with a child, but before his dream-self dies he feels immense guilt and roars like a wounded animal. The glass apparatus seems to be a reference to alchemy, a symbol for the work Jung is doing, his intellectual child; it suggests that his love affairs are destroying not only his lover and himself but also his work. The

46

next dream has a similar atmosphere. It is set in India where he is attending a ceremony where there are two widows who, rather than being burnt, have their right hands cut off. "Horribly real and cruel", he says (*BB 7*, p. 175, n. 71). Toni Wolff, with whom Jung had a relationship until her death in 1953 (Sherry, 2008, p. 44), was to effectively become his second wife and so this dream is clearly referring to the sacrifice that both she and Emma Jung are having to make through their relationship with him. Losing their right hands may be interpreted as his dream-self's comment on them losing their own agency through their association with him, as they both were to prove their worth as psychoanalysts in later years.

In July 1918 Jung again raises the problem of women with his soul and she tells him that his relationship with the "black one" is tainted with an evil spirit due to the fact he has not released Salome from her. Salome is "the spirit of the earth that dances poisonous dances, that bewitches and intoxicates, that drinks blood and causes magical sickness", she says (*BB 7*, p. 186). In other words, he has been projecting his dark anima, that this argument proposes was originally based on the ritual encounter with the evil Salome in his childhood initiations, onto Toni Wolff. His soul describes Salome as her other half, her opposite, and urges him to engage with Salome and force her to give him answers, just as he had repeatedly forced her to answer him, even though it filled him with frustration and rage. He takes up the challenge and calls on Salome, allowing her to speak to him, as his other main automatised characters have done. The ensuing long and fractious conversation they have is filled with her accusations of his weakness and threats to torture him with physical and emotional pain. But he remains steadfast in his rejection of her, noticing her fear, until she recognises that Philemon is behind his shift towards her. "This is Philemon's work!" she cries (*BB 7*, p. 189).

By threatening to torture him, Salome is reminding Jung of the initiatory ordeals, while her reference to Philemon as the manipulator behind the scenes suggests that he represents the overarching controller of the ritual experiences. As we saw in *The Red Book*, Philemon first appeared as an ageing and feeble-minded magician, but as the active imaginations progressed, he was shown to be a devilish fraudster engaged in black magic, with the intention of entrapping Jung in a master-slave relationship (Brunet, 2019). Towards the end of

47

Scrutinies Jung realises that the words he had been hearing throughout his fantasies were those of Philemon and when he depicted him in Image 154 as a medieval knight with outspread wings Jung states that he venerates him, despite the fact that Philemon had deceived him. Jung's veneration for Philemon, even though he seems to have been behind the whole series of initiatory ordeals, suggests that even towards the very end of the journals Jung is still under his spell.

All along, Jung has been trying to understand who these inner characters are and what they mean and yet, as the previous study has proposed, they appear to be related to the initiatory scenarios carried out in Masonic contexts (Brunet, 2019). In the following entry, on July 31, 1918 (*BB 7*), the conversation between Jung, Salome and his soul now develops into another complicated and obscure metaphysical argument with Salome rejecting the notion that she is a mystery; instead, she wants to be seen as representing pure sensation. In the final entries in 1918 Salome is still protesting and threatening to keep disturbing and irritating him.

Even towards the end of the *Black Books* Jung's focus on the problem of the women in his life persists. In early January, 1922 there are several entries dealing with this issue. On January 4 he asks his soul for advice about Toni Wolff. She tells him that Wolff is the emissary of the Great Mother but is not aware of it, and reads a series of runes with strange hieroglyphics on them that are magical-sounding but make no sense. His soul concludes that as the Great Mother she deserves to be treated roughly and should submit to him; in other words, he is to treat her misogynistically (*BB 7*, p. 210). His soul's suggestion that he denigrate her as a representative of the Great Mother may be reflected in an observation made by the historian of religion, Mircea Eliade (1958/1995, p. 80). In a discussion of puberty rites within ancient secret societies Eliade notes that the denigration of the mother plays a key role in traditional initiation practices. In warrior cultures it is intended to sever the connection with the mother and rebirth the young boy into the patriarchal context where toughness, the ability to dissociate from pain and the capacity to suffer humiliation are the marks of survival. Here, again, we see that the voice of Jung's soul is promoting attitudes that reflect the initiatory practices he appears to have undergone earlier in his life.

On January 6, 1922 his soul tells him that he must let Toni Wolff go and focus on rebuilding his relationship with his wife, creating a new house for them and celebrating peace, beauty and the love between them, to which Jung answers: "Can it lie in this shocking simplicity? Why then my errancy? Why my seeking?" Clearly, such a directive to return to marital harmony is not the answer to the complex inner turmoil that Jung is suffering from, but his soul replies that through this long process he has now paid for the sins of the father and has "discharged [his] guilt down to the last penny" (*BB 7*, p. 213).

Jung's problems with the women in his life appeared in his first journal entries in 1913, and his dream identification with the apothecary of Chamounix, a character laden with marital guilt, suggests that his active imagination process partly began with unacknowledged feelings of his own marital guilt. But the simple solution of abandoning his affairs and reconnecting with his wife did not satisfy Jung. Rather, he is determined to try to make sense of the complex mystical or philosophical problems that his active imaginations describe and so in this entry his soul urges him to look into himself, to the "thrice-holy Isis" that he has only seen in women until then (*BB 7*, p. 212). She describes an African scene and Jung is reminded of a dream of a divine youth that he had in Africa, two years before. In this dream he was in a casbah in an Arab city where he wrestled with an aristocratic Arab youth and they both fell into a moat where he pushed the youth's head underwater to make him unconscious (*BB 1*, pp. 76–78). Then he was in an octagonal room in a citadel where there was an open book containing magnificent calligraphy and an exotic script from West Turkestan, which Jung identified as *his* book. The young prince was again present and Jung's dream-self patiently persuaded the youth to read it. Jung's African dream seems to be telling him to connect more directly with his youthful self and gently supports him to do this. Again, we may be seeing a difference between the dream characters, as Davies suggests, who are relatively quiet and are there to serve a function, as opposed to the vociferous and infuriating nature of characters like Salome and his soul, who appear to be introjected perpetrators.

On January 7, 1922 (*BB 7*) Jung sees strange hieroglyphic messages and his soul's explanations of these signs and symbols become increasingly obscure. In a discussion of the symbols in this message she states that the third sign is difficult and talks of Egyptian themes and the word FANDRAGYPTI, the pheasant of the Egyptians Isis, Osiris and Nephthys.[4] She names Jung, Emma and Toni as a triumvirate bearing these symbols and aligns Toni with the god Nephthys, the Egyptian goddess of the dead and sister of Isis and Osiris. Here again, we seem to be looking at themes from Cagliostro's Egyptian Rite, which involved the worship of Isis, along with the role taken by an innocent young boy (pupille) or young girl (colombe):

> The boy or girl would kneel in front of a globe of clarified water placed upon a table, covered with a black cloth embroidered with Rosicrucian symbols, and Cagliostro, making strange mesmeric passes, would summon the angels of the spheres to enter the globe; whereupon the youthful clairvoyant would behold the visions presented to his or her view ... This is what is called 'crystal vision' by students of psychical research, although the object employed is usually a ball of rock crystal and not a globe of water, such as Cagliostro used ... The crystal is used to promote hypnosis, also to visualize the images that appear in the mind. Undoubtedly Cagliostro was an accomplished mesmerizer ... But, like many mediums who have such gifts, he sometimes resorted (if his enemies are to be believed) to trickery and sleight-of-hand to accomplish results when the real power was not forthcoming (Evans, 1919, p. 7).

Evans describes the room in which the séances took place as having statuettes of Isis, Anubis and Apis, while the walls and Cagliostro's black silk robe were covered with hieroglyphics. He says he wore a turban of gold cloth and a chain comprised of emeralds, metal scarabs and cabalistic symbols around his neck. We see a similar personage in the twentieth century figure of Aleister Crowley (1875–1947).

A similar atmosphere pervades Jung's African dream as well as the vision of the hieroglyphic messages he is now being shown by his soul in 1922. The presence of crystal vision appears in a number of his earlier active imaginations, which he incorporated into *Liber Primus*: in "Descent into Hell in the Future" he experiences the sensation of descending into a cave where he must reach a six-sided crystal. In "Mysterium Encounter", where he first meets the prophet Elijah, he sees an image of Eve, the serpent and Odysseus projected onto a bright stone, the colour of water. In "Instruction" he is again in the company of Elijah and Salome and sees a fire in a shining crystal, along with several religious figures. Then in "Resolution" Elijah tells him to step over to the crystal where he sees a frightening vision of Christ on the cross and experiences the feeling of being crucified himself. All of these encounters appear to be examples of hypnotic or trance-like visions induced using crystals or a globe of water along similar lines to those in Cagliostro's Egyptian Rite.

Throughout the entries of January 1922 (*BB 7*) Jung's soul puts forward a series of complicated mystical interpretations, their meaning masked with obscure symbolism, and relates them to his relationship with his wife and Toni Wolff. She talks of the moon and sun, the masculine and feminine and the four functions, and then to fish, fishing rods and stars. She relates Jung's position in regard to these signs and states that he is out of balance (*BB 7*, p. 214). Turning to Albert Pike's *Morals and Dogma* we find that these symbols are repeatedly discussed in the lectures and relate to the Zodiac and the soul's journey, as well as the Egyptian myth of Isis, Osiris and Horus. Persian notions of the Zodiac, he says, contain the concept of the soul's ascent and descent, to and from the heavens. Moving through the first six signs, from Aries to Virgo, it is fortunate and happy, while in Libra, the seventh sign, the soul begins to be sensible of evil, regarded as the Balance. The last five signs, from Scorpio to Pisces, is where the soul enters the realm of evil and darkness. "It lost its felicity by means of the Balance", he says, "and regained it by means of the Lamb [Aries]" (Pike, 1871, p. 352). Jung's soul's reference to being out of balance and to the moon, sun and stars appears to be reminding him of the wording of this lecture that may have accompanied some form of training in Masonic astronomy.

The mention of the four functions and fish also finds its parallels in *Morals and Dogma*. Pike notes the role that the stars and constellations played in the journey of the twelve tribes of Israel through the desert. He cites the symbolism of the number four in the layout of the Hebrew camp and the four great Royal Stars, including one, Fomalhaut, meaning "in the mouth of Pisces", a brilliant star near Pisces, the constellation symbolised by two fishes (Pike, 1871, pp. 331, 332). He describes Fomalhaut as being the most malignant of signs, indicative of violence and death, and states that when the Egyptians expressed

51

anything odious or evil in their hieroglyphics, they would paint a fish. In the entry of January 7, 1922, it is noted that years later in *Aion* (1951) Jung recognised that the two fish were related to the astrological sign of Pisces and discussed it in terms of the Ages of Pisces and Aquarius, the Christ and Antichrist. His soul also states that Toni Wolff "has the calling to receive the two fish" (*BB 7*, p. 214). According to Albert Pike this would symbolise her association with the darkest position in the journey of the soul.

Now, in this entry, we learn from his soul that Wolff is to be seen as Nephthys, the sister of Isis and Osiris and that she, Jung and Emma are to form a triumvirate. In *Morals and Dogma* Pike refers to Nephthys as Nephte and describes the relationship between these divine siblings with Osiris and Nephte producing the child Anubis, whom Isis searches for and nurtures as her own protector (1871, p. 273, 345). Jung has already been told by his soul on January 4, 1922 that Toni Wolff is an emissary of the Great Mother (or Isis in ancient Egyptian terms) but that that she is being forced against her will in taking on this role and is suffering under this burden. In 1926 Wolff recognised that her own psychology was bound up with ancient Egyptian themes: "It fits like a glove", she says (*BB 7*, p. 215, n. 181). Such a statement begs the question of whether Toni Wolff was also a product of Masonic abuse and was carrying the burden of initiatory trauma just as Jung was. As Shamdasani notes, "[Wolff] was experiencing a similar stream of images … she was disorientated and in the same mess" (Jung, 2009a, p. 204; 2009b, p. 38). Could it be that just as he was the "pupille", was she the "colombe" used in an Egyptian-style ritual? And could this explain Jung's reaction to his dream of the two doves, of bringing Toni Wolff so much into his life, because he knew unconsciously that they shared a similar initiatory background?

According to his soul, the triumvirate these three individuals are to form are embodied in the word "Fandragypti", meaning pheasant of the Egyptians (*BB 7*, p. 215). This is one of the words in a series of hieroglyphics that accompanies the debased magic practices within these exotic rites revealed a few days before. "Wigalda, wigamma, widrofit fialtomari fundragypti remasse", his soul says are vaguely related to "[making] a sublime husband" (*BB 7*, p. 210). She then reminds him that he once wanted to learn Arabic (*BB 7*, p. 212). Throughout *Morals and Dogma* there are a number of Arabic words used and, in relation to astrology, Pike states: "the old libraries are full of Arabic books on this pretended science" (1871, p. 333). Pike was a gifted linguist and he states that he searched in vain in the Hebrew and Arabic for some word used in the Masonic rituals but found them to be utterly absurd and not legitimate words from these languages (1871, p. 351). It seems that the wording Jung records here has nothing to do with making a sublime husband and belongs to this category of the absurdly fantastic, created only to add to the luridly occult atmosphere of the Egyptian-style ritual that he appears to be recalling. However, the reference to the pheasant of the Egyptians, meaning the peacock, is a far more accessible symbol. In Egyptian symbolism the peacock's fan-shaped tail covered with "eyes" is associated with the all-seeing eye of Horus and, along with the mythical phoenix, is a symbol of rebirth; the phoenix was one of the symbols used in Cagliostro's Egyptian Rite (Evans, 1919, p. 15).

In January 1922 the entries record a few more occasions where Jung asks his soul for her advice about the women in his life but he finds her answers unsatisfying. On January 8 his soul urges him to talk to his wife, but he finds that difficult, saying that he shies away from people's emotions. On January 27 he asks his soul why she deprives him of sleep and she answers that his sleeplessness is a result of his own injustice and again encourages him to part with Toni Wolff, as the suffering this situation is causing is great. Acting now as the voice of his conscience, his soul is commenting on the damage his affair with Wolff is inflicting on them all. But in the following entries Jung does not address this criticism; instead, he moves to further meditations on the African dream.

At this point in *Book 7* there are now very few references to Jung's problems with women, only a handful of dreams and realisations that take up only a small space in the entries. One of these realisations concerns a dream from December 24, 1923. This is where he interprets the dream as dealing with the death of the anima in response to the death of his mother. He describes his decision to go with the anima as misguided with bad results, which seemingly means his choice to maintain his affair with Toni Wolff. However, in this entry he notes that his anima has fallen silent since the death of his mother and he finds this meaningful, but does not explain why he sees it this way. A further dream, on November 20/21,1926 includes the wording "I play childish games with a few women" (*BB* 7, p. 237), while on December 3/4 of that year Toni Wolff appears in a dream. But neither of these dreams is very revealing in regard to his relationships with women.

We do know that Jung regarded his mother, Emilie Preiswerk Jung, as having a second personality like himself, an uncanny one "like a priestess in a bear's cage" which emerged during the night hours, and that she encouraged Jung's interest in the occult (1963, pp. 59–60). When in this state she would say unexpected things to him that would leave him stunned to the core of his being. But without more details about his actual interactions with his mother it would be difficult to say whether her personality was also introjected into his psyche in a way that would manifest in the types of conversations with his soul throughout the *Black Books*. It is quite possible, though, that his mother may have undergone early traumas associated with the occult that rendered her psyche split in similar ways to her son's.

Jung is now entering a phase where his entries are becoming shorter and more infrequent and contain more dreams than previously. He also records the deaths of friends and patients in the last journal and on May 23, 1927 he writes of a dream about Emma and cancer, which turns out to be prophetic, as it was the very condition from which his wife eventually died. But what makes this dream difficult for Jung is that his soul challenges him by suggesting that he wished for his wife's death, producing an immediate response of outrage. "You gallows bird, stop your monkey chatter", he protests, but then concedes that he has said this himself. He then ponders whether his marriage is hopeless and decides that he must continue to suffer it, "as one who bears an incurable disease" (*BB* 7, p. 243).

Is this some recognition that his need for polygamy is, in fact, an incurable illness? Given the argument here, is it one of the long-term sequelae of the multiple injuries to the soul that the initiatory process has produced during his youth? And is he not following the advice of the initiatory doctor, to look to polygamy as a balm as women know how to heal sick children?

So, what is Jung's soul and what role does it play? His soul is definitely not one thing but something comprised of multiple parts and, as we have seen in this chapter, its representation changes throughout the course of his journal entries. It first appears in the form of a girl child, a puzzling concept for Jung, but one that might relate to his first encounters with the child who was to become his wife. This girl child visits him in his dreams and is comforting and reassuring, presenting his soul in a positive light. She then turns into the more clichéd notion of the dove, but then splits into two, a boy dove and a girl dove, which, as we have seen, is closely related to the presence of children in Cagliostro's Egyptian Rite. It suggests that the dream is encouraging him to remember an early initiatory experience along these lines. Later, Jung is able to make psychological sense of the division into the two doves as the split between the part of himself that suffered the "crucifixion" and the part that flew into dissociative bliss in order to escape the trauma. This leaves him with a deep feeling of bitterness towards the part of him which escapes. We then see a black-haired girl child depicted in a tableau amongst religious figures that this argument suggests may be a memory of an initiatory scenario. This black-haired girl transforms into Salome, the femme fatale of the Christian story, whom he is told is his own soul, another initiatory trick. Salome's character as dark anima is then projected onto Toni Wolff. But Salome recedes into the background and the female shade who urges him to eat the liver of a dead child comes forward as his soul's representative, which Jung himself recognises as a theatrical trick. After acknowledging that he may be a sick child who is turning to women for comfort, his soul as evil temptress now morphs into a more positive maternal figure, promising a more constructive relationship with his anima.

These various female figures merge into an overall representation of his soul as female, becoming both his adviser and manipulator, imparting confusing metaphysical arguments designed to endlessly frustrate him, but also reminding him to face his memories and eventually to alter his attitude to his marriage. She becomes part conscience, part internal critic, and the part trying to urge him to look more closely at and connect with his child or youth selves, which he never fully achieves in the course of the journals. While giving enormous time and energy to his conversations with her, allowing her to speak voluminously, he rarely gives his child or youth self a voice so that he can tell *his* stories and his perception of what has occurred. On one of these occasions, towards the end of *Book 7*, his soul introduces him to a divine youth who speaks to him and wants Jung to tell him who he is, but Jung cannot relate to him. This episode will be discussed in Chapter Five.

Twenty years after these entries Jung would write about the soul and the concept of multiplicity in the psyche, turning to the terminology of consciousness and unconsciousness, which was better suited to the language of his profession. In a discussion of *double consciousness*, a phenomenon debated amongst his colleagues, he writes:

> This is an age-old experience of mankind which is reflected in the universal supposition of a plurality of souls in one and the same individual. As the plurality of psychic components at the primitive level shows, the original state is one in which the psychic processes are very loosely knit and by no means form a self-contained unity. Moreover, psychiatric experience indicates that it often takes only a little to shatter the unity of consciousness so laboriously built up in the course of development and to resolve it back into its original elements (Jung, 1947/2001, p. 71).

The shattering of the psyche into many parts appears to be one of the consequences and even aims of the initiatory abuses. Enacted on a child or youth, where a sense of self-contained unity is by no means yet established, the multiple psychological attacks on the child's understanding of reality are bound to fragment his sense of self into myriad forms. In this same publication from 1947 Jung then puts forward a tantalising subtitle, "The Unconscious as Multiple Consciousness", promising further answers to the phenomenon of multiplicity in the psyche. However, this is where he launches into an extensive discussion of alchemy, the direction he took in his research after *Book 7*, leading to a further layer of his work that will not be addressed here. Remaining with the content of the *Black Books* this study will now turn to the various belief systems and their accompanying gods that appear in his active imaginations and in further discussions he has with his inner parts.

Notes

1 In *The Red Book* there is, however, a note inserted by the editors citing this statement in *Book 3* (Jung, 2009a, p. 290, n. 149: 2009b, p. 322).

2 For those interested in the scientific terminology, the brain areas involved are the medial temporal and frontal lobes, posterior cingulate, retrosplenial cortex, and lateral parietal and temporal areas (Schacter et al, 2012, p. 677).

3 The "old brain", sometimes known as the 'reptilian brain' is the part of the brain that develops in utero. Along with the limbic system, which develops in early childhood, these two brain areas are engaged when confronted with a threat to initiate the fight or flight response. Van der Kolk describes these two areas working together as the "emotional brain" which in situations of danger has "first dibs on interpreting incoming information" before the analytical mind comes into play (van der Kolk, 2014, p. 61).

4 The use of capital letters in FANDRAGYPTI is Jung's.

3

"In which underworld am I?" *(BB 2, p. 159)*

In his journal entry for November 26, 1913, in a statement not included in *Liber Novus*, Jung asks: "In which underworld am I? It is dark and black as death!" (*BB 2*, p. 159). Over the previous four nights he had found himself groping in the dark on a path that was leading him on an internal journey; it was as if he was wandering blindfolded into a strange kind of underworld. As the journey unfolded, he became aware that this underworld bore many similarities to the myths, belief systems and cult practices of ancient and classical civilisations, as well as the medieval world. Prior to beginning the record of his active imaginations in the *Black Books* Jung had been reading scholarly works on mythology, folklore, ancient religions and philosophy, a fascination that had begun in his youth, and these themes had culminated in his publication of *Transformations and Symbols of the Libido* in 1912 (*BB 1*; 1963/2019). But the context in which he frames these themes in his journals is different: it is often highly charged with intense emotions of anger, outrage, confusion and terror, accompanied, in the early stages, by suicidal ideation. This suggests that the traditions he is describing have impacted him on a deeply emotional level and are not the product of disinterested scholarship, but something else. The studies here argue that these intense states, coupled with the similarity between his fantasies and Masonic rites, suggest that Jung appears to have undergone a complex initiatory process in childhood and/or youth incorporating spurious versions of the Masonic rituals (Brunet, 2019). This chapter will demonstrate that Jung's search to try to understand the cult beliefs of the ancient world were driven by his long-forgotten initiatory experiences and their accompanying teachings.

Children born into these cult-like contexts can be selected quite early for particular roles and vocations. In a questionnaire for survivors of various organised and non-satanic ritual abuse, including Masonic abuse, the interviewees were asked if they remembered being taught explicitly about the beliefs of their abusers (Scott, 2001, pp. 86–89). Some described classes where religious lessons took place, where they would copy the teachings out or learn them by rote. From the responses to this survey, it appeared that this formal teaching took place fairly early in childhood as many of the descriptions were childlike and lacked theological sophistication. Scott concludes that in the cases she examined the sole purpose of using these religious themes was to frighten the children. However, for a child who is selected for a leadership position, such as we may be looking at in Jung's case, a deeper knowledge of the cult's belief systems would be required. It is interesting that Murray Stein, in an interview about *The Red Book* in 2010, made the observation that Jung's fantasies initially looked like "a regression to Sunday School", but then transformed into more complex philosophical themes as they progressed (cited in Henderson, 2010, p. 95).

Being taken repeatedly to "the realm of the gods" can be part of the religious training in ritual abuse (Miller, 2012, pp. 66, 83–84). A survivor of these secret cult practices, Trish Fotheringham, underwent a range of abuses right throughout her childhood in the 1960s and 1970s. At the age of 10 and 11 this incorporated being taken to the realm of the gods through a combination of hypnosis, holographic projections, movies and scenarios acted out by actors on a stage. This training was to teach her to preach at public events and to "speak the words of the gods", leading her towards helping the "great leader" and his followers to save the world, which even at this age, she rebelled against (Fotheringham, 2008, p. 514). Throughout the *Black Books* Jung is repeatedly taken into this realm where he is forced to incorporate the gods he meets into his psyche as inner parts or alter personalities.

By focusing on Jung's active imaginations in the *Black Books,* and in particular on the material that was not included in *Liber Novus*, this chapter will examine the various beliefs that accompany the initiatory scenarios or appear in Jung's conversations with his inner parts. Examining the philosophical themes encountered in the journals as well as the different gods that Jung confronts, it will explore the ways in which these ancient traditions were used to contribute to the trauma, pain and confusion of his inner journey. It will demonstrate that the framing of these philosophical discussions often mirrors similar discussions throughout Albert Pike's *Morals and Dogma* (1871), a handbook for members of the Ancient and Accepted Scottish Rite (AASR), which the previous study found to be one of the Masonic rites most frequently associated with Jung's active imaginations. Throughout the discussion it will trace Jung's developing understanding of the true nature of these experiences, which becomes more apparent in the additional material found in the *Black Books*.

"... and I groped along my path." (*BB 2*, p. 149)

In the original manuscript of Jung's first journal there is an undated paragraph facing the first entry. This paragraph, which was not included in *Liber Novus*, translates as: "A huge task lay before me – I saw its enormous size – and its value and meaning escaped me. I got into the dark, and I groped along my path. That path led inward and downward" (*BB 2*, p. 149). The concept of groping in the dark appears again on December 22, 1913 (*BB 2*) where he describes feeling his way from stone to stone and contemplates the need to let go of all previous knowledge in order to enter this world of darkness in poverty and humility. This section of the entry, comprised of four paragraphs, is not reproduced in *Liber Novus*.

The expression "groping in the dark" to represent a search for meaning is commonly used to describe the initiate in the first degree of Freemasonry where he is known as the Entered Apprentice. All Masons must undergo this ritual. Walter Wilmshurst (1932/2008) was an English Freemason and contemporary of Jung's and from a reading of his Masonic writings it is clear that he celebrates the legitimate rituals of Freemasonry and spurns any spurious use of the rites. Wilmshurst wrote a manual of instruction for Masons who had recently completed their first degree in which he outlines the general principles and various stages of initiation. The intention of this initiatory process, he says, is to symbolise the transformation of the candidate's mind and soul from his state of darkness, called the Hall of Ignorance, where he is groping about for light and wisdom, leading to an expanded state of spiritual consciousness

(Wilmshurst,1932/2008, Part 1:3). Whatever the candidate's prior learning, he says, either academic, scientific or philosophical there is something much more for him to learn. The candidate, at this stage is called a child. Such a description is not dissimilar to Jung's sense that there is some huge task ahead of him and that his scientific and philosophical knowledge is of no use on this path. At the beginning of *Black Book 3,* for example, there is a paragraph not included in *Liber Novus* where he describes how he has been led away from his firm foundation in science while on this "truly hard way", where he says: "I feel that a large chunk of science has broken off" (*BB 3*, p. 99).

Wilmshurst's manual then explains that the initiatory path will involve a spiritual adventure and voyage of the mind where the candidate will undergo a gradual transformation and renewal of his mind and outlook, but this will not involve doing any violence towards himself. He describes the modern ritual as peaceful and free of commotion, but the dangers encountered in the rites of the ancient Mysteries, he says, would have been far more realistic and frightening, putting a candidate through severe trials to test his mental stability and moral fitness (Wilmshurst, 1932/2008, Part 1:3).

By the end of his first journal Jung has already recorded a series of fantasies involving an atmosphere of cruel mockery and scornful laughter as well as excruciating ordeals, suggesting that his initiatory path is more akin to that of the ancient Mysteries and to a more abusive version of initiation than the official rituals of modern Freemasonry. On November 28, 1913 (*BB 2*) he finds himself wandering aimlessly in a desert, experiencing it intensely with all the accompanying bodily sensations. Then, on December 12 he feels he is falling into a cave where he hears the noise of a thousand voices and sees a thousand serpents lining the walls. This is followed by a journey to Hell, "all frightfully muddled" and the feeling of being attacked by magical beings leading him to feel as if a "hellish magic" has changed him into a monstrous animal (*BB 2*, p. 171). In a statement not included in *Liber Novus* he asks: "Can you hear the uproar of outrage in me?" (*BB 2,* p. 172). This is not the response of a disinterested scholar but the deepest expression of raw feeling. Two nights later he dreams that he has murdered the hero Siegfried, leading him to thoughts of suicide. The previous study identified the plots of many of these fantasies to be closely resembling those of specific rituals from the AASR (Brunet, 2019). It also argues that the practice of hypnosis may account for the intensity and strange unreality of these initiatory scenarios.

In Albert Pike's *Morals and Dogma* there is a discussion of the Eleusinian Mysteries in which he describes initiation as a mystical death, involving pain, terror and shock, aimed at producing an altered state of consciousness in the candidates. He also uses the concept of groping in the dark:

> The first scene was in the προναος, or outer court of the sacred enclosure, where amidst utter darkness ... the candidates were overawed with terrific sounds and noises, while they painfully groped their way, as in the gloomy cavern of the soul's sublunar migration; a scene justly compared to the passage of the Valley of the Shadow of Death. For by the immutable law exemplified in the trials of Psyche, man must pass through the terrors of the under-world, before he can reach the height of Heaven (Pike, 1871, p. 284).

So why is it that Jung chose not to use the expression "groping in the dark" in *Liber Novus*, instead replacing the initial paragraph facing the first entry with a more elaborate and sermon-like entry entitled "The Way of What is to Come"? It appears that in his first journal entries he has already begun to make connections, possibly based on his reading, that these fantasies are describing some kind of initiatory path, although one that he is struggling to identify. In the first few days, for example, he recognises that the words he is hearing are not his own. In a statement not included in *Liber Primus*, he says: "It is not even my <u>language</u> that ~~flows~~ speaks through my pen" (*BB 2*, p. 155);[1] while on December 20 he says how astonished he is that his soul is wanting him to write down all these words, as they deal with such secrets and riddles (*BB 2*, p. 179). The underworld he is in seems like meaningless nonsense and feels like torture, governed by "cowardly ear-whisperers" who are contaminating him with their poison (*BB 2*, p. 153). But despite these torturous experiences, and even his own inner resistance, Jung nevertheless yearns to understand what lies behind these fantasies and by December 11 he describes how impatience is overwhelming him and he wants to know what this is all about.

His entry of December 21, 1913 (*BB 2*) may provide a clue. It was transferred to *Liber Primus* as "Mysterium Encounter" and describes Jung's initial meeting with the Old Testament prophet Elijah and the beautiful, but evil, New Testament Salome. Most of the journal entry matches the final version but there are a few added comments in the journal that cast a new light onto Jung's experience of this encounter. The previous study discussed "Mysterium Encounter" as an allegorical mystery play with the scenic qualities of a Masonic Tracing Board (Brunet, 2019, p. 41). It suggests that Jung appears to have been present at a Masonic-style initiation where he meets two individuals dressed as these biblical characters and is told a confusing narrative about their relationship, one contrary to the accepted Christian meaning of their roles in biblical history. The discussion notes that there are indications of trauma in this entry and the sense that Jung is describing the fantasy from the perspective of a child. It also notes that Jung avoids addressing the emotional depths of this encounter, preferring to intellectualise some of the themes it represents.

In the journal, however, he makes a few comments that imply that he may have come to a dreadful realisation, one which he chooses not to share in the final version. He has been having fear-filled sleepless nights leading up to this fantasy and the entry contains several comments in parentheses which demonstrate his fears. He first describes a descent into the depths, accompanied by a nauseous feeling, implying that something deeply disturbing may be emerging from the unconscious. Then, an old man dressed in an Oriental robe appears, accompanied by a black serpent. In parentheses Jung states: "(I obey– no resistance)" (*BB 2*, p. 179). A young maiden follows and she takes Jung's hand, entering a house where he sees a crystal which radiates colours that entirely surround him. But with this there is another parenthetical statement: "(Now it gets difficult)". He describes images within these colours: Eve, the tree and serpent, along with Odysseus and his crew aboard their famous ship, and then a further parenthetical statement: "(frightful–but it must be)". A poster picture of an old man with a child appears and his comment is "(disgusting– survived)". The entry then proceeds with the discussion between Jung, Elijah and Salome that appears in the final version and where Jung struggles with the riddle that these two figures propose.

Jung had already written to Freud in 1907 revealing that he was a victim of sexual assault in his boyhood (Freud, Jung & McGuire, 1974, pp. 94–95), but here, six years later, he seems to be realising, with feelings of disgust, that he has survived a fearful encounter in a ritual setting, possibly with a man dressed as the biblical Elijah. The story of Elijah and the child is found in 1 Kings 17: 21–24. During a period of drought Elijah is sent by God to a widow where he performs a miracle, creating more than enough food for the household. He then heals the woman's gravely ill son who was no longer breathing. He takes the child from her arms and carries the boy to a bed; there "he stretched himself upon the child three times", praying to the Lord until "the soul of the child came into him again, and he revived". In Masonry "the widow's son" is a euphemism for a Freemason (Mackey, 1882, p. 202), based on the fact that Hiram, the architect of Solomon's Temple, was the son of a widow of the tribe of Naphtali (1 Kings vii, 14). Coupled with the reference to the Odyssey in Jung's fantasy, a well-known symbol of initiation, the story of Elijah and the child could be read allegorically, in Masonic terms, as a symbol of the death and rebirth of the initiate. However, Jung's spontaneous expressions of fright and disgust suggest a more disturbing scenario: a traumatic encounter, one which he survived, that was seemingly of a sexual nature or at least the semblance of it.

The entry of the previous evening, December 20, 1913, contains a grandiose speech based on Christ's parable of the mustard seed and is directed to the birth of the "miraculous child", but the language used is a shocking parody of Christ's message and is full of mockery and degradation. It appears to have been spoken by his initiators (Brunet, 2019, pp. 38–39). Jung transferred it to "The Conception of the God" in *Liber Primus* and attributed it to the spirit of the depths. But there are several paragraphs in the journal entry that are not included in the final version where the language used matches the feelings of disgust described above. Two expressions, "ice-cold hands of steel murderously grasp after you" and "one would like to slobber over you in heat" convey decidedly disturbing connotations (*BB 2*, p. 177). At the beginning of this entry Jung appears to be piecing together both the images he is seeing and the words he is hearing in these fantasies, and wonders whether he should remain in this new world as "semi-unrealities [develop] into horrible realities" (*BB 2*, p. 176). Such a statement suggests that he was becoming aware of some

64

traumatic encounter in childhood, seemingly of a sexual nature, and that these two fantasies seem to be confirming his feelings.

The first four paragraphs of the entry of December 22 are not included in *Liber Novus*. Here he finds himself entering a gate and groping in the dark. A set of instructions defines the attitude that he must take on this path: former value judgments and knowledge, along with any accompanying arrogance, must be shed and he must enter "poor, pathetic, humble [and] ignorant" (*BB 2*, p. 185). He must look at what he sees without desire or passion and turn all anger against himself, focusing only on hope as his support.

Such a description is similar to that provided by Wilmshurst in his manual for newly initiated Masons. He cites a prayer used by Freemasons, beginning, "from the unreal lead me to the Real" (Wilmshurst, 1932/2008, Introduction), not unlike Jung's statement two nights previously, although Jung's experience of the Real is entirely repulsive. Wilmshurst's exhortation for the candidate to put aside all previous knowledge, as noted earlier, matches Jung's wording in this entry, while the concept of the newly initiated Masonic candidate ignorantly groping in the dark is not unlike Jung's description of his movements in this entry. However, the exhortation in Jung's fantasy to turn all anger against himself is not included in Wilmshurst's manual. This implies that the wording he is recording, along with the already harsh initiatory scenarios, are not those of a sanctioned version of Freemasonry but something far more damaging, involving undue physical and psychological violence towards him, accompanied by self-castigation.

By this stage Jung seems to be becoming aware of the possibility that he has been initiated in a manner not dissimilar to that used in the initiatory rites of the ancient world. In this entry he reveals that he knows that these fantasies involve mystery plays: "The mystery play is delicate as air and thin smoke", he writes, suggesting how difficult it is to grasp (*BB 2*, p. 185). Even in the first two months of recording them in his journals Jung already seems to know that his active imaginations are describing mystery plays, similar to, though not the same as those of the ancient Mysteries. However, at this point he refrains from conveying this realisation in *Liber Primus*.

On Christmas Day, 1913 he records a longer entry, which is transferred to "Resolution", the last entry of *Liber Primus*. It begins with a paragraph that is not included in the final version, which contains a reference to a secret that is to be kept "virginally" (*BB 2*, p. 190). Given the implications in the previous entry this secret may be read in several ways: that initiatory secrets in general must never be shared with outsiders; that he must never share his own personal initiatory experience or even admit it to himself; or, if it actually was a sexual encounter in a ritual context, that there was no actual rape involved. Nevertheless, the experience, when being relived, was enough to make him feel terrible fear and disgust. In the rest of the entry he meets the prophet again and is shown various images: a black and a white serpent engaged in battle and a temple of the sun where he meets a dwarf who calls himself Mime. He is then directed to go and look at a crystal where he sees further images, including a child holding two serpents. He describes the strangeness of this experience and the sense that he was hallucinating and wonders if he really was meeting Elijah and Mime. He says he has doubts about what this really is, but does not mention this in *Liber Novus*. This experience seems to be another example of a trance-like state induced through crystal-gazing.

The final part of this entry describes a torturous bodily sensation where he takes the position of the crucified Christ, with the serpent coiled around his body, mentioned in the previous chapter. Here Salome tells him that he *is* Christ and lays at his feet in rapturous devotion. The extra sentences in the journal, where he mentions the crystal, convey his doubts about the reality of this visionary experience, and that it may be a hallucination of some sort, but he nevertheless feels a sense of completion. Even so, Jung's experience of imitating the crucified Christ meant an excruciating descent into near madness, only forestalled by his research into the Mithraic Mysteries. Included in the last chapter in *Liber Primus*, "Resolution", is a reference to a seminar Jung gave twelve years later where he discusses this vision, stating that he had a peculiar feeling of being put through such an initiation and identifies the extensive role of Mithraism in its symbolism (Jung, 2009a, p. 252, n. 211; 2009b, p. 197). His further comments relate these experiences to the ancient Mysteries but he makes no connection to modern practices, such as the Masonic rites being identified in these studies.[2]

A paragraph inserted into *Liber Novus* that does not appear in the *Black Books* may tell us more about the context in which Jung's terrifying initiatory ordeals may be taking place. In the commentary for "Splitting of the Spirit" his final paragraph states:

> Everything that becomes too old becomes evil, the same is true of your highest. Learn from the suffering of the crucified God that one can also betray and crucify a God, namely the God of the old year. If a God ceases being the way of life, he must fall secretly. The God becomes sick if he oversteps the height of the zenith (Jung, 2009a, p. 241; 2009b, p. 160).

In the *Draft* version Jung had added "this is what the ancients taught us" (2009a, p. 241, n. 109; 2009b, p. 160). While this could refer to his reading about the ancient religions, it might also be another example of language that was spoken in the Masonic training. Given the argument here, one wonders whether "the ancients" might refer to the elders conducting the initiatory rituals that Jung is recalling and that this was one of the teachings that were included. For this reason, it needs to be read in terms of the complex relationship between Christianity and Continental Freemasonry in the 19th century.

As Guy Liagre notes, in Switzerland at the beginning of the 19th century Freemasonry and Protestantism were intertwined and the L'Union des Coeurs Masonic lodge in Geneva was at the centre of a Protestant religious awakening that incorporated a new form of mystic-theosophist Freemasonry (2014, p. 168). In this context Bible societies in Switzerland were founded with the help of pastors and their Masonic lodges. At the same time the Swiss lodges had been placed under the aegis of the Grand Orient de France, considered the mother lodge of Continental Masonry, from 1801. In France Protestants and Freemasons had a common enemy, the Roman-Catholic Church, but after the European Revolutions of 1848 more of the Continental lodges became focused on republican ideals and the complete secularisation of society, and were more anti-religious generally. In 1878 the Grand Orient agreed to delete all references to the Bible and any religious dogma from their rituals. This led to a rupture between the French lodges and the Anglo-American and some of the German lodges, placing the Grand Lodge of Switzerland in an awkward position due to its friendly relations with the Grand Orient de France (Gruber, 1913, p. 774).

It is possible that in Swiss Freemasonry this mixed position towards Christianity may be what lies behind Jung's final paragraph in "Splitting of the Spirit" and the confusing references to Christian themes in his fantasies. On the one hand, Freemasonry and Protestantism had co-habited well, but on the other, the various rites used within the Swiss lodges might have expressed different views. A proclamation made in 1902 by Senator Delpech, the president of the Grand Orient de France, demonstrates a position similar to that expressed in Jung's concluding paragraph cited above. It states:

> The triumph of the Galilean has lasted twenty centuries. But now he dies in his turn. The mysterious voice announcing (to Julian the Apostate) the death of Pan, today announces the death of the imposter God who promised an era of justice and peace to those who believe in him. The illusion has lasted a long time. The mendacious God is now disappearing in his turn; he passes away to join in the dust of ages the divinities of India, Egypt, Greece, and Rome, who saw so many creatures prostrate before their altars. Bro. Masons, we rejoice to state that we are not without our share in this overthrow of the false prophets. The Romish Church, founded on the Galilean myth, began to decay rapidly from the very day on which the Masonic Association was established (cited in Gruber, 1913, p. 782).

The author who cited this speech was Hermann Gruber (1851–1930), a German Jesuit and Masonic scholar whose position in the opposite camp undoubtedly influenced his research. However, the similarity between Jung's final paragraph in "Splitting of the Spirit" and this one should not go unnoticed. As Gruber observes, the claims made by the Grand Orient were highly exaggerated but he does state that the Grand Lodge Alpina of Switzerland was one of the allies of the Grand Orient in this undertaking. Jung's grandfather was elected Grand Master of the Grand Lodge Alpina in 1850 (Bair, 2004, p. 12), the period directly after the 1848 revolutions when this shift in sentiments began, suggesting that such attitudes might lie behind some of the confusing comments around Christianity in Jung's active imaginations. However, in

Jung's entries the Christ does not disappear altogether but his role gradually alters to allow the introduction of new gods.

"All this is Mithraic symbolism from beginning to end."

(Jung 2009a, p. 252, n. 211).

By 1925 Jung had looked back on his active imaginations and realised that the cult of Mithras, celebrated amongst the Roman legions, had played a major role in them. The ordeals of the ancient mystery cults were intended to produce altered states of consciousness resulting in an experience of intense bliss, mystical light, or an overwhelming sense of the Divine. But the methods used often involved pain, fear, humiliation and exhaustion. In a warrior context, scenes of brutality and the fear of imminent death could result in a soldier experiencing a blissful state of release and a sense of immortality. Ancient warrior cults like the one dedicated to Mithras sought to reproduce these experiences in a ritual setting, while beliefs in the transmigration of the soul, or reincarnation, encouraged the soldiers to sacrifice themselves in battle (Malcolmson, 1999, p. 57; Green, 1992, p. 86). Modern Masonry adopted Mithraic themes into its teachings and may have given rise to speculation about its secret practices. One example of this is a comment made by the Masonic author M. P. Hall in which he states that in this cult: "children of the male sex were initiated long before they reached maturity" (1928/2004, p. 51). Whether Hall's comment was based on fact or not, the belief amongst the fraternity that boys might have been initiated into Mithraism may be of significance in terms of Jung's experience and the "irregular" use of Masonic rites.

The characteristics of the sun god Mithras and of the settings and doctrines of this cult appear throughout *Liber Novus* and many of these are discussed in the previous study (Brunet, 2019). In the final part, *Scrutinies*, where the religious or philosophical underpinnings of the initiations are being explained, Jung is confronted with the devastating results of his accumulated initiations: he has been led to believe that he has made a series of choices to rebirth a new god into his soul. On December 13, 1915 (*BB 5*), he records a conversation with a female shade where he questions her about the meaning of various symbols and concepts encountered on this path. But his questions express intense anxiety, confusion and outrage at the methods used to inculcate these new beliefs. She answers him sternly: "Christian shrouds have fallen ... Let your feelings whimper like puppies. The ears on high are deaf ... there is only one road, the military road of the Godhead" (*BB 5*, p. 252). In other words, she is saying that his Christian beliefs, with their concern for the more tender feelings, have been undermined throughout these initiations and incorporated into the much harsher belief system of Mithraism.

In *Books 6* and *7*, in those entries not used in *Liber Novus*, Mithraic themes re-emerge on several occasions, particularly around Christmas time. According to the myth, Mithras was born during the winter solstice, on December 25, the same day as Christ's birth, so it is not surprising that Jung's thoughts might turn in this direction during the festive season. His reveries, though, are not filled with joy but with pain, horror and the deepest regret. On Christmas Eve 1916 he writes:

> Our Lord was born on this night ... The fire broke out of the old earth. Its innards were affronted. The son of the fire went away and reached the light and the light went pale ... a new sun broke away from the flaming body of the primordial mother. A dragon crept up and spat out the new sun ... Oh abyss of wisest folly! Oh heaven's mountain of foolish wisdom! You light that climbs higher, don't snatch us up! ... You iron of the innermost, of the primordial and firm, do not draw us down! ... I melted once, I burned once. I have now become solid (*BB 6*, p. 271).

What is different for Jung is that there is now a new sun, a new god in the heavens for him. The day when Christ was born has now become Natalis Solis Invicti, the birth of the Unconquered Sun, a celebration of the birth of Mithras; and the festive season is now filled with reminders of the excruciating process that smelted his psyche into a new form through a series of terrifying and traumatic initiations. In terms of the psychological process of alter formation it seems that whenever Jung cites the emergence of a new sun it appears to signify the painful birth of a new alter personality.

It is not surprising, then, that further reminders of this shift might return around the Christmas/New Year period. As the gaps between his journal entries gradually widen, he writes of disturbing dreams around this time of year. On December 30, 1921 (*BB 7*) such dreams are filled with overwhelming fear and he asks his soul what is going on. On Christmas Day 1922 he writes of similar dreams disturbing his sleep and on December 24, 1923 after a hiatus of eleven months, he records another dream. He first illustrates it in a sketch, showing a frog-headed figure in a cartouche, surrounded by smaller figures. Then on Christmas Day he explains the dream's narrative: it takes place when he is on military service in a wood in Canton Zürich where there are Roman antiquities. Here, he comes to a crossroads where he sees a large stone frog or toad without a head and a boy with a toad's head, as well as two busts with anchors hammered into their heart region, one of a Roman man and one from 1640, along with mummified corpses. A woman appears, who is both dead and alive and he recognises her as a member of the nobility.

Jung provides no analysis of this dream at the time and only comments on it three years later, on December 16, 1926 (*BB 7*), in a short entry where he regards it as dealing with the death of the anima as a response to the death of his mother. But he feels that his attempt to go to the anima has not worked well; he calls it misguided, producing bad results, and she has now fallen silent. However, this dream could also be read in terms of the Mithraic themes that permeate his active imaginations. Compulsory military service was, and still is, required of young men in Switzerland and Jung participated in his share of these training missions, so the dream's context is close to reality. Set in an ancient Roman site it suggests a Mithraic connection, while the Roman bust with the anchor hammered into its heart implies that the beliefs of this cult, or at least a modern version of it, have been brutally implanted into his own heart. The Toad God or God of the Frogs appears in the "Seven Sermons to the Dead", where it is also known as Abraxas. The term Abraxas first appears in the writings of the early Christian Gnostic, Basilides, whom Jung considers to be the author of the Seven Sermons (2009a, p. 346, n. 81; 2009b, p. 508, n. 83).

Basilides, Abraxas and the role of the Mithraic cult all appear throughout Pike's *Morals and Dogma*. Even in the first chapter, aimed at the newly initiated Apprentice of the First Degree, there is a basic outline of the Mithraic Mysteries, describing Mithras as a Sun-God and noting its seven degrees based on the seven planets and its central doctrine of the transmigration of the soul, symbolised by a ladder of seven steps. In this same lecture Pike also introduces Philo Judaeus (1871, p. 12), who is mentioned in Jung's fantasies in *Book 3*, to be discussed shortly. In a later lecture Pike talks of the level of cruelty in the trials of this cult and the fact that they were banned by the Emperor Hadrian, but then were re-introduced by the emperors Commodus and Constantine and then spread throughout the Roman Empire (1871, pp. 278, 304–305). This early mention of Mithraic themes in the Masonic initiatory path aligns with Jung's sense that even in his initial fantasies there was already an indication of the Mithraic nature of their symbolism. Pike then introduces Basilides' theory of the attributes of the Deity and the mystic word Abraxas, designating God as represented in 365 manifestations in his lecture for the 17th Degree or Knight of the East and West and expands on this in the lecture accompanying the 26th Degree (1871, pp. 197, 397–398). A study of Mithraic worship by C. W. King in 1887, when Jung would have been twelve years old, also identifies the continuing influence of Mithraism and its relationship to Freemasonry. He states:

> with their penances, and tests of the courage of the neophyte, [the Mithraica] may be said to have been maintained by an unbroken tradition through the secret societies of the Middle Ages, then by the Rosicrucians, down to that faint reflex of the latter, the Freemasonry of our own times (King, 1887, pp. 116–117).

As we have seen in *Book 2*, Jung admits that what he was writing was not even his own words and in the Seven Sermons he affirms this by stating that the sermons are written by Basilides and not by himself. The question is: is Jung unconsciously repeating a series of lectures based on Pike's *Morals and Dogma*?

The frog-headed god in Jung's dream has an older lineage in ancient Egypt, which may have further bearing on the argument that we could be looking at initiatory themes in this dream. Heqet was the Egyptian goddess of fertility, represented in the form of a frog, a symbol of the fecundity of the Nile. She appears in the Osiris myth where she breathes life into the new body of Horus and was the wife of Khnum, who was depicted at his potter's wheel fashioning a child figure (Wilkinson, 2003, p. 229). This goddess was invoked for the protection of mother and child during physical birth, but she was also associated with rebirth or resurrection, as well as the underworld, suggesting the concept of remaking the psyche of a young person through initiation. Here, we are reminded of modern fables concerning the "making" of a boy such as the story of *Pinocchio* by the Italian Freemason Carlo Collodi (1883; Hamill & Gilbert, 2004, p. 198).

The location of Jung's dream at a crossroads is also significant in terms of initiation. In the Greek Mysteries Hecate was known as the goddess of the crossroads. But ancient scholars and more recent ones have suggested that the Egyptian goddess Heqet (Hkt or Hqt) was the source of the Greek Hecate (Bernal, 2008, p. 133). Here, it is noted that the crone goddess Hecate was central to the Eleusinian Mysteries and that there is one clue that she had a connection with Heqet in Aristophanes' play, *The Frogs*, a parody of Eleusinian initiations. Heqet is not mentioned in Pike's *Morals and Dogma*, but Hecate is; she appears in his description of the initiation rites of the Eleusinian Mysteries in his lecture for the 24th Degree or Prince of the Tabernacle (1871, p. 311).

In Jung's dream then, his drawing of the toad-headed figure in a cartouche tells us we are in the Egyptian underworld, but the fact that he encounters it at a crossroads may indicate that this dream is also associated with the Greek underworld. The transposition of the toad's head to the boy would then signify Jung's initiatory transformation where he has been made to believe that he has taken on the form of an ancient god. The mummified corpses, another reference to Egypt, could signify the many ritual deaths he has undergone in order to achieve this status. In some earlier Masonic rituals the candidate is made to look like a mummy. Henry Melville describes a section of a Royal Arch initiation where: "The aspirant at this time receives a blow on his forehead, and is suddenly wrapped in a winding sheet, like an Egyptian mummy, and sinks backwards into a sarcophagus or coffin" (1864, p. 7). In a vision recorded in January 27, 1922 Jung sees a gloomy image of "a man in a white robe with a black face, like a mummy" and his soul tells him that it is an image of himself (*BB 7*, p. 220). In my own case, in an initiatory scenario in a Masonic lodge at the age of seven, I was loosely wrapped in wide strips of bandaging like a mummy (Brunet, 2007, p. 261). From these comments, it seems that Jung might have undergone something similar to my own experience.

There are other symbols in this dream, which Jung has sketched, that connote other themes: a symbol of a cross in a circle appears four times. This symbol was given prominence in his painting for "The Three Prophesies" in *Liber Secundus,* where it is depicted in brilliant red and gold. While it is an ancient sun symbol, the previous study also identified it as a reference to the Templar degrees in the Scottish Rite and the Order of the Red Cross, a grade within the Masonic Order of Knights Templar (Bogdan, 2007, pp. 91–92; Harwood, 2006, p. 69; Brunet, 2019, p. 124). Knightly themes appear throughout *Liber Novus* and in Continental Freemasonry they are ubiquitous. The second bust in Jung's dream is from 1640 and this date is mentioned by Albert Mackey, where he notes that an edition of a history of the crusades was published in London in that year (Mackey, n.d./2019, "Guglielmus Tyrius"). It was originally written by the medieval historian and archbishop of Tyre, Guglielmus Tyrius (c. 1130–1186) and contains many references to the Knights Templar. It is possible that Jung might have come across such an edition or that his dream is recalling a reference to it from the initiatory lectures. So, besides Egyptian, Greek and Roman themes being represented in this seemingly simple dream, Jung is also being reminded of the most famous of the medieval warriors, the crusading knights.

The final element of the dream involves a woman, whom he recognises as a member of the nobility and who is both dead and alive. This could be referring to the goddess Heqet or Hecate, from cultures long dead, but who are still "alive" in these rituals. In the drawing there are two simplified figures in dresses that suggest female forms. The one on the left has two of the cross symbols at her feet and the one on the right is a stick figure holding two more of these cross symbols, each hanging from a line below her feet. As two suns they suggest the two gods, Mithras and Christ, who now occupy Jung's internalised heavenly realms, but they are not represented as if they are in the sky. Their position below the women's feet is a reminder of the ordeal where Jung felt that he was hanging upside-down and a new sun was rolling beneath his feet in the chapter "Death" in *Liber Secundus.* In the previous study this scenario was related to reports of abuses where the children are hung upside down during the rituals (O'Donovan, 1994, p. 3; Lacter & Lehman, 2008, p. 90; Miller, 2012, p. 65; Noblitt & Perskin Noblitt, 2014, pp. 62–63). In Jung's case it suggests the possibility that the rolling sun was a theatrical device seen from an upside-down position (Brunet, 2019, pp. 68–69).

This dream from 1923 brings all of these different underworlds into Jung's present where, in his late forties, the memory of his military service would not have been very distant. In someone who has been initiated in a spurious version of the Masonic rites and who has internalised Mithras alongside their Christian beliefs, such as we see here, the psychological shift from the Christian emphasis on the more tender emotions to a readiness for war could be called up in an instant if necessary. But Jung was never required to fully activate Mithras in his psyche due to Switzerland's status of neutrality. While the Grand Orient de France might have been deleting references to any gods in their rituals in support of a move towards a purely secular society, the Freemasons in Switzerland, if Jung's experiences are to be given a political slant, clearly saw the need to retain the gods in theirs.

Jung began asking his soul which underworld he was in on November 26, 1913 (*BB 2*), when he was only a few weeks into the process of recording his active imaginations; two months later, on January 23, 1914 (*BB 4*), he asked her if they had moved beyond the in-between world or were yet to arrive. But he does not include either of these entries in *Liber Novus*. Further experiences in his active imaginations take him through several different underworlds and on the way he has discussions with some of the characters he meets. These meetings provide more insight into the philosophical themes underpinning his initiations and, as we shall see, are very similar to those outlined by Albert Pike in *Morals and Dogma*.

"But what else did those anchorites of the first centuries of Christianity do?" (*BB 3*, p. 99).

In Jung's fantasies the beliefs of the early Christian Gnostics are espoused by the anchorite Ammonius, a third century Christian philosopher whom he meets on December 30, 1913 (*BB 3*), in another experience in the desert. Over two nights their discussion ranges from how to read holy books, the meaning of the Word, and the philosophy of Logos in the ancient world. Ammonius mentions Philo Judaeus, whom he argues made complex abstract views on the nature of the Divine, but complained that Philo was a slave to words. This surprised Jung, who had understood Philo to be a serious philosopher and great thinker and finds the anchorite's views puzzling and not what he would have expected. Ammonius then talks to him about the process of "unlearning" before conducting Jung to the entrance of an Egyptian stone grave where he must sleep for the night. This suggests that Jung has something to unlearn about the Christian beliefs and classical philosophy that he was originally taught.

The following morning, on January 1, 1914, Jung wakes at sunrise and ponders the previous day's discussion, wondering whether Ammonius was actually a Gnostic. He then finds himself praying to the sun, thinking of Helios, the Greek god of the sun, and worshipping a scarab, a symbol of ancient Egyptian beliefs. This creates an inner state of exultation, but he eventually shakes it off, feeling that he is talking nonsense and worshipping an animal. The discussion between them resumes and Ammonius relates the story of his first encounter with the concept that God had become flesh in the man Jesus Christ. Ammonius was originally from Alexandria in Egypt and he equates the characteristics of Christ's birth, death and resurrection with the myths of the Egyptian gods Horus, the son of Osiris, and Seth, the brother of Osiris. He proposes a number of philosophical questions, asking whether Christianity was a Jewish transformation of the Egyptian beliefs and whether in the history of all religions there is some final goal. He concludes with an example of an African slave who had heard neither of Osiris nor Christ but who understood the symbolism, as it mirrored the beliefs of his own tribal upbringing. Ammonius concludes by stating: "It is a worldly error to believe that religions differ in their innermost essence. Strictly speaking, it's always one and the same religion. Every subsequent form of religion is the meaning of the antecedent" (*BB 3*, pp. 112–113).

Similar conclusions are reached by Albert Pike in *Morals and Dogma*. At the beginning of his lecture for the Third Degree he writes, "All religious expression is symbolism" and proceeds to expand on this theme and discuss the dangers of confusing the symbolism of words, or the sign for the thing signified, leading to superstition (Pike, 1871, pp. 48–49). He also talks of the way in which religious philosophy began to resort to complicated definitions and formulas leading to disputes over the meaning of words, an argument similar to what Jung's Ammonius says about the philosophies of Philo Judaeus. By the end of the lecture Pike reaches a similar conclusion to that spoken by Jung's Ammonius, stating: "Humanity has never really had but one religion and one worship", and criticises the Christian view that all other religions are a deception (1871, p. 75). He also delves into the philosophies of the Gnostics, citing the doctrines of Philo Judaeus, and discusses the Essenes and Therapeuts (Pike, 1871, pp. 183, 189). Here, he describes the life and manners of these mystical groups, in particular their prayers at sunrise.

Pike's lectures for the Third and 17th Degrees clearly parallel those in Jung's fantasy in the desert where he meets the anchorite, suggesting that the philosophical discussions between them may have been based on Masonic teachings, possibly delivered during an initiation or in some form of religious instruction. As the previous study suggests, these same themes also appear in other degrees from the Scottish Rite, as well as in other rites such as the Rectified Scottish Rite and the Ancient and Primitive Rite (Brunet, 2019). The Jesuit scholar Hermann Gruber summed up the overall role of Masonic philosophy and symbolism, saying:

> Many Masonic authors in the Latin countries …and some of the principal Anglo-American authors (Pike, Mackey, etc.) declare, that Masonic symbolism in its original and proper meaning refers above all to the solar and phallic worship of the ancient mysteries, especially the Egyptian (Gruber, 1913, p. 779).

Jung's desert experience where he finds himself in an Egyptian stone grave, worshipping the sun and hearing the teachings of the ancient Mysteries suggests a theatrically represented version of Masonic philosophy and symbolism. His final comment in this entry, when he feels he is suddenly in the twentieth century and no longer in the "multicolored in-between world" (*BB 3*, p. 113), creates the impression that he has emerged from the memory of this initiatory experience back to his present-day adult self.

However, there are examples in Jung's active imagination that suggest that the teachings from Pike's lectures concerning Gnostic doctrines are being deliberately distorted in order to create confusion for him. In the entry of December 21, 1913 (*BB 2*), where he meets Elijah and Salome, Jung learns that the "blood-thirsty ~~and~~ horny monster" Salome is Elijah's daughter, and is completely shocked by this distortion of biblical roles (*BB 2*, p. 182).[3] He is told that they have been "companions since time immemorial" and is led to believe that he must love Salome, a thought that terrifies him. In the next entry Salome tells him she is his sister and their mother is Mary, a concept he describes as "a devilish spell" and an "unnamable horror" (*BB 2*, p. 189).

This confusing episode may have its basis in Pike's treatise on the 32nd Degree or Sublime Prince of the Royal Secret, where he mentions the teachings of Bardesanes, a Gnostic whose doctrines were embraced by Syrian Christians. Bardesanes uses the term the unknown Father and his companion, the Mother of Christos, Son of the Living God and then describes the Holy Spirit as the Son's sister and spouse, who "unites herself with him as his primitive Companion" (Pike, 1871, p. 397).[4] In Jung's case, the substitution of the evil Salome for the concept of the Holy Spirit seems to be a deliberate corruption of the Gnostic beliefs by his abusers in order to make his experience even more nonsensical and confusing. Coming directly after the experience where Jung describes his disgust at the image of an old man and a child, a possible scene of sexual abuse, this deliberate distortion of Christian teachings is another of the practices described in reports of contemporary ritual abuse (Miller, 2012, pp. 57–72). In these contexts, a traumatic experience such as rape or near-death torture is used to induce a programmable tabula rasa state in the child prior to the installation of the new distorted teachings (Lacter, 2011, p. 62). This is not unlike the practices used in archaic puberty rites where, according to Mircea Eliade, the novices undergo terrifying ordeals in order to facilitate the disintegration of the personality and the creation of a tabula rasa state before the inculcation of a new identity (1958/1995; pp. 72–73).

Towards the end of *Book 7*, on January 27, 1922, Jung is still struggling with the confusing nature of all of these interrelated philosophies and beliefs and asks his soul: "Why do you make this damned confusion?" (*BB 7*, p. 221). On this occasion she answers: "This perplexity is necessary. Everything must be mixed up together", an answer that confirms the intent to confuse in these abusive versions of the Masonic teachings. As we are seeing, many of these philosophical discussions with his soul about ancient belief systems are not unlike those presented in Pike's *Morals and Dogma*. But Pike was not a scholar and the way he discusses all of these different ancient belief systems in his lectures is sometimes rambling and disorganised, such that the statement "everything must be mixed up together" could sometimes apply to the lectures themselves. The confusion, for Jung, though, does not only concern the teachings and belief systems, but the fact that through them, he is forced to incorporate into his psyche a series of gods who make further excruciating demands on him. The next god who makes his appearance is the Orphic god Phanes, who will eventually take up a position in Jung's internal cosmology.

"This is where Phanes appears and he, the golden bird, flies ahead."

(*BB 6*, p. 261).

The appearance of the Greek god Phanes in *The Red Book* is fairly brief and Jung illustrates him in Appendix A as the symbol of a young boy in a winged egg in a diagram entitled "Systema Munditotius", the system of the whole world. However, in later journal entries not included in *Liber Novus,* Phanes and the Orphic Mysteries take a prominent role, occupying his attention from September 1916 to March 1919. Jung had a copy of a text dealing with ancient beliefs in which he underlined the section on the Orphic god Phanes (Jung, 2009a, pp. 301–302, n. 211; 2009b, pp. 358–359). But his interaction with this god in his journals is marked by the release of a torrent of pain, frustration, anger and confusion before he reaches the point where the god Phanes is born as an image of the divine child (*BB 6*, p. 260, n. 267). This process is not unlike the struggle he had with the gods Mithras and Abraxas. It seems as if he is being subjected to a further long and painful process of initiatory transformation under the guise of yet another god.

The Orphics were a mystical initiation society flourishing in Greece around the 5th century BCE. Orphic initiations dealt with the death and rebirth of the personality and its doctrines included a belief in metempsychosis (Boechat, 2016, p. 88, n. 8). Their beliefs included the myth of Zagreus, the divine child of Zeus and Persephone, which is regarded as a retelling of the murder of

Osiris, which Pike discusses in *Morals and Dogma* (1871, pp. 421, 424). The myth begins with the divine child Zagreus being declared the new king of the cosmos. But the Titans were jealous of the child and lured him with toys, slaying him, dismembering him and cutting him into pieces. They then boiled his limbs and tasted them. His heart was saved by Athena and taken to Zeus who brought the child back to life as Dionysos, while the limbs were collected by Apollo and taken to Mount Parnassus. Zeus punished the Titans with a thunderbolt and from their ashes the human race was born. The myth was regarded as explaining the twofold nature of humanity, the divine represented by Dionysos and the wicked by the Titans, who nevertheless contained Dionysos within them, as they had eaten him (Chrysanthou, 2020; pp. 85–88). While the myth may represent the broader theme of the co-existence of good and evil in humanity, it could also be read as a description of the initiation of a child. Being eaten by the Titans and then later reborn has an unmistakable resemblance, in psychological terms, to being put through a terrifying initiatory ordeal by a group of all-powerful elders, resulting in the fragmentation of the child's identity in response to severe or life-threatening trauma.

As Anthi Chrysanthou demonstrates, the mythical character Zagreus/Dionysos had the same attributes as the Orphic Phanes: they were both identified with the sun and were regarded as the creator of the cosmos and everything in it. Jung referred to the symbol ☉ and connected it with the god Phanes and Orphic theogony in *Liber Novus* (2009a, p. 301, n. 211; 2009b, p. 358). As the previous study points out, this symbol has great importance in Freemasonry, where it is termed "the point within a circle" (Mackey, 1882, pp. 54–56; Brunet, 2019, p. 115). Albert Mackey relates the Masonic use of this symbol to the Orphic sect and also discusses the symbol's relationship to the worship of the phallus in antiquity and the sculptured representation of the *membrum virile* or male organ, noting that this worship was said to have begun in Egypt in relation to the myth of the murder of Osiris. Jung's dream-like encounter with a phallic symbol like this at the age of three or four is discussed in the previous study (Brunet, 2019, pp. 15–18).

Pike's *Morals and Dogma* also mentions the beliefs of Orphism, including the Orphic egg, a mystic symbol of the world, and its link to the ancient Egyptians. Pike notes how this mystic egg appears in several ancient religious contexts, both eastern and western, including between the horns of the Mithraic Bull. Phanes, he says, the Light-God of the Orphics, was to emerge from the egg of chaos entwined with a serpent, much like the god Mithras (Pike, 1871, pp. 288, 339, 355, 477). Metempsychosis, or the ancient concept of the human soul's descent from and ascent to the divine source during the cycle of birth, death and rebirth, also appears throughout *Morals & Dogma*. Here, it is related both to the biblical story of Jacob's Ladder and the mystic ladder in the Mithraic Mysteries.

The first appearance of Phanes in Jung's later entries occurs on September 28, 1916. Here, he is conversing with his soul, who describes Phanes arriving in the form of a golden egg-bird flying from the "tree of six lights" which has grown out of the head of Abraxas (*BB 6*, p. 261). The individual, his soul says, is striving towards the tree of seven lights, which symbolises the individual uniting with Abraxas. Jung finds these concepts very difficult to understand and in the following week his soul tells him more about these lights, but still in a very confusing and coded form. "The most dangerous enemies of the large lights are the small lights ... Science belongs to the small lights", she says (*BB 6*, p. 265). His soul also tells Jung that he must dig up what has been buried, implying that Jung may have already known this material and must recall it. In the context of the argument here this would suggest that Jung may have once heard these concepts in the initiatory experiences of his youth.

The symbolism of the six lights is directly related to Freemasonry and since the eighteenth century the Order has embraced a concept of three greater and three lesser lights, which have taken on various meanings over the centuries (Mackey, 1914, p. 447). In the Scottish Rite the three greater lights are represented as the Holy Bible, Square and Compasses, while the three lesser or Sublime Lights are the Sun, the Moon and the Master of the Lodge (Pike, 1871, p. 13, 14). Throughout *Morals and Dogma* Pike traces the extensive use of numerical symbolism within Freemasonry, and the numbers three and seven have multiple meanings. But it seems that the Masonic symbolism is being used here not to enlighten Jung but to deliberately confuse him with its ambiguity and false profundity.

In this fantasy Jung's soul suddenly stops relating these teachings when the spirits of Elijah and Salome reappear. Jung had seen these two figures in a dream on May 3, 1916 (*BB 6*) where they seemed to be suffering and he converses with them and tells them that the concept of the one God had been replaced amongst mankind with a multitude of gods and daimons, which to Elijah is blasphemous. Jung then describes how both God and his own soul had become multiple. In a fantasy on October 6, 1916 (*BB 6*) Jung meets the two spirits, Elijah and Salome, again. This time they are very distressed at being abandoned by the living, but are having trouble crossing over to the other side and want to learn about life after death. Salome is as cold as a corpse, so she asks him to remove some large stones away in order to find her warmth. There, to his horror he finds a corpse and realises that it is himself, or brother-self, and wonders how this could have happened (*BB 6*, p. 267). He is furious with Salome, feeling that she was behind his brother-self's death, but then she urges him to climb the tree again to reach the light. He is not sure that he wants to and thinks it would be better for him to remain earthbound and let the golden bird fly. His soul then tells him that he dies as a man, becomes an earthworm and then Phanes arises from him, another description that encapsulates the formation of another alter in the psyche.

In this argument and throughout the previous study Jung's brother-self is described as the part of him that, due to dissociation, has remained internally connected to the initiatory traumas behind a wall of amnesia, and is therefore "dead" to the conscious mind. Bessel van der Kolk, describes *dissociation* as "a compartmentalisation of experience ... [in which] traumatic memories are characteristically stored separately from other memories, in discrete personality states" (1996, p. 306). Jung's discovery that a part of himself has died therefore goes part way towards bringing the traumatic initiations to consciousness, and the recording of them in his journals allows him to question their purpose. A similar sudden awareness also appears in "Nox Quarta", in which he describes this part as "the dead that cried the loudest, that stood right at the bottom and waited, that suffered the worst" (Jung, 2009a, p. 304; 2009b, p. 369), which the previous study suggested could be referring to rape or its simulation (Brunet, 2019, pp. 117–118). Jung's determination to record every minute detail of these active imaginations allows him to view them critically. While he yearns to understand them, at the same time he feels his soul is actually making fun of him as all he can feel is suffering and pain. He senses that he has been tricked and calls her the "most diabolical of all temptresses ... [seducing] me into the madness of holiness, into stupid and unjust arrogance" (*BB 6*, p. 270). By December of this same year, he feels he is in a bath of poison and is disgusted with himself and sick of his soul, calling her "dirty animal!" (*BB 6*, p. 271).

Their quarrel over these teachings lasts into January 1917, where Jung continues to rage against his soul and experiences states of anxiety and horror. His soul then calls upon another entity, Abraxas, whom Jung has met before, but this time he is described in his earthly form and as a hermaphrodite who can unite what is separated and bring joy. Jung becomes angry at these pagan teachings but in answer his soul tells him: "Unify yourselves, and thus become whole!" (*BB 6*, p. 279). This directive implies that Jung's psyche has become fragmented into multiple parts and that he needs to unite them. At this point Jung invokes Phanes, asking for light. Then, in another visionary encounter on February 19 he hears the voice of Phanes telling him that disunity has been removed from him and he can now enjoy a secure and level way.

Here, we may be looking at an example of pseudo-integration where the abusers trick their victims into believing that they are now integrated and no longer multiple. In fact, many internal parts can still remain cordoned off from everyday consciousness. A survivor of ritual abuse and therapist, Wendy Hoffman, who has documented the process of unravelling her own traumatic memories in great detail, discusses the concept of *pseudo-integration,* stating:

> I believe a fairly good rule of thumb is not to believe anything the perpetrator group says ... From my experience, integration causes a strong interior physical response. You don't need anyone from the outside to tell you it's happening. You know. After my first integration, my brain spasmed for days, but I have an old brain. The danger in all this is that programmers put different and miscellaneous sections in victim's brains. It is possible to have a good integration in one dominant section but not be aware that other sections of the same brain remain fragmented. Abusers will bypass the integrated section(s) and target the others. So you have to plow through all the sections to find

all those other hidden parts (Personal correspondence, October 7, 2023).

Jung's invocation suggests that he may have converted to Orphism and to these pagan practices that he seems to despise. But the following day he recants his invocation to Phanes. "I invoke no one", he says, and seems to be doubting the purpose of his encounter with yet another god (*BB 6*, p. 280). He asks his soul what she is gaining from his destruction, but then she admits to diverting his attention away from the subject, saying that she wants to drive him to women, discussed in Chapter Two. This entry concludes with Phanes claiming that Jung's misery allows *his* star to shine, reinforcing Jung's sense that these seemingly religious processes are in fact taking his strength away from him.

By March 1917 we see the result of all these stressful interchanges between Jung, his soul and the god Phanes. He reports the deepest depression, the "deepest barometer level of the last fifty years", and asks what is going on (*BB 6*, p. 281, n. 312). In this entry he records the words of his soul, which direct him to undertake an internal process related to the Cabiri, a process that will be addressed in the next chapter. In the following entry, three weeks later, he states that he has followed these directions and Phanes appears, bringing all things beautiful: brightness, fragrant flowers, springtime and a time of rest, as well as a set of instructions for Jung to follow. But this so-called brightness has an opposite effect on Jung: he is physically sick, deeply introverted and "completely frozen" (*BB 6*, p. 283, n. 316). In April he says he has followed Phanes' instructions but asks if it was magic, and then describes a mystical fire that sits above him; however, this causes him to suffer from anxiety, numbness and sleeplessness. These references to magic will be discussed in Chapter Four.

On May 20, 1917 (*BB 6*) Jung says he wants to know about Phanes, the luminous one, but also Philemon, the riddlesome one. Philemon then appears and says he has become Phanes, "not a man but a flame of God", and that he embodies other characters such as Atmaviktu, Izdubar and Elijah (*BB 6*, pp. 297–299). Philemon has been present periodically right throughout the active imaginations and some years later Jung notices that he and these other characters embody phases of the master. In *Liber Novus* Jung often becomes suspicious of Philemon, identifying him as deceitful, a practitioner of black magic and a charlatan. It seems that the character, Philemon, may have been Jung's chief initiator and has taken on different disguises, perhaps enacting the role of Master throughout the initiation rites. In reports of ritual abuse one survivor described the accompanying religious lessons to be "where [you learn] to be obedient [and learn] to have a Master and know who your master was and do as you were told" (Scott, 2001, p. 88). Jung's painting of Philemon (Image 154 in *Liber Novus*) suggests a conflation of roles enacted in some of the degrees of the AASR, such as the 28th Degree or Knights of the Sun, where the members are addressed as knights and some of them represent the seven angels who, according to the ancients, governed the five planets, the sun and moon (Blanchard, 1950/2002, Part 2, pp. 203–217; Brunet, 2019, p. 136).

There is no more on Phanes in the journals until September 11, 1917 (*BB 7*) when Philemon delivers a further sermon. This time it is a eulogy celebrating Phanes as a god of light who embodies all that is benevolent in nature and the positive aspects of life, light and human potential. On October 11 Philemon again praises the qualities of Phanes and then follows this with a sermon that is a variation on Christ's Sermon on the Mount, with several inversions of some of Christ's key sayings. At the completion of his sermon, he performs an action used previously in *Scrutinies*: he bends down and touches the earth and asks its forgiveness for delivering a teaching. Finally, he enters a way-side chapel and asks forgiveness from Christ for altering his words, calling him "brother" and crying, and then kisses the icon's rigid hand. This segment appears to be a memory of another of Jung's initiatory experiences where a lecture or sermon is being delivered by the Master of the lodge, whom Jung has named Philemon.

The performative actions at the end of Philemon's sermon appear to have a symbolic purpose that again may be related to Albert Pike's lectures. In these lectures there are multiple references to the earth. In his extensive lecture for the 28th Degree or Knights of the Sun Pike focusses on the power and wisdom of Nature and the inspiration that grand forms like mountains have on thoughts of the Divine. In the context of delivering a sermon he states the following:

> Nature is full of religious lessons to a thoughtful man ... Familiarity with the grass and trees teaches us deeper lessons of love and faith than we can glean from the writings of Fénélon and Augustine. The great Bible

of God is ever open before mankind ... The great sermon of Jesus was preached on a mountain, which preached to Him as He did to the people, and His figures of speech were first natural figures of fact (Pike, 1871, p. 512).

It would seem that Philemon's gesture of touching the earth is a reminder that these spiritual lessons are intermingled with an understanding of nature. The fact that Philemon apologises for his sermon honours the earth as the original repository of all spiritual teachings. The second of Philemon's actions, an apology towards Christ, emulates Pike's immediate coupling of the reference to Nature's teachings with the Sermon on the Mount in the Knights of the Sun degree. Philemon's reference to Christ as "brother" also entails concepts put forward in Pike's lecture for this degree. Here, Christ is promoted as an example, supremely worthy of imitation, but Pike concedes that not all Masons follow the Christian creed. He describes an alternative view of Christ as an inspired human and member of the Essene community, as opposed to something divine, but acknowledges that his teachings are nobler than those of all other philosophers, moralists and reformers (Pike, 1871, p. 516).

On July 31, 1918 (*BB 7*) Jung records Phanes speaking in sermonic form of the four paths and four streams of the rivers of Eden. He talks of the joy of suffering and two nights later his sermon continues, celebrating the joy, beauty and perfection of completion. The first sentence of this entry reads: "Truly, I am the sacrifice: completion is the I am sacrifice" (*BB 7*, p. 193). The crossed-out phrases suggest that Jung is hesitating to admit to himself that *he* has been sacrificed in the process of bringing Phanes into existence. Then in March 22, 1919 Jung's soul reminds him of his torturous Christ-like experience on the cross, calling it his Golgotha, while Philemon joins the conversation and tells Jung that he has given birth to Phanes. Jung then questions the need for him to die for the sake of the gods but nevertheless concludes this entry by saying, "I see the inevitable" (*BB 7*, p. 198). In the argument here, this scenario appears to be a spurious initiatory situation in which one or more of the Masons are acting in the leading roles to convince Jung that his heavy sacrifice has enabled the birth of a new god in his soul, or in psychological terms, the creation of a new alter in his psyche.

Amongst Jung's mandala paintings in *Liber Novus* there are two that appear to
be related to these two sermons delivered by Phanes that may tell us more about
their purpose. Image 121, painted in November 1919, accompanies the chapter
"Nox Quarta". It depicts a central octagonal form that Jung describes as the
Lapis Philosophorum, surrounded by four blue rivers of Eden; sixteen green
segments and sixteen petal shapes surround this central symbol; the central
form has the appearance of a cut stone with many faces. References to the
symbolic role of the Garden of Eden and its four rivers can be found in *Morals
and Dogma* where Pike discusses the symbolism of the number four (1871, p.
45). In his extensive lecture for the Knights of the Sun degree he then deals
with the alchemical symbolism of the philosophical stone, describing it as "the
foundation of the Absolute philosophy, the Supreme and unalterable Reason"
(Pike, 1871, p. 557). Albert Mackey refers to the term "Lapicida", sometimes
used in Masonic documents to denote a Freemason and derived from the Latin
lapis, for stone and caedo, to cut, thus denoting Freemasons as stone cutters
(1914, p. 426). Given the theme of completion in Phanes' sermon this central
form in Jung's painting suggests the completion stage of his psychological
fragmentation through the many traumatic ordeals he has undergone, creating
a newly formed psyche comprised of many different "faces", alters or parts.
Jung's preoccupation with stones right throughout his life is therefore
understandable in terms of the centrality of stone symbolism in Freemasonry,
the organisation that appears to have played a key role in his psychological
formation.

The second painting relevant here, created in 1927, is another geometrical
mandala, Image 159. It accompanies the entry "The Magician" in *Liber
Secundus*, where Jung first meets Philemon and may inform Philemon's
version of Christ's Sermon on the Mount. This mandala was based on a dream
of an island where a Swiss lived in the centre of the dirty city of Liverpool (*BB
7*, pp. 239–240). The design has a luminous flower in the centre, surrounded
by a city map and then eight gates leading to eight stars, each surrounded by
eight segments. Jung realised that *he* was the Swiss who lived on the island and
that there was no way in or out of the gates. A recent Masonic discussion of the
octagon relates it to the eight-pointed cross worn on the breasts of the Knights
Templar, describing it as the real cross of initiation, as well as the significance
of the triangle and lozenge shapes in building the Templar cipher (Grand Lodge

of British Columbia and Yukon, 2023, "Templar Cipher"). Jung's design is filled with triangles and lozenge shapes and the fact that he recognises that he, himself, is locked inside this structure raises the red flag of organised group abuse (Miller, 2012, p. 46). In this type of abuse these internal geometrical structures are created by the perpetrators through traumatising the young children; the structures are then elaborated over the years to systematically locate alters mentally within them and install codes to activate them. Located in Jung's dream in a 'dirty' city is a giveaway comment on the corrupt use of this knowledge as a programming method.

So here we see parallels between the philosophical themes surrounding the appearance of Phanes in Jung's fantasies and those discussed in Pike's *Morals and Dogma*. However, Pike's lectures, while complex and interwoven, are not espousing evil. They are not, for example, suggesting in any way that these ancient belief systems are to be used to traumatically indoctrinate a child. But it does appear that Jung's initiators *were* using these lectures this way, especially to reinforce a deep state of confusion. In his middle years, as Jung struggles to make sense of these continuing fantasies, the effect on him is a roller-coaster of intense emotions, both sickening and confusing, then seemingly ordered but never fully resolved. From March 1919 in *Book 7* we do not hear of Phanes again.

"Once more I forgot that post-Christianity has begun." (*BB 6*, p. 252)

Throughout the *Black Books* Jung makes many statements that suggest that he is looking for what lies behind his active imaginations. The above statement referring to post-Christianity captures the apparent intention of these initiatory strategies: to replace Christianity with a system based on various forms of the ancient Mysteries in the psyches of the young. In the ritual of the Knights of the Sun degree the candidate is taught a summarised history of the ancient Mysteries and their connection to Freemasonry. The lecture states that while Masonry imitates the ancient Mysteries, it does so in a modified or reduced form due to the continual alterations the Masonic rites have undergone (Blanchard, 1950/2002, Part 2, p. 220). It appears that the focus on the various ancient mystery cults and their accompanying gods in Jung's active imaginations was in the service of this gradual shift to move beyond Christianity. But in Switzerland this shift was not to be a sudden one; it was not aimed at fully supplanting Christianity in the souls of those raised in it. Instead, Jung's experience suggested that it involved a gradual transition, firstly from the Christ to Mithras, an ancient god with many similar characteristics, and then to other gods, as we have seen in this chapter. But the disturbing methods used to re-form the psyche of a young person raised in Christianity is what is at issue here, and one which is being addressed throughout these studies.

At the beginning of *Book 7* Jung inserted some notes on a dream that appears to be confirming this aim of employing the ancient Mysteries in a move towards post-Christianity. His dream concerns the felling of a tree that he interprets as the biblical king Nebuchadnezzar, which he associates both with the Attis myth and with the giant Izdubar who initially appears in the entry "First Day" in *Liber Novus*. Jung connects Izdubar with the rising sun as well as with other sun gods such as Mithras and even Christ as "novus sol" (*BB 7*, p. 147, n. 1). He then extends these connections to the modern papacy, regarding the pope as the human personification of the sun and "the big tree" who, like the biblical character Nebuchadnezzar, must be felled. He interprets his dream to be telling him that this is his job. He also notes that there is an old woman who interferes with him and a secret assembly that has already become known to the entire world, with the Americans "weighing in", adding "and the world's delegate appears in the consistory" (*BB 7*, p. 147, n. 1). He says that he enters this assembly through the rear door and is already too late.

Jung's Izdubar fantasy was discussed in the previous study, noting that when the Gilgamesh epic was first translated it was thought that the central character, a mighty warrior originally named Izdubar, was describing the Babylonian King Nimrod, regarded as one of the founders of Freemasonry (Mackey, 1914, p. 513; Brunet, 2019, p. 75). The Chaldean Nebuchadnezzar was a later king of Babylon, having conquered it and many other nations. He reigned 630 years before Christ and appears in the Masonic Royal Arch system where there is an account of his armies leveling Jerusalem to the ground and, along with it, King Solomon's Temple (Mackey, 1914, p. 508). The connection between Nebuchadnezzar, Nimrod and the felled tree is associated in Freemasonry with the role played by the cedars of Lebanon which were employed to firstly build Noah's ark, then the Temple of Solomon and then, after Nebuchadnezzar destroyed it, the Second Temple. This theme appears in the 22nd Degree of the AASR, the Knight of the Royal Axe (Blanchard, 1950/2002, Part 2, p. 88, n. 260). In *Morals and Dogma* there is repeated mention of the Attis myth, although Pike spells it Atys. He likens the Phrygian myth of Attis and Cybele to the Egyptian Osiris and Isis, the Persian Mithras and Asis, and the British Hu and Ceridwen, remarking that they all represent the sun and moon and that their similar adventures have been incorporated into the ceremonies of initiation amongst all these mystery cults (Pike, 1871, p. 272). So, even though the Attis myth, Izdubar/Nimrod and Nebuchadnezzar have no connection historically, the fact that Jung connected them in his interpretation of his dream points, again, to the possibility that his dream was recalling Masonic references, including the themes that appear in Pike's *Morals and Dogma*.

This dream may also be symbolic of the political motives behind Jung's initiations in his own time. Jung likens the figure of Nebuchadnezzar to that of the Pope and the old woman who interferes with him, as the church. He interprets the dream as saying that his work is to bring down the papacy, which would accord with the aims of Continental Freemasonry. He then mentions the convening of a secret assembly, which appears to be a reference to the role of a secret society already known to the entire world. This may refer to Freemasonry more generally, but his comment on the consistory may tie it more specifically to the Scottish Rite. According to Pike (1871, p. 595), the final two degrees, namely the 31st or Grand Inspector Inquisitor Commander and the 32nd or Sublime Prince of the Royal Secret, are classed as the Consistory.[5] Albert Mackey describes the Consistory as the meetings of members of the 32nd Degree that confer the 31st and 32nd Degrees (1914, p. 175).

It has been long acknowledged amongst Freemasons themselves that there are both 'true' and 'false' versions of the Scottish Rite. The Masonic authors Fred Pick and Norman Knight note that the Scottish Rite is to be found "working regularly and irregularly, in virtually every country in which the Craft operates" (Pick & Knight, 1955/1991, p. 104). The Masonic author A.C.F. Jackson notes that as far back as 1766 various degrees related to the Scottish

Rite (sometimes known as Rose-Croix in England and Australia) were given negative criticism by the Council of Knights. Of the Kadosh degrees, amongst the higher Rose Croix degrees, the Council accused it of being "false, fanatical, detestable, not only because it is contrary to the principles of Freemasonry but also because it is contrary to the principles and duties of the State and Religion" (Jackson, 1980, pp. 35, 38). But this situation is not confined to the eighteenth century. Writing in the Australian context in 1980 Jackson (p. 207) notes that the rapid expansion of the Rose Croix Rite in this country and the presence of spurious versions has posed problems of control and supervision. While these Masonic authors are open as to their sentiments about the Scottish Rite, they remain true to their pledge of secrecy by not stating what is meant by these contraventions of morality.

Jung's comment that he came too late to this secret assembly and entered it by the rear door is concerning. It implies that he may know more about the role of this secret society than he is openly admitting. Does it mean that by 1917 he had worked out that he had been admitted into this secret assembly "by the rear door", that is, through his initiations in childhood? And why does he say it is too late? Has he realised that this secret assembly is so powerful already that the world's delegates are already involved with it? These questions may not be answered in the *Black Books*.

This chapter has focused on the various underworlds that Jung has entered in his active imaginations, the characters who have lectured him on the associated philosophies and the gods that have wielded their power over him during his sojourn there. The themes discussed in the philosophical sections, as we have seen, are frequently very similar to those found in Pike's *Morals and Dogma,* suggesting that Jung's initiators may have been drawing on this text for the philosophical aspects of his initiatory training. However, the distorted use of these lectures suggests that the aim of his initiators was not simply to educate him in all of the ancient traditions but to use their narratives in a twisted manner in order to subjugate his will and take his soul captive, the most extreme use of power over others that Pike himself warns against (1871, p. 56). This was achieved through a shattering of the psyche into multiple fragments through repeated initiatory traumas and the installation of alter personalities or separate self-states in the name of each of the gods he meets.

Jung recorded this process in great detail in order to try to understand what it was all about. In a discussion with Cary Baynes in 1917 he talked about the fact that there were various figures speaking in his active imaginations but that he saw them as phases of the master (*BB 6*, p. 298, n. 345); in other words, the various Master Masons or lead figures conducting the initiations he appears to have undergone. His own goal was not to identify with these characters but to remain the observing psychologist with the aim of understanding the process. The next chapter will examine further aspects of this journey, including his attempts to understand the role of magic in his experiences, his encounters with other characters and several more of his dreams.

Notes

1   The underlining of the word <u>language</u> and crossing out of the word ~~flows~~ is Jung's.
2   In the *Black Books 1913–1932*, published in 2020, this same footnote (now *BB 2*, p. 191, n. 221) is reduced and the reference to Jung's feeling that he had been put through such an initiation is deleted.
3   The crossed out ~~and~~ as well as the word 'horny' does not appear in *Liber Novus*.
4   The capitalisation of these roles is Pike's.
5   A lecture for the 33rd Degree or Sovereign Grand Inspector General is not included in *Morals and Dogma* but the ritual for this degree is included in Blanchard (1950/2002, Part 2, pp. 465–480).

4

"I warned you about magic.
Devilish stuff gets into you." *(BB 6*, p. 263)

On September 28, 1916 Jung approached his soul, saying that he wanted to
tackle something that was dark to him: the magical (*BB 6*, p. 259). He assumes
that she can teach him but she protests that these matters are dark to her also
and explains that she can only help him to uncover what he already knows
himself, material that exists in his "beyond" that he has not yet been able to
grasp. She seems to be talking about her role in helping him to bring his
repressed memories to consciousness. At this point she describes a vision of
something hazy in a dark forest and begins to reveal a series of inexplicable
symbols to him. She says he has picked up something that does not belong to
him, something magical and poisonous that he says makes him feel tipsy. "I
warned you about magic. Devilish stuff gets into you", she says (*BB 6*, p. 263).
References to magic, both black and white, appear throughout *Liber Novus* and
the previous study has already discussed many of its features, but the journal
entries from June 1916 in *Black Book 6* and those in *Black Book 7* are not
reproduced in *Liber Novus*. These later entries involve lengthy and complex
conversations about magic between Jung, his soul, Philemon and other
characters such as Atmaviktu, Ha and Ka. While the philosophical aspects of
Jung's active imaginations, as we have seen in the previous chapter, were
confusing enough for him, the magical themes take obfuscation and the
nonsensical to new heights.

As the French sociologist and anthropologist Marcel Mauss observed, the
creation of a sense of confusion and chaos is central to the way magic works
(1902/2005, pp. 67–70). He cites mythical spells, the invocation of gods,
demons, onomatopoeic muttering of a phrase, prayers, and meaningless ritual

words as the traditional elements of magic rituals. The use of magic practices, including black magic, is also a noted feature of the ritual abuse of children in the present era (Finkelhor et al, 1988; Smith, 1993; Becker, 2008; Miller, 2012; Noblitt & Perskin Noblitt, 2014; Lacter, 2021). Here, the children are easily tricked with stage magic, made to believe that they have magic powers themselves, or told that their abusers' spirits have been placed within them during sexual abuse or otherwise abusive rituals.

This chapter will examine the content of the last two *Black Books* for further material concerning the use of magic in Jung's indoctrination process. It will demonstrate that, once again, Albert Pike's *Morals and Dogma* (1871) may play a role. As was noted in Chapter One, Pike was a gifted linguist and was able to draw on a wide range of material in several languages, often without acknowledging these sources. In the case of his lectures that involved magic themes, such as the one for the 28th Degree or Knights of the Sun, Pike has drawn extensively on Lévi's *Dogme et Rituel de la Haute Magie*, which was first published in French in 1855. This chapter will demonstrate that Pike's Masonic teachings have again been used in a distorted manner to create a bewildering atmosphere of evil magic. Incorporated into the discussion will be some of the present-day knowledge of how magic themes are used in the context of ritual abuse.

"I recall that you are not a human but a half-daimon." (*BB 6*, p. 259)

By the time Jung is writing *Black Book 6* he is well aware that his soul contains daimonic characteristics. On February 2, 1916 (*BB 2*), in an entry not reproduced in *Liber Novus,* his soul has been pressing him to serve her, but he rejects this vehemently and protests that he does not want to be a serf and that she should not dominate him, just as he does not want to dominate her. By now his careful documentation of all of his fantasies, including the intense discussions and arguments he has had with his soul and other inner characters, has given him a degree of insight into the internal dynamics of his multiple soul-state. However, he does not yet have enough of a language to describe it, unlike the situation today where there is a body of research into ritual abuse that has been developed over the last few decades. But the stage he is now

94

reaching could be likened to that part of the survivor's progress where they are beginning to understand what has been done to them. As Ellen Lacter notes:

> ... once the victim recalls how these 'abuser personalities' (or introjects) were induced to form, the abuse that they endured, the directives they were given, that they were coerced against their will to perform functions they never would have chosen to perform of their own free will, etc., these parts can now make their own decisions about what they believe, who they are, and how they wish to live their lives (2021, Type 5. "Abuser personalities").

These realisations, though, do not occur suddenly or in one conclusive moment; they are often approached in a circular manner, where the survivor may need to revisit the ordeals and question or challenge the lies and trickery involved before the pain of the memories finally dissolves. It can take years for the meaning and purpose of each of the introjected elements to be fully revealed. Jung recognised that approaching the unconscious had to be negotiated cautiously and that the process of circumambulation was a preferable way to deal with it. He was to employ this approach with his patients when dealing with their dream material (Jung, 1964; pp. 203, 222). Again, he may have been drawing on memories of its use in the Masonic context as the Rite of Circumambulation is an important part of the rituals and is borrowed from the customs of ancient sun-worship (Bogdan, 2007, p. 51). The symbolic journeys through the desert, for example, are enacted in this circular manner and symbolise an ordeal.

Jung is his own analyst here and he has discovered that, despite the tremendous fear that has accompanied many of the fantasies, he is capable of putting up a strong resistance to the indoctrination process. But he also knows that he needs to explore every aspect of it, even if it is painful and terrifying, in order to reconnect with those parts of himself that were lost. The use of magic in his ordeals is an area that involves several hidden corners that he has only partially explored. Now, despite his awareness that his soul, as an introjected abuser personality, is part of the problem, he still knows that he must enlist her help in order to attempt to make sense of how magic has been used to try to enslave him.

The theme of the Cabiri and the Samothracian Mysteries is one of the concepts that Jung revisits on several occasions that contains seemingly magical elements. He had copies of scholarly works about them, so was obviously trying to understand their significance and relevance to his active imaginations (Jung, 2009a, p. 320, n. 310). They appear in the chapter "The Magician" in *Liber Secundus* and are discussed in the previous study (Brunet, 2019, pp. 131–134). In *Black Book 6* Jung provides further information about this theme that is not included in *Liber Novus*.

The entry of September 29, 1916 (*BB 6*) is strangely bewitching, and here his soul describes a series of symbols. She weaves a chilling and mysterious atmosphere around them, describing them as entangled, like a knot of serpents or ropes, which Jung illustrated in Image 71 in *Liber Novus*. She asks Jung where he could have learned them and how they came to him. She also describes them as "so chilly and northerly – so maritime" (*BB 6*, p. 262). In his journal he draws the symbols freehand and they are reproduced in the translation with similar freehand drawings. They include a sign that means "an upper and a lower one, divided lengthwise, [making] four", two fiery circles, "like eyes, empty sockets of fire", then "two tears of glowing glass, burning upward", a grave that is empty suggesting someone has risen up from it, and a fork shaped letter "Y". His soul acts as if she is protecting him from "a disgusting swindle [and] hellish sorcery" and wards this "devil's filth" away, telling him he must purify himself through his hard work "so that the light becomes completely pure and white" (*BB 6*, p. 263). Each of these symbols and the accompanying expressions have a meaning in Freemasonry.

Jung's soul's description of a chilly, northern and maritime quality of the symbols is a direct reference to the Cabiri, minor Greek deities who were thought to offer protection to sailors and vessels at sea. Their Mysteries were established on the island of Samothrace in the northern Aegean Sea and involved an enacted myth of the murder of Cadmillus, the youngest of the Cabiri, by his three brothers. The Masonic author R. H. Brown (1882/2002, p. 16) states that they were derived from the Egyptian Mysteries of Osiris and Isis, while Albert Mackey (1914, pp. 125–126) likens their central myth to the Hiramic Legend of the Third Degree of Freemasonry, where Hiram Abif, the architect of Solomon's Temple, is murdered by three fellow workers. The

Hiramic Legend is central to the Masonic teachings and is referred to in many of the higher degrees. The Cabiri are also mentioned throughout *Morals and Dogma* and Pike states that children of a tender age were initiated into the Cabirian Mysteries (1871, p. 307); although, not being a scholar, he does not provide a source for this claim. But rather than explaining these references, Jung's soul continues to confuse him with the cryptic manner in which she talks of these ancient practices. As his internalised abuser, she seems to delight in dropping hints about his initiatory experiences, which he cannot yet fully face, despite his search for answers amongst scholarly works.

Morals and Dogma may provide answers to the symbols Jung is being shown here. In his lecture for the Third Degree or The Master, Pike includes a section on ancient words linked to sun worship in a variety of languages including ancient Egyptian, Parsi, Hebrew, Phoenician and others (1871, pp. 58–62). He makes a series of connections between the various words for the sun in his detailed discussion, but it is his descriptions that match the wording in Jung's journal entry. The Parsi word Khur, the literal name of the sun, he says, also means "the socket of the eye", accounting for Jung's soul's reference to eye sockets. This leads Pike to the word Khora, the ancient name for Lower Egypt, explaining Jung's first symbol of upper and lower divided lengthwise as a representation of Upper and Lower Egypt alongside the Nile. From here Pike arrives at the Hindu name for the sun, Hari, which includes the concept of fire or flame. This leads him to the ancient festivity of Mal-Karth, the winter solstice where the sun god is reborn from a pyre on December 25, linking Jung's symbol of the flame with the grave. In Egypt, it was Horus, he says, who was buried three days and regenerated, just as the Masonic hero Hiram Abif was murdered and remained for three days in his grave before being uncovered, thus answering Jung's soul's comment about the one who rose from the grave. Pike then talks of the hieroglyph of the elder Horus as "a pair of eyes", and the festival of Epiphi, when the sun and moon are in line with the earth, called "the birth-day of the eyes of Horus", tying it to Jung's symbol of the two fiery circles or sockets of fire. He then discusses the Hebrew letter Yōd, progressing to the "mystic character Y ... the sacred word of the Hindoos [sic]", explaining Jung's forked symbol. Pike also mentions the word Khūr, as opposed to Khur, saying that it means white or noble in Syriac, tying it to Jung's soul's directive that he must become completely pure and white.

It appears that Jung's abusers have drawn on Pike's lecture for the Third Degree in order to create a false atmosphere of evil magic. They even represent the symbols in a similar order as their explanations appear in the lecture. But rather than clarifying the real nature of these symbols his soul exaggerates their mysterious and evil quality, building the horror and using it to manipulate him into further dependency on and obedience to her.

There are several more symbols in this entry: a severed head, a grill, a loop, a prison, and a cock (*BB 6*, p. 262). Their meaning is also obscure but may be related both to Jung's fantasies and to the themes in *Morals and Dogma*. The severed head recalls Jung's meeting with Salome and her demand for the head of John the Baptist. In Pike's lecture for the 17th Degree or Knight of the East and West, he discusses the Essenes and argues that John the Baptist preached a similar doctrine to this sect and was likely to have been an Essene (1871, pp. 190–193). R. H. Brown suggests that the Cabirian Mysteries, along with the Dionysian, continued to influence initiatory societies into the time of Christ and were shared by the secret society of the Essenes (1882/2002, p. 19). So, it is possible that Jung's symbol for the prison, and even the symbol of the grill, would not only be related to John the Baptist's incarceration but also to the Gnostic doctrine of the soul's sojourn on earth as a period of imprisonment, a belief shared by the Essenes. Jung's loop symbol could then be read as the soul's journey from the godhead and its return. But as a loop, rather than a figure-of-eight or symbol of infinity, it suggests that this need not be an endless process, unlike the concept of continual rebirth that Pike describes as "the purgatory of Metempsychosis" (1871, p. 283). Pike also raises the question of whether Christ was an Essene, and argues that the Essenes were not worshipping the sun as a god in their solstice festivals, but rather as a symbol of light and fire (1871, pp. 190, 193). Jung's symbol of the cock, a bird that heralds the morning sun, may then be a reference to Christ's impending death and betrayal by his disciple Peter. Read in these terms, the symbols in this entry are not necessarily indicators of evil magic, but rather a visual way of representing Gnostic beliefs using Pike's wording. However, what *is* evil is Jung's abuser's manipulation of these teachings in order to confuse and terrify him.

On March 8, 1917 Jung's soul gives him more instructions about how to create the mystic light and she again mentions the Cabiri. She tells him that he must utter words and continue building what the Cabiri have started, laying stone upon stone. He must pass what he has learned through the highest lights of science and art; wheat must grow from the mud and the fire must be kindled. This involves work and putting aside everything else besides the completion of this work. On March 30 his soul tells him he must undergo the birth pangs of what is to come, a beautiful springtime or "wedding of souls"; but for now, he must look towards the rocks that salvage him and the child. She then asks him if he hears the bell, and whether he has money on him. He must put it away, find water and drink it, and then kindle the fire, his sword ready for the arrival of Phanes, the mystic light. She asks him if he is weary, and tells him to rest, stay quiet and wait for what is to come. In the next entry, ten days later, Jung says he has rested and done what he could. "Was that magic, a wish to force things?" he asks (*BB 6*, p. 284).

These mysterious preparations seem like magic to Jung but, again, they appear to be a deliberate muddling of Masonic ritual and the accompanying teachings in order to create an atmosphere of confusing nonsense. They are, in fact, a blend of two degrees, the Third and the 18th, along with elements of the Cabirian Mysteries, which in Freemasonry are seen to have similar symbolism to the Third Degree. The mention of words, as the editor reminds us (*BB 6*, p. 282, n. 313), is a reference to the New Testament, John chapter one. As the previous study points out, this is the biblical text read out by the Prelate in the 18th Degree of the Scottish Rite; while the search for the Lost Word is a motif that appears in many degrees (Brunet, 2019, p. 24). The Cabiri and the laying of stones are discussed by Pike (1871, p. 265), who states that the Cabiri of Samothrace were thought to be the same as the gods of Britain who were worshipped by the Druids, reflecting a belief held in the nineteenth century and debated by scholars that Druidism and the Samothracian beliefs were one and the same religion. Their worshippers were builders and their temples, as Pike notes, were enclosures of unhewn stones similar to the stone circles of Britain. Jung's soul's comment, where she mentions the rocks that salvage him and the child, is another hint that he must look to the initiatory experiences of his childhood in order to understand this material.

His soul's instruction to pass what he has learned through the highest lights of science and art relates to a previous conversation with her on October 6, 1916, where she tells him that science corresponds to the sun, and art to the moon. Wheat growing from the mud relates to the Cabiri as described in *Morals and Dogma* (Pike, 1871, pp. 274–275, 306, 363). Alongside their role as the protectors of sailors and ships, the Cabiri were also gods of fertility and agriculture. Pike notes that the goddess Ceres was one of four deities worshipped at Samothrace. She was traditionally associated with corn, but at a later point Pike relates her to the constellation of Virgo, symbolised by a woman holding an ear of wheat. He notes that Masonry has preserved the ear of wheat as a symbol in relation to both Ceres and Persephone who were goddesses who brought the civilising effects of agriculture to men, to "soften their savage and ferocious manners" (Pike, 1871, p. 274). The fragrance of flowers can be a reference to the final celebratory stage of some of the Masonic degrees, where the Lost Word is found; in some versions the lodge can be decorated with red roses. In the 32nd Degree, for example, the candidate is told "a true Mason … gathers at last the Masonic rose" (Blanchard, 1905/2002, Part 2, p. 433).

His soul's question, "have you money on you?" and instruction to put it away (*BB 6*, p. 284), recalls the preparation of the candidate in Masonic initiations. Prior to his initiation the candidate is told to divest himself of any metals, including money, in order to enter the Holy Temple, symbolising that a man's wealth plays no role in Freemasonry (Mackey, 1914, p. 482). The instruction to find water and drink was mentioned by R. H. Brown in his discussion of the Samothracian Mysteries. He states that the Cabirian candidate was made to drink from two fountains: "the one called *Lethe* (oblivion) and the other *Mnemosyne* (memory), by which means he lost the recollection of all his former crimes, and preserved the memory of his new instructions and vows" (Brown, 1882/2002, pp. 16-17). Brown's explanation corresponds with the discussion of the Cabirian themes in the previous study, where Jung's action of bringing down his sword to cut the devilish knot that entangles him is equated with the destruction of the memories of his initiations and then the building of a "new tower" (Brunet, 2019, p. 132). Amnesia towards one's crimes may have been useful in ancient warrior cultures in order to preserve the sanity of their soldiers, but in Jung's case we seem to be looking at a similar process applied to a child, who has been made to falsely believe that he has committed a series of egregious crimes.

In the entry of March 8, 1917 (*BB 6*) Jung is told that the first bell strikes and a call goes out over the land; his soul asks him if he is weary and tells him to revive himself as the time of rest begins. She has also told him that others must participate in the work. At this point Jung's soul ceases the instructions; he asks her what he is supposed to do with her dark words, but is told to stay quiet. Here, Jung gives no indication that he is able to relate these words to any memories of an initiation or mystery play.

In an earlier study the author put forward a psycho-physiological interpretation of some of the key myths and symbols of Freemasonry, arguing that some of them may be symbolising the impact of trauma on the brain and psyche (Brunet, 2007, pp. 62–88). The Second Degree, it argues, appears to emphasise the rewards of patient spiritual development that can eventually produce a highly enriching mystical experience. However, the Third Degree may be suggesting the dangers that can accompany attempts to shortcut this process, particularly through the use of shock. It contains the legend of Hiram Abif, the architect of King Solomon's Temple (Mackey, 1914, pp. 329–330). In its ritual enactment the architect is approached by three brothers, Fellow Craftsmen, who pressure him for the secret Word. When he refuses to tell them they each attack him with a blow to the head. The first blow is to his left temple and he falls to his right knee, the second is to his right temple and he falls to his left knee, and the third is to his forehead and he collapses, dead. The traitors then bury the body unceremoniously in a shallow grave. After three days the body is found by the searching Masons, but it is decaying and when they pull on the corpse's hand it slips. It takes the Masons three attempts to retrieve the body through the Five Points of Fellowship, a symbol of brotherly love and support. The body is then returned to the king for decent burial. At the conclusion of the ritual the Master's Word is whispered into the candidate's ear.

This legend can be viewed as an allegorical representation of trauma as the psyche's reaction to an encounter with death, but one that includes the added element of betrayal as Hiram is murdered by three brothers. Betrayal trauma, as Jennifer Freyd (1996) argues, is one of the forms of trauma most difficult to accommodate and therefore most associated with repression. The three blows to Hiram's head that make him fall to the opposite knee emulate the series of shocks applied to the initiate. In neurological terms, they may relate to the crossed neural control of the brain hemispheres on the body, while also representing the effect on the cognitive functions of the pre-frontal cortex, which are sent offline during traumatic shock (van der Kolk, 2014, pp. 55–73). The familiar Masonic symbol of skull and cross bones could also be interpreted in this light. The rough burial of Hiram Abif could then be regarded as the role of repression that pushes the experience just below the surface of consciousness. This initiation, if interpreted in psychological terms, could then be seen as a controlled application of shock to immerse the candidate in the liminal state and then carefully return him to his normal state at the end of the process. In the Third Degree the restoration of the candidate involves a reversal of the murder when the body is retrieved. However, it takes several efforts for the corpse to be disinterred as the hand slips when the Masons try to grasp it. This suggests that the sense of touch and "bodily memories" may be the first indicators of buried trauma, but the memories are often too painful to be addressed and can slip away from consciousness as one attempts to grasp them. Finally, the Five Points of Fellowship used to restore Hiram's body suggests a mirror-image between the conscious mind and the unconscious material, rather like Jung's sense of his "brother self" that has been buried in the unconscious. The Five Points of Fellowship may also be a reference to the five senses, as the retrieval of repressed memories can restore a more balanced relationship between body and psyche.

In the Third Degree the Master's Word whispered into the candidate's ear is Mahabone, described by one member of the Order as signifying where the secret is buried, like marrow in the bone, as well as the concept of rotten or decayed, almost to the bone (Wells, 1978, p. 15). In his discussion of the 18th Degree, which also appears in the instructions to Jung in this entry, the Masonic author A. E. Waite describes it as a memorial of loss and recovery, and an elaboration on the Hiramic theme of the Third Degree (1925, p. 15). Consequently, these two Masonic rituals, read in terms of traumatic memory, may be a symbolic way of describing the profound nature of repression and the accompanying psychological decay that can occur if the memories are not retrieved. The search for the Lost Word, which appears throughout many

Masonic rituals, could therefore be viewed as the search to find words for the traumatic experience, implying the retrieval of the repressed memories. This suggests that as far back as the early eighteenth century, long before the disciplines of psychiatry and psychology were able to explain the mechanisms of psychological trauma in neurobiological terms, the Masons were enacting it allegorically in their ritual for the Third Degree.

"I see: the castle has three towers …" (*BB 6*, p. 285)

Jung's entry of April 17, 1917 takes him to the next stage in this process where he experiences a fire above him, which he relates to his accompanying dreams and to the sense of his brain being "open to heaven, to receiving the spirit" (*BB 6*, p. 284, n. 320). His soul relates this fire to the north and cold, another possible reference to the Cabirian Mysteries, and then talks of a book from the fire, which he must learn to read. Jung interprets this as a reference to a secret script, but his soul stresses that his intellect is not of use here. Instead, she provides him with a description of a castle with three towers using the colours blue, green, red, white and gold, while the holy one (Phanes) sits in contemplation, dressed in white. The castle appears to be on clouds of fire in blue skies. Jung is asked whether he wants to go through the gates of the castle, but desists, allowing his soul to enter for him, where she describes what she sees in terms of various colours: a gold serpent, a red cave, a white gate and so on, all leading to a bridge of threads traversing from star to star, in search of the source of the fire. She then states that Jung has drawn this astral fire down into himself, but asks why evil has taken her away from him and why she had gone into the eye of evil and to the stars. He answers that she did not believe in him, but he feels that the source of the fire is within him, as Phanes has arisen in him, and now he has the highest wisdom and lives in its splendour.

The creation of imaginary internal structures in which to "house" the separate memories of traumatic ritual experiences and the accompanying alter personalities that were formed through them is one of the strategies used on children in present-day ritual abuse. Here, the children can be told that "the building we showed you is in your mind"; in some cases, a child may be shown a castle and is told that this castle is within her (Lacter, 2011, pp. 61, 85, 95).

In Jung's fantasy this structure is also an imaginary castle, emerging from the clouds, an apt representation given the knightly themes of Continental Freemasonry. These imaginary structures are then used in a form of *programming* defined by Alison Miller as "one of the words that organised abusers use to refer to their splitting a child's mind and training different parts to perform various tasks they assign them, tasks that would be abhorrent to their conscious mind" (cited in van der Merwe & Sinason, 2016, pp. 25, 26). These parts are then locked away in imaginary internal prisons. Colour and number symbolism can be used in these programming methods and in Jung's case, as we shall see, may be directly associated with Albert Pike's *Morals and Dogma*.

In the entry the next day, after Jung again expresses his distrust of his soul, she launches into a description of the castle involving a further system of colours and numbers: "Thrice five towers surround the castle. Thrice six gates are in the walls. Thrice seven great halls are in the castle. The green stream flows below", then caves stacked with gold, and so on (*BB 6*, p. 287). Then she says that the castle is empty, apart from Philemon, who is in "the golden house of splendor" and says everything is ready but no one comes (*BB 6*, p. 288). This is due, she says, to the fact that there is no bridge to the castle and she urges Philemon, as the pontiff, to build a bridge "of rare and precious stones" and she will help him.

Morals and Dogma is filled with references to the stars and the system of the Zodiac, interpreted in relation to the transmigration of the soul through the spheres, and incorporating colour and number symbolism. In his lecture for the 19th or Grand Pontiff Degree Pike discusses the symbolism of the various primary and secondary colours, including the colour black, as well as the sacred numbers found within the ten Sephiroth of the Kabbalah (Pike, 1871, pp. 234–235). In the Grand Pontiff lecture, he describes the jewels of the lodge as "the symbols and emblems of the virtues required of all good Masons" (Pike, 1871, p. 237). The term Grand Pontiff refers to the concept of a high priest, drawn from the Latin "pons, pontis", meaning "bridge", implying that a high priest's role is to form a bridge to the Divine. Jung's soul's reference to Philemon as the pontiff, who must build a bridge of precious stones, is again the rearrangement of Pike's wording and the symbolism of the 19th Degree to create more mystery for the ever-perplexed Jung.

The symbolism of the number three has multiple applications in Freemasonry and appears throughout Pike's lectures. In his discussion for the 23rd Degree or Chief of the Tabernacle Pike states that there are three movable and immovable jewels and three pillars in Masonic symbolism and when he mentions Indian forms of initiation, he describes the initiate "invested with a cord of three threads, so twined to make three times three and called *zennar*", which, he says, is related to the Masonic cable-tow, a cord tied around the candidate's neck or waist (1871, p. 261). Later in the lecture for this degree Pike describes Gothic Mysteries using the word "thrice" a number of times: "Every thrice-three months thrice-three victims were sacrificed to the tri-une God" (1871, p. 266). So, the concept of the bridge of threads and the repeated use of 'thrice' in Jung's entry have clearly been drawn from Pike's lecture for the 23rd Degree. His soul's admission that she went into the eye of evil might also be drawn from the lectures. At the conclusion of the lecture for the 14th Degree, or Grand Elect, Perfect, and Sublime Mason, Pike warns the members to beware of being tempted to evil and states: "Break not into the house of innocence, to rifle of its treasure; lest when many years have passed over thee, the moan of its distress may not have died away from thine ear!" (1871, p. 159). This sounds like a very clear directive to the Masonic members to desist from using their knowledge to abuse children and steal their innocence, the very thing that Jung's perpetrators seem to have done to him when he was young.

In the entry of April 18, 1917 Jung says he does not feel completely himself, while his soul states that she is mentally ill and that Jung has forgotten much: "You don't recall a single instance", she says (*BB 6*, p. 287). On the other hand, his soul says that she has experienced a great deal of "unbelievable things", but the fact that the rooms of the castle are empty, apart from the presence of Philemon in one of them, may signify the fact that Jung cannot remember any of them. Today's survivors of ritual abuse describe many different ordeals which they have undergone, but they are often so far removed from concepts of normal society that they come across as unbelievable. Their experiences of pain, suffocation, electroshock and other forms of torture are not only carefully hidden from the general community but are also hidden from the victims themselves in internal self-states through the power of dissociation and amnesia. These self-states then perceive themselves as trapped behind, within, or attached to the internal structures created for this programming purpose (Lacter, 2011, p. 61).

Colour programming appears in the Reversed Kabbalah, a training system based on a distortion of the ancient mystical tradition which traditionally uses codes to draw down divine energies (Katz, 2012, pp. 91–117). The reversed form substitutes demonic entities for angelic beings and its practices are based on torture rather than meditation. Stella Katz, a self-confessed ritual abuse survivor who became a trainer in Reversed Kabbalah, notes that the modern-day use of this practice includes colour programming that can begin in babyhood. Here, the child is hurt in ways that leave no mark while being shown different colours and magical symbols. Early internal splits are created through constant annoying sounds, being jabbed with needles or receiving small electric shocks, and at the right moment the new child alter is named and assigned a colour and a magic symbol. Accompanying this, the child is taught how to place coloured dolls into their corresponding pockets, thus laying the groundwork for the abusers to call out alter personalities at will through colour and/or number symbolism. Katz also points out that those children who fight back and are the hardest to break are considered to be high priest material. While Jung's journals do not tell us whether he ever underwent such a practice so early in life, the appearance in April 1917 of a castle structure with many rooms suggests that he might have undergone something like this at some point in childhood. The information provided by Katz begs the question of whether Jung's resistance to indoctrination, apparent throughout his journals, was seen as an attribute qualifying him for some form of senior role in the cult.

Jung's entry of April 25, 1917 (*BB 6*) begins with his soul describing a black bird and a white serpent, a reverse coloration of the two creatures that have already appeared in *The Red Book*. But accompanying them is the skeleton of an elephant, its flesh eaten by ants, an animal not seen before in *Liber Novus*. His soul asks Jung: "Do you feel this in your body? Probably not, it happened a long time ago" (*BB 6*, p. 288). This reference to an elephant is particularly obscure and is not explained by his soul, but the serpent begins to speak and says he has come from the great cave below, where he has lived for thousands of years. As the editor notes (*BB 6*, p. 289, n. 331), the way he describes himself resembles the symbol of the Ouroboros. If we return to Pike's lecture for the 23rd Degree we will see that this is another appropriation of his wording where he discusses the Indian Mysteries (1871, p. 261). He says that their initiations were conducted in caves and describes the vast Temple of Elephanta, where the candidates would long wander, searching for Light. References to the symbolism of the serpent appears right throughout *Morals and Dogma* but in the lecture for the 23rd Degree Pike relates them to the many ancient temples, some of which "were in the shape of a circle to which a vast serpent was attached" (1871, p. 265). Albert Mackey (1914, p. 237) describes the cavern of Elephanta, on the island of Gharipour in the Gulf of Bombay, as dedicated to phallic worship and only accessible to the initiated.

The statement that Jung probably does not remember this elephant because it happened a long time ago (his memories eaten by ants) may be referring to his childhood dream, at the age of three or four, of the giant phallus in the underground temple (1963, pp. 25–27). Young children can enter trance states more easily than older ones (Lacter, 2011, p. 72), and so this suggests the possibility that Jung may have been hypnotised and taken imaginatively into this underground space in his early years. Hypnosis is used in pediatric medicine today to calm the children before beginning a medical procedure that could frighten them (Anbar, 2021). For children of the age of Jung's dream this can involve tapping into the child's natural imaginative abilities and love of stories. Another way to induce a trance-like state in a young child, according to Anbar, is to set up a situation to confuse the child and while the child is trying to process "what is wrong with this picture" he is distracted from what is happening to him. In Jung's childhood dream he is confronted with a strange object that makes no sense (the tree trunk with an eye on top) and then he is told by his mother that this object is a man-eater, an even more confusing concept. For Jung, this memory was never fully erased and he puzzled over it even in his eighties, attesting to the persistence of early traumatic memories that, elephant-like, might never fade.

The exchange between Jung's soul and the white serpent and black bird includes multiple references to different colours: the green one, the black stone, grey rocks, white marble and so on. The serpent says that she has seen the "green one ... nailed to the rocks, like a garment with no one in it. I saw it because I was blind. One who sees cannot see it" (*BB 6*, p. 289). Given that Pike's wording has already been linked to the wording in these entries the only reference to green that appears relevant here is contained in a sentence from his lecture for the Third Degree: "the greenness of unripe intellect ... a schoolboy's smattering of knowledge" (1871, p. 51). Pike also states that the ancients worshipped the sun in the form of a black stone called Elagabalus, or Heliogabalus. He adds that the faithful are promised a white stone, known as the Philosophical Stone that is related to the Table of Emerald, a Hermetic text that is the foundation of alchemy (Pike, 1871, pp. 557–558). The reference to being able to see only if one is blind is likely to be code for an initiate, blindfolded but aware of the initiatory nature of this symbolism.

Jung records wearing a green garment, which bursts into leaf in "The Red One" in *Liber Secundus*. He also illustrates a figure in a green and blue garment in Image 45, accompanying the chapter "First Day" in *Liber Secundus*. This figure is holding up a circular structure in an architectural setting that the previous argument suggests may have been symbolically representing a practice known as the Middle Pillar exercise used in Ceremonial Magic (Brunet, 2019, p. 80). However, the variation that Jung depicts suggests that its effects on the psyche can be dangerous. The occultist and ceremonial magician, Israel Regardie, warns that while these magic practices can be uplifting, they can also be used by those practising witchcraft or demonology (1938/1945, p. 17). Jung states in the next chapter, "Second Day", that he is concerned with going blind from the brilliant white light of mystical illumination, which in his accompanying painting is illustrated as a large black star at the top of the circle. The reference to a green garment, nailed to the rock with no one in it, could then be read as the devastating effects of such an exercise on a young person, which, along with the multiple initiatory traumas, leaves only the outer shell, the everyday "front" personality, while other parts of the psyche remain entrapped in dissociative states.

Jung's soul then asks about Atmaviktu and the serpent answers that he *is* Atmaviktu and became him after passing through many different human and animal forms where he forgot who he was in all these different states (*BB 6*, pp. 288–291). Jung depicts Atmaviktu as a many-legged green dragon in

Images 117, 119 and 123 and in the previous study it is discussed in terms of the dragon in Mozart's Masonic opera *The Magic Flute* (Brunet, 2019, p. 119). Then the serpent describes Atmaviktu becoming a man for the purpose of healing but dying several times and reverting to these various animal forms. Such a description implies multiple initiatory ordeals that have created many inner parts, personality states or fragments that through dissociation have been lost to amnesia.

In *Memories* Jung describes his childhood fascination with stones where he would talk to stones and sit on them, wondering whether he was the stone himself, imaginatively shifting his identity in and out of the stone (1963, p. 33). At the age of ten he carved a little mannikin and placed it in a box with a stone and hid it in the attic where it became a source of comfort when he was distressed. After a year of doing this, he said he felt that he had come to the end of his childhood. But at the age of thirty-five his unconscious provided a name for this mannikin: Atmavictu, calling it the "breath of life", which he related to the fearful tree of his childhood dream (Jung 1963, p. 35).[1] So the reference to Atmaviktu in this entry is now indicating a particular time in Jung's childhood when some of these initiatory processes might have occurred. In Pike's discussion of the Indian Mysteries, he mentions that children could undergo initiation at eight years of age (1871, p. 261).

Finally, in this entry of April 25, 1917, the serpent opens the gate of splendour where Philemon, the lover, stands in a green garment. Jung's soul says that Philemon is not a man but "truly the self" (*BB 6*, p. 292). Given we are looking at Masonic rites, the term "the lover" here may be a reference to the motto of "Brotherly Love, Relief, and Truth ... the three great tenets of a Mason's profession" (Pike, 1871, p. 19). For Philemon to now appear in the green garment suggests that concealed within the everyday personality of Jung's youthful self is Philemon, the magician who has now become his main perpetrator introject. In the previous study it was suggested that Jung's painting of Philemon as a medieval knight in Image 154 with a wide set of wings was a conflation of the knightly and angelic figures of the 18th and 28th Degrees and therefore a representation of the powerful master of his initiatory ordeals (Brunet, 2019, p. 136). According to Stella Katz, in ritual abuse an angel figure at the end of the path is a guard and reaching this angel in memory recovery or therapy can mean getting too close to the core and the risk of setting off a dangerous booby trap that can lead to self-harm or suicide (2012, p. 114). So, it seems that Jung's determination to comprehend these strange internal states is leading him towards the core of this inner structure.

In the following entry of April 28, 1917 (*BB 6*) Jung asks for answers concerning the skeleton of the prehistoric elephant and his soul asks why the bones remain in front of the gate, blocking the way to Philemon. The serpent states that the elephant's bones represent the primordial past and an old instrument that needs to be replaced. The use of the term "primordial" implies that the initiatory processes may have started very early in Jung's life. At this point, the serpent notices that Jung is writing this information down and says that he should learn to see these things himself, rather than depend on his soul to describe them. But in the next entry of April 29 Jung states that he can see nothing, so his soul again intervenes. The serpent then explains that the elephant was in existence before Atmaviktu even imagined being a man, when men did not build castles and lived wild, suggesting a state of childhood before the formation of an inner castle structure to house Jung's alter personalities. The serpent then encourages Jung to destroy the bones, that is, the past and therefore the memories of his childhood initiations; she says he must use unnatural means or certain ascetic exercises, in order to do this. The elephant or mammoth, a powerful primordial animal famed for its extensive memory, is an apt symbol for the nature of traumatic memories that time will not wear down and only exercises that will destroy or push the memories down further will dispose of the bones. What these exercises are will remain to be seen.

"This man is a star seed – where did he come from?" (*BB 6*, p. 296)

Two weeks later, on May 14, 1917, Jung asks his soul to investigate as there is dissension in the air. She talks to Philemon and he tells them that he and Atmaviktu have united and as a consequence Philemon now has eternal youth; this took place when he entered the castle and had a meal with the white serpent who created the light above his head. Philemon describes the man Jung as "earth" who has seen everything and has come close to the eternal fire, but now is fulfilled and released and peace will now come to him. He says this man,

Jung, has been a vessel for him to reach the God and describes himself as a fire or flame, having passed through this man and surpassed him. He also says that he is not Jung's soul nor his God. Instead, he describes Jung as a "star seed" that has fallen from "the indeterminate", and says that Jung is foreign and will never really belong to the earth and its laws, but is illuminated from a distant star (*BB 6*, pp. 295–296).

As Mircea Eliade (1958/1995, p. 92) notes, in initiations in agrarian cultures the seed plays an important symbolic role, as opposed to the role of bone in initiations amongst hunting peoples. In *Morals and Dogma* references to the seed in initiation rites appear frequently, most significantly when Pike is describing Egyptian beliefs as they relate to Freemasonry. The Blazing Star or l'Etoile Flamboyante, he says, is one of the most important symbols in Freemasonry, and is associated with Sirius, the brightest star in the heavens whose presence preceded the annual rising of the Nile, a seasonal indicator for Egyptian farmers (Pike, 1871, p. 15). The myth that arose out of this early agricultural knowledge was the story of Isis and Osiris, the gods who personified these natural processes. Citing Julius Firmicus, Pike describes Isis as the earth and Osiris as the seeds of fruit that died in winter and then came to life in spring with the help of the natural heat of the sun. The son of Isis, Horus, was to symbolise the sun which Pike describes as "the inexhaustible source of life, spark of uncreated fire, universal seed of all beings" (1871, p. 15). Later, Pike states that these original agricultural phenomena became linked to the nature of the human soul, stating: "The soul of man was as the seed hidden in the ground" (1871, p. 423). In his lecture for one of the highest degrees, the 28th or Knights of the Sun, Pike then arrives at an alchemical interpretation of these earlier myths stating that the Sun in the Hermetic Emerald Tablet is "the universal magic power ... the secret fire, living and philosophical ... the Universal Seed" (1871, p. 557).

So here again, Jung's initiator, speaking as Philemon, is drawing on Pike's lectures to create another confusing explanation for what Jung has undergone and what is coming next for him. But at this stage its meaning is fairly nonsensical; in the first part of this entry Jung is told that he belongs to the earth, then that he is earth, but at the end he is told that he does not belong to the earth and is foreign (*BB 6*, pp. 295, 296). This muddled version of the

Masonic teachings might not be easy to interpret but its emotional intent is very clear: it reinforces that the young Carl Jung is somehow very different to others, as if, internally, he has fallen into this world from a far distant star. But as the Masonic author Albert Mackey notes:

> In the 28th Degree of the Ancient and Accepted Scottish Rite, the explanation given of the Blazing Star, is, that it is symbolic of a Freemason, who, by perfecting himself in the way of truth, that is to say, by advancing in knowledge, becomes like a blazing star, shining with brilliance in the midst of darkness (1914, p. 106).

On one level, then, Philemon is saying that Jung's association with Sirius is an indicator that he is a Freemason, even if he does not know it. This aligns with his paternal grandfather's alteration of the family's coat-of-arms to include Masonic symbols, claiming membership of the Order for the entire family (Jung, 1963, p. 220; Brunet, 2019, p. 2). The naming of Jung as a "star seed" implies that he is not only the offspring of a Freemason but also a product of Freemasonry. Jung is told that "the star seed in you is immortal" and it is also referred to as "the grain of gold, that fell into your eye" (*BB 7*, pp. 148, 149).

At this point we see the re-appearance of the mystic fire, which Jung had previously encountered on January 18, 1916 (*BB 5*). This time, Jung sees a vision of fire and smoke as if the earth is on fire but in the middle is a flower blooming, comprised of gold and precious stones. It is possible that he may have related this vision to the impact of World War I, as this was the reality at the time, but there may be another interpretation. In the previous study, it was suggested that this mystic fire relates to the awakening of the Kundalini serpent and its progression through the spinal chakras which Jung appears to illustrate visually in the series of paintings accompanying the terrible shock of "The Sacrificial Murder" (Brunet, 2019, pp. 97–107). The manipulation of the chakra energy centres through some form of profound shock is one of the techniques associated with the ritual abuse of children (Miller, 2012, p. 100). These chakras can then be triggered to bring out alters in the body related to the different initiatory ordeals.

As *Book 7* begins, we see Philemon raising himself up, his head in the blazing fire and burning upward towards the heavens, as if undergoing a mystical experience, but he feels weighed down by the burden of the body. Jung is told that, in order to fully achieve this mystical state, he must offer further sacrifices. This entry occurs on June 3, 1917, but it is four months until the next entry where Jung states that he has brought offerings showing his willingness and submission. During this period he was on military service and it seems that he was referring to carrying out his soul's advice regarding Toni Wolff and Maria Moltzer. At this point a figure appears whom his soul describes as Ha, a black magician, satanic sorcerer and "spirit of deception" (*BB 7*, p. 148). Ha seems to be another introjected personality in Jung's imagination. His soul then engages in a lengthy conversation with Ha, which becomes very complex and the manner in which they speak is argumentative and melodramatic, like a piece of theatre. At the beginning Jung's soul addresses him as "you innocent one", suggesting that Jung is being spoken to as a youth, so it is possible that Jung may be remembering, in detail, a performance from his initiatory experiences involving these characters. As we shall see, this long conversation and series of so-called magical incantations are again drawn from the wording of Pike's Scottish Rite lectures, principally from the Third and 28th Degrees.

The character of Ha, the black magician, appears as a representative of satanic evil. He says he is necessary, but suffers from the exposure to too much dazzling light. He feels he wants to strangle someone and Jung's soul identifies him as "the one who hid himself in the black ape who wanted to kill the harmless one" (*BB 7*, p. 149). In his lecture for the Third Degree Pike (1871, p. 76) discusses the concept of Satan as being not a black god, but the negation of god, not a person but the concept of free will that was created for good, but could also serve evil. So, Ha's comment that he is necessary is based, in Pike's lecture, on the concept of Satan as free will. Pike also reminds the members that every moral characteristic of man can be found represented in the animal kingdom; he notes that there are humans who resemble "the apes that imitate and chatter" (1871, p. 57). The concept of apes in Masonic ritual goes back to the magical séances of the Egyptian Rite developed by Count Cagliostro in the late eighteenth century, which became a scandal (Schuchard, 1995). Apes or monkeys of various types were seen to represent the debased, bestial or animal nature of human beings, and their opposite was deemed to be the angels. In

113

these rituals they were represented either with men dressed in animal suits or with the presence of real monkeys, chained up and enacting sexual or vicious behaviour, "while the hypnotized participants gazed into their magical glass bowl and clouds of incense obscured the animal 'spirits' in the darkened lodge" (Schuchard, 1995, p. 188).

The statement about the black ape may also refer to a practice used in ritual abuse, where perpetrators can dress up in animal costumes to frighten the children. In my own case, as the daughter of a Freemason, I was put through similar frightening ordeals in my father's Masonic lodge. On one occasion, at the age of four, I was being held by two men in costume, one dressed as a bear and the other as a gorilla. They were pushing my head into papers on the black and white tiled floor, telling me I could never write about these experiences; then they would lift me up to look at a painting, saying that I could make paintings. Throughout my art career I produced images of gorillas and many of bears. For one exhibition, entitled *Screen Memories*, a play on the Freudian term, I used stills from old King Kong movies in which the gorilla carries a fainting woman. In Jung's case, could his child-self have been similarly frightened by a man dressed as an ape, who might have pretended to strangle him? (*BB 7*, p. 149).

Ha has a grain of gold that has fallen into his eye and burns him, and so he wants to get rid of it and is willing to bargain with Jung's soul, who will take it from him. In exchange, Jung's soul asks for Ha's science and "knowledge beyond Philemon" (*BB 7*, p.150). Ha claims that Jung's grain of gold fell into the dirt, that Jung does not like the dirt but that he does, as he loves dung and nurtures the scarab there. Another obscure passage, this appears to be a further example of the deliberate distortion of Pike's lectures to create a perplexing riddle.

In his lecture for the Third Degree, Pike states: "Gold, to the eye of the Initiates, is Light condensed" (1871, p. 76) and so if we substitute the word "light" for "gold" throughout Jung's passage to do with Ha it takes on the more usual meaning of the Freemason's search for light. Earlier in the lecture Pike had referred to the Hebrew word for gold, Zahab, meaning light. Asking "what is light?" he cites the science of the day that had shifted from its understanding of light as luminous particles, shot from the sun, to that of luminous waves (Pike, 1871, p. 57). This is one explanation which partially answers Jung's soul's request for Ha's science, but it is more likely that the answers she seeks are contained in a higher degree, the 28th, which involves the science of alchemy, thus explaining the request for "knowledge beyond Philemon". In his lecture for this degree Pike mentions the medieval alchemist, Raymond Lulle, who uses the term "seed of gold" as a necessary ingredient to the alchemical production of gold. Pike then states:

> The Great Work of Hermes is, therefore, an operation essentially magical, and the highest of all, for it supposes the Absolute in Science and in Will. There is light in gold, gold in light, and light in all things ... in all maladies of soul and body ... a single grain of the divine powder, is more sufficient to cure him (1871, pp. 557–558).

It appears, then, that the term "seed of gold" is a reference to alchemy, which in Pike's lecture proceeds from describing the attempts to chemically produce the metal gold to its symbolic role in terms of the transformation of the soul. The seed of gold falling into the dirt can then be seen as a symbolic way of representing Pike's wording in the Third Degree lecture, where he discusses the ancient concept of the soul, its divine nature and the need for it to experience the "sordidness and sin" associated with its attachment to the body (1871, p. 58). In his lecture for the 24th Degree, or Prince of the Tabernacle, Pike describes the meaning of the scarab for the ancient Egyptians as a symbol for "New Life out of Death and Rottenness – to them the greatest of mysteries" (1871, p. 312).[2] So, the dirt to which Ha refers is the sordidness and sin of earthly life and the dung and rottenness that the scarab symbolically transforms.

At this point Ha has been overcome by the torment and pain of the burning gold in his eye and accedes to Jung's soul's pressure. She tells him to spit out the secret and he will be released. In order to have the painful seed removed Ha chants "Kara–kara–krama–kras–tel–ham" and then describes a tree laden with golden and delicious fruit, full of seeds (*BB 7*, p. 151). Jung is ordered to get the book and read out the incantations that will help to release the seed from Ha's eye and Ha says that he is weaving an impenetrable mystery around him, while Jung's soul complains of a suffocating stink. Ha then declares that Philemon is not a man and neither is he; "I'm just a remnant", he says (*BB 7*, p. 151).

As this argument suggests, Philemon is not a man but an introjected alter personality. But Ha's statement that he is a remnant suggests that he is not a fully developed alter like Philemon, but may be a part or fragment that holds a painful experience. In some Masonic rituals from the nineteenth century the mysterious dazzling light created around the candidate was produced by igniting gum camphor kept in an urn on the altar (Duncan, 1866, p. 239). Camphor burns intensely and rapidly, producing a flare effect and its toxic smoke can cause coughing and wheezing and serious eye irritation, needing an immediate eye-wash or medical attention (Camphor Safety Data Sheet, 2014). Substituting the word "light" for the seed of gold in Ha's eye and the pain it inflicts may be a description of a chemical injury involving severe eye irritation from the toxic fumes of a sudden intense flash of light used in one of these rituals. The exposure to blinding lights has been documented as one of a series of cruel practices used on children in contemporary ritual abuse (Rutz, Becker, Overkamp & Karriker, 2008, 73).

Ha's chant in this entry also appears to be associated with Pike's lecture for the Third Degree. A gifted linguist, Pike provides several words in Sanskrit. While none of them exactly match the chant that Ha makes, the words Heri, Khur, Khirah and Aum, which he does mention, have a similar cadence (Pike, 1871, p. 61); their effect is certainly magical. So, again, the oddly arranged themes in Jung's active imagination here are drawn from Pike's lectures and given a deliberate twist to make them even more obscure and meaningless. The tree laden with the seed-filled golden fruit appears to be a reference to the biblical fig, the tree of the knowledge of good and evil, which when eaten "your eyes will be opened, and you will be like God, knowing good and evil" (Genesis 3:5). But as Alison Miller notes, in ritual abuse the introjected parts that are deliberately created during some form of trauma can be instructed that they are the perpetrator or a younger version of him, "born from his seed" (2012, pp. 51–52; 2018, p. 112). As we have seen in the previous chapter, Jung has been taken through many processes to raise him to the level of a god through experiences that could only be described as evil, each one of them creating another alter personality to add to his poly-fragmented psyche.

"... I crawled out of a stone ..." (*BB* 7, p. 151)

In this same entry of October 7, 1917 Ha then launches into a complex process involving mother, father, two cones and a series of runes. It begins with him crawling out of a stone and he says how this stone is shaped like a sharp block or cone: "It's beautiful, it's pointed above and completely round underneath and evenly proportioned" (*BB* 7, p. 151). This process takes place over several entries throughout September 1917 and Jung illustrates them visually in a number of his paintings in *Liber Novus*.[3] Image 72, for example, depicts six of these cones with the rounded ends fractured as if to depict a series of coloured diamonds.

In the Masonic initiatory process, the candidate is represented by the symbol of the rough ashlar, "a stone taken from the quarry in its rude and natural state" to be gradually transformed into the Perfect Ashlar, the stone that has been worked into a cubical form by the workmen; Pike also talks of the diamond concealed in the rough dark stone (1871, pp. 8, 534). So, Ha's description of the beautiful cone appears to be referring to a diamond, as in image 72. This interpretation is confirmed in Image 121, Jung's painting of a mandala with the shape of a faceted diamond at its centre. Masonic initiation, then, is represented as a gradual process of refinement, but Ha's metaphor of "crawling out of the stone" conveys a different concept: while it implies something emerging out of this process, the verb "to crawl" conveys an image of exhaustion or suffering and the sense of having to learn everything all over again from the very beginning, like an infant.

In his lecture for the 25th Degree or Knight of the Brazen Serpent Pike expands the concept of the journey of the soul in the Mystery tradition (1871, pp. 314–317). Originally, he says, the soul was regarded as dwelling in the heavenly realms, but lured by the desire of animating a body it undergoes the journey from the heavens to earth, where it will be imprisoned in matter. On its way the soul supposedly passes through the constellations represented by the signs of the Zodiac; these were called "gates". Note here the gates of Jung's fantasy castle and the "gate of splendor" where Philemon stands (*BB 6*, p. 292). In this process, Pike says, the soul loses its spherical shape, "the shape of all Divine Nature, and is lengthened into a cone, as a point is lengthened into a line" (1871, p. 315). Then the soul experiences the disorder of matter but forgets the many journeys it has undergone, seemingly the memory of former lives. In this philosophy life on earth is equated with the death of the soul, and the symbols of initiation are all related to the Masonic interpretation of the astronomy of the ancient Mysteries (Pike 1871, p. 317; Brown, 1882/2002). Later in this lecture Pike refers to the cone again, in relation to the sun and moon in Egyptian mythology, which were regarded as the two great Gods, the male Osiris and female Isis, or in Jung's fantasy, the father and mother. He now refers to the cone in terms of the shape of the shadow that the earth projects, which produces night (Pike, 1871, p. 337). In the context of ritual abuse, the symbol of the cone can then be seen to represent the imprisoned soul and the cone shaped like a diamond, the soul that has been refashioned by the hardening process of the many traumatic initiatory ordeals. It is a process undertaken in the shadows and what is forgotten is the memory of each of the excruciating ordeals that this process has entailed.

Ha describes the diamond shape of the black mother stone hardened to such an extent that she can no longer feel: "She can't laugh and can't cry and is totally like hard stone", he says (*BB 7*, p. 151). He says he hates his father who concocted this and even though he loves everything to be regular and straight, he cannot help but disturb things, to make things bent or distorted. Ha, then, is describing himself as an internal part or fragment that cannot feel joy or grief due to the horror of the initiatory ordeals. Consequently, he acts as a disruptive force, producing erratic responses in the man Jung, so that he acts weak and indecisive when he should be "strong and fireproof" (*BB 7*, p. 152). Much later, in 1958, when he was contemplating the sorting of the black and gold seeds, Jung realised that he, himself, was the shaman and that the character of Ha was healed (*BB 7*, p. 149, n. 5). This suggests that by remembering and recording these bizarre machinations, despite their strangeness, that he has gone some way towards healing this internal part. However, it could also indicate that he felt that he had imposed all of these dark psychological changes onto himself; that he is responsible for them and not his initiators.

118

In this and the next seven entries there is a series of hieroglyphic-style phrases that appear to be some form of imaginary language rather than an identifiable one. In *Morals and Dogma* there are many references to hieroglyphs. Pike talks of an obscure text in a mysterious language, the Divine tongue, whose hieroglyphics few can decipher and says that only through initiation can one learn to decipher it (1871, pp. 18–19, 260). Jung's hieroglyphs involve serpent-like shapes and in one there is a circle with a cross. In the lecture for the 25th Degree Pike discusses hieroglyphic characters on the Rosetta stone that involve snakes and the four quarters of the world divided by a cross, so there is a similarity there (1871, p. 355).

But Ha's bewildering explanation of these hieroglyphs only adds to the mystery. They contain two suns, upper and lower cones, a serpent winding its way around the suns and various arrangements of parallel lines and spirals. At certain points the sun is imprisoned and then freed, and contained within prisons above and below, and there is a quadrilateral shape, "which you call thoughts, a door-less prison with thick walls", which accords with the observations about programming methods that involve creating internal structures for the containment of alter states (Miller, 2012, p. 46). These actions create splits, "instead of one, you are 4, and split", and are then re-formed back into the one again (*BB 7*, pp. 152–154). These strange steps with all their permutations of movements continue until October 11. They conclude with Ha saying "Ha-Ha-Ha–a jolly name–I am clever" and he talks of the magic of the white man, Christianity (*BB 7*, p. 157). Jung dismisses these convoluted instructions as a fairytale and a monotonous magic spell with no meaning, while his soul feels sick with nausea at Ha's nonsense. However, Philemon describes it as the truth, seen from behind, and teaches them a song celebrating Phanes (*BB 7*, pp. 157–159). Philemon's claim that it is the truth may indeed be valid as Ha appears to be describing a complex programming system that is not unlike those used on victims of ritual abuse today.

The previous study examined Jung's series of nineteen paintings accompanying "The Sacrificial Murder" in *Liber Secundus* (Brunet 2019, pp. 97–107). These paintings contain the elements of the black and gold seeds, the cones and the Blazing Star and images 89 and 90 include hieroglyphs similar to those in *Black Book 7*. The analysis of these paintings linked them to the practice of Kundalini, themes from the Kabbalah, symbols associated with Goetic or Ceremonial Magic and grimoires such as *The Lesser Key of Solomon*, which involves the conjuring of demons. The Freemason, A. E. Waite, decried the use of these black magic practices, describing them as travesties of occult doctrine and a debased application of the Kabbalah (1898/1913, pp. 9–12, 14). As Stella Katz notes, at a later stage in their training in the Reversed Kabbalah, the child is taught a higher form of black magic and demon spell work (2012, p. 113). This is what Jung appears to be remembering. So, while Ha's description of himself as Ha-Ha-Ha suggests that everything he says is a game or joke, it is possible that his obscure instructions could be describing some type of programming as they seem to suggest the locking up of Jung's inner parts or alters in some systematic way in different parts of the psyche.

"…the black magician's brother. He prowls around me." (*BB7*, p. 163).

On October 22, 1917 another character appears; this is Ka, who describes himself as the other side of Ha and the commencement of the soul. Ka is a concept that appears in the *Egyptian Book of the Dead*. Wallace Budge (1936, p. 86) describes it in terms of the death of Osiris where Horus embraces him and transfers his own Ka, meaning his own power, in a doubling action. Ka's description of himself as the other side of Ha also implies some sort of doubling or mirroring action and could be seen as another reference to the splitting of the psyche that can occur in the context of a highly traumatic experience. He appears to be a further introjected personality in Jung's imagination. In *Liber Novus* Ka does not speak, but Jung depicts him artistically in Image 122. His mottled face is a cross between a human and a goat and he has a long beard; it is set against a painted background of sedimentary rocks embedded with fossils. As the previous study suggests, the face appears to be a theatrical mask (Brunet, 2019, p. 121). The prehistoric setting suggests that we could be looking at another frightening episode for the child Jung, possibly in early childhood, where a masked figure like this might have appeared.

From October 1917 through to July 1919, Jung records many conversations that include this character, some of them intense arguments between Ka and

Philemon. Ka claims to be Philemon's shadow, his dark side. When Philemon states that he does not care that he has "dipped [his] robe in the blood of this man" (meaning Jung), and asks coldly what is innocence to him, and then preaches about the consoling powers of Phanes, Ka is outraged and protests: "The red of your mantle is blood ... It cries of crimes against the innocent" (*BB 7*, pp. 165–166). Ka is not hoodwinked by Philemon, which suggests that Ka represents a part of Jung who knows that he has been tricked and criminally abused during his childhood, as this argument suggests. Then Philemon, himself, admits his guilt: "My hand is red from the blood of the guiltless. I tore the eternal good from his flesh", he says, but adds that it was for the purpose of connecting him to the splendour and imperishable gold of a mystical state (*BB 7*, p. 166). However, Ka names Philemon a liar, swindler and thief who stole from Jung when he was a minor and made him into a slave for the sake of his own lust for power. Jung is then asked to respond to this situation but feels pulled between the two extremes of heaven and the realm of Phanes, and earth, represented by Ka. He decides to leave the situation as it is, stating that this is his life and that *he* is the seed between the shadow and the light. Philemon and Ka bless him for choosing this approach, but his soul then questions his decision, implying that he is still being controlled by these inner characters. So, at this stage, it seems that Jung wants to retain the connection with the mystical states he has experienced, despite the fact that they were orchestrated through torturous procedures in childhood. Having been born into this situation, seemingly a cult that practices this interpretation of ancient beliefs, this *is* his life and all that he really knows.

In the following discussions between these inner characters Ka continues to dwell on the harsh reality and pain associated with these beliefs and describes Philemon's focus on their beauty and wonder as a "divine work of delusion" (*BB 7*, p. 169). He says how Jung's eyes were blindfolded, a direct comment on initiation, and applies the metaphor of the tree and its leaves and their decay to critique Philemon's teachings about immortality and Gnostic beliefs in metempsychosis (*BB 7*, p. 169). Ka's discussion of the life and death of trees amounts to a general meditation on death and he then applies the metaphor of the seed and the speck of dust to a rather confusing passage on the vastness of the heavens and immensity of the soul.

121

These subjects, again, appear to be drawing on themes throughout *Morals and Dogma*, but in a deliberately confusing manner. In a discussion of human pride Pike describes man "stalking through infinite space in all the grandeur of littleness! Perched on a speck of the universe, every wind of Heaven strikes into his blood the coldness of death ..." (1871, p. 32). Pike then refers to the soul as growing like an oak and describes every leaf and every blade of grass holding secrets within them; in a later lecture he talks of the decay of vegetation and the falling of leaves as an emblem of the power that changes life into death and then back again (1871, pp. 86, 158, 350). He lectures the members on Socrates' notion that the right pursuit of philosophy is studying how to die and the concept of death as the great mystery; a little later he describes the Indian Mysteries and their doctrine of Metempsychosis (Pike, 1871, pp. 283, 308). In one of the last lectures, for the 28th Degree, Pike describes the theory of atheism where death is the end and again uses the metaphor of the speck of dust (1871, p. 465). So, whoever delivered these speeches to Jung originally, was again drawing on the Scottish Rite lectures, but by deleting the context and melding the opposing philosophies together it results in a confusing message embedded in seemingly profound language.

In February 10, 1918 Jung's soul states that Ka is the brother of Buddha, another curious comment. The explanation for this also lies in *Morals and Dogma* where Pike notes that the Freemasons regard Buddha as "the first Masonic legislator ... who, about a thousand years before the Christian era, reformed the religion of Manous" (1871, p. 202). Despite the historical vagueness the Buddha is seen as a brother Mason, thus explaining why Ka is regarded as Buddha's brother here. When Ka asks Jung for a response to all of this and to decide whose truth he wants, Jung states that he must find his own answers:

> What do I know of Philemon's truth, or yours? I know that you speak of your truth and you contradict one another. So my truth decides. The second principle of my truth goes: I don't know. You know your truth and Philemon knows his. I don't know mine. That is the truth (*BB 7*, p. 171).

This statement suggests that Jung is thinking independently of the influence of these inner characters, and yet it may also be the case that he is following the directives of the Masonic lectures even here. In his lecture for the 10th Degree Pike describes the positive qualities of the true Mason who follows the Masonic path, one of which is where: "He accepts what his mind regards as true, what his conscience decides is right, what his heart deems generous and noble; and all else he puts far from him" (1871, p. 120).

By February 28, 1918 (*BB 7*) Jung is still wondering how he can solve the question of Philemon and Ka and their seemingly opposing views, but his soul tells him that Philemon has been captured when he painted his image, and Ka has been accepted. Nevertheless, the two characters still argue and cause problems for Jung. His soul tells him that he has imbued them with too much power and that they give him a false splendour, suggesting a false sense of mystical illumination, and a false shadow, meaning the powerful feelings of guilt that were artificially generated through the initiatory ordeals. The solution to these extremes, his soul implies, lies in the mediating aspects of everyday life, an explanation that Jung finds astonishing, presumably because it is such a simple explanation for these complex problems.

On March 1, 1918 (*BB 7*) Jung's soul launches into a lengthy and confusing discourse on the nature of God and the attitude which Jung should take towards him. The seed metaphor appears again, but in another confusing manner where his soul describes God as not knowing himself as the seed. Jung admits that these concepts are too difficult and that he does not follow them; he describes them as "a Danaid's barrel of endlessness and meaninglessness" (*BB 7*, p. 180). Jung's soul then mentions the Buddha again. In Pike's lecture for the First Degree he discusses the role of prayer in the Masonic ceremonies along with the nature of God and faith from a Masonic perspective. Immediately after this he turns to the symbol of the two pillars between which the Apprentice enters, representing the entrance to Solomon's Temple. These pillars are crowned with a bronze decoration of pomegranates which "appear to have imitated the shape of the seed-vessel of the lotus or Egyptian lily, a sacred symbol of the Hindus and Egyptians" and proceeds to discuss the "universal seed of all beings" (Pike, 1871, pp. 11, 15). He then outlines the ten commandments for Freemasons: the first refers to God as having various qualities including immutable wisdom and supreme intelligence, and when he mentions Buddha in a later lecture, he refers to him as "[comprehending] his own person", that is, knowing himself as a god (Pike, 1871, p. 61).

Jung's soul's complicated version of these Masonic teachings is therefore portraying the opposite attitude to God to that represented in the Masonic lectures, again intended to thoroughly confuse him. Jung's reference to the Danaids can also be found in *Morals and Dogma* (p. 275) where, in his lecture for the 24th Degree, Pike mentions the daughters of Danaus whose crime was that they had shown contempt for the Mysteries of Eleusis and were punished in Tartarus. Even though Jung is still trying to understand these concepts he is able to identify the deliberate attempts at obfuscation when he asks his soul if she has been struck by a foreign spirit. She answers that she is under a spell from a foreign power and tells him he must take over with his science, suggesting that he must work on these themes rationally from now on. Stating that her work is done, she bids him farewell.

But on April 15, 1918 (*BB 7*) his soul returns with more confusion about Ka, Philemon and the god Phanes, as well as ramblings about inner and outer roads and confusing explanations about how to differentiate the I from the self. She concludes this section, which vaguely describes balancing the inner and outer, with the word "Amen" and states that this is the usual word to use after such mysteries. "I hate all mysteries", she ironically says (*BB 7*, p. 183). The final lecture in *Morals and Dogma* is for the 32nd Degree or Sublime Prince of the Royal Secret. Here, Pike discusses the importance of balance in the Masonic life and of maintaining equilibrium in all things. He concludes his lecture with a capitalised Latin phrase: 'GLORIA DEI EST CELARE VERBUM. AMEN', "it is the glory of God to hide the word" (Pike, 1871, p. 621). It appears that Jung's soul (the introjected voice of one or more of his initiators) is using the Scottish Rite lectures almost to the last one, which is the 33rd Degree, but at the same time mocking their secrets by muddling the themes to such an extent as to make them appear even more impenetrable than they already are.

At this point Philemon and Ka reappear, still bickering. Ka demands to know why he should be condemned to a "dark, solitary, joyless existence" while Philemon deceives the world with his "hypocritical golden haze" (*BB 7*, p.

184). Ka claims that Philemon now has a broken wing and is no longer effective, but the children, "the titans", have heard Ka's words and now "shake the foundations." This entry suggests that there might be a shift in Jung's understanding of what has happened to his child self. Viewed in terms of dissociation, Ka would then represent the part of the self that experiences the pain of the abuse that is pushed downwards into the earth and into darkness, while another part of the psyche rises upwards to the heavens, towards a glorious mystical state of release from the pain. Six weeks later, Jung's soul reinforces the beneficial effects of Ka as a symbol for Jung's connection to the earth and to the people he loves, but she also warns that this is a limitation. Philemon, she says, fears this link to the earth and knows how to fly, saying "he sees the serpent among the roses and wants to be a butterfly" (*BB 7*, p. 185). This reference to the serpent and roses recalls the 18th Degree of the Scottish Rite or Rose Croix, where in Jung's fantasy of his experience of Christ's crucifixion he includes the sensation of the Mithraic serpent wrapped around his own body, with the butterfly a common symbol of the psyche, as its Greek origin suggests.

Jung's next journal entries in July and August 1918 are primarily focused on his relationships with the women in his life, as discussed in Chapter Two. But during this period, he is also hoping for some sort of completion to this difficult process: "Is the I born?" he writes (*BB 7*, p. 185). However, according to Jung's soul in the entry of July 10, 1918, completion involves further complexity involving Toni Wolff, discussed previously, and the repeated use of the number four: four sufferings, four joys, four winds and four streams. At this point Phanes reappears and delivers a sermon-like speech containing the symbolism of the number four, and then proceeds to describe the nature of completion. The symbolism of the number four is addressed multiple times throughout *Morals and Dogma* and in the lecture for the Second Degree Pike cites its biblical use including the four streams in the Garden of Eden, the four winds of Heaven, the four creatures seen by Ezekiel, and so on. In his lecture for the Third Degree he refers to the four words that are abbreviated in the Kabbalah that "[express] the synthesis of the whole dogma and the totality of the Kabalistic science" (Pike, 1871, p. 77). There are many more references to its significance in Pike's lectures and Phanes' reiteration of the symbolism of the number four appears to draw on these same repeated references to it in *Morals and Dogma*.

It is not until January 25, 1919 that the theme of magic reappears with the opening sentence, "a heavy sacrifice has been brought", accompanied by a disturbing image of Philemon, now called the Chinese magician, raising a child up and then throwing him to the ground (*BB 7*, p. 195).[4] Magical chains are mentioned and Philemon and Ka react in their characteristic ways: Philemon scurries away to higher spheres, dissociating from the violence, and "Ka rumbles, shaking on the rocks" as if he feels this violent action bodily. The question is: is this simply a metaphor or a memory of something Jung has witnessed in his childhood, even some violent action towards another child? Jung's soul says that she saw it and says that he must let "everything distant [come] to pass" (*BB 7*, p. 196). In other words, she seems to be telling him to allow the memories to emerge. Witnessing extreme cruelty towards other children or small animals, whether real or simulated, is another practice used in ritual abuse, aimed at demonstrating the power the abusers have over life and death (Rutz et al, 2008; Noblitt & Perskin Noblitt, 2014).

In the next entry, on February 2, Ka tells Jung that he thinks too much and so he has deliberately covered him in sorrow. "You should not think, but procreate", he says (*BB 7*, p. 196). Read in one way, Ka seems to be encouraging Jung to let go of his intellectual attitude towards these experiences and to feel them more; by truly connecting with his pain and sorrow this will allow him to work through it more creatively and imbue him with more strength. But the term "procreation" could also mean the creation of more alters in the psyche, so Ka's advice may be reinforcing the programming. Ka also says that Jung has become "psychically feminized" by Salome and needs to become a man (*BB 7*, p. 197). At this, Jung asks his soul why she has kept this from him, but she protests that she does not know what Salome is doing, but Ka does; she says her focus is on the light, not on the activities in the shadows.

The phenomenon of alters being unaware of the existence or experience of other alter personalities in an individual was first noted by Pierre Janet in 1886. He called them "nuclei of consciousness which can continue to lead lives of their own" in a patient named Lucie/Adrienne (cited in Somer, 2016, p. 94).

These separate internal states can be trauma-induced through overwhelming situations, but also hypnotically induced (Noblitt & Perskin Noblitt, 2014; van der Hart, 2016). We have seen these two methods of splitting the personality in Jung's active imaginations. Discussing clients with trauma-derived DID the psychotherapist Phil Mollon (2016, p. 213) notes that those clients with more complex and severe symptoms appear to have endured deliberate childhood torture by abusers. These intentional practices can produce individuals who can function normally in conventional roles in society, work and family, but have no memory of other more clandestine experiences or roles that they have played. Until his confrontation with his own unconscious Jung was functioning conventionally in these other areas of his life and was totally unaware of this other side of his life and its extreme complexity.

On March 22, 1919 Jung reports how hellishly difficult this process is. He asks his soul for help but she criticises him for his soft heart, as Ka had done, and relates this to his tendency to suffer through the suffering of others. "Do you want me to plunge myself into the heat of eternal procreation?" she says (*BB 7*, p. 198). This appears to be a comment on Jung's psychology practice, where, by being too involved with the pain of others, he may be exposed to too much vicarious trauma and to the risk of creating more internal alters in himself. She reminds him of his Golgotha, a direct reference to his personal crucifixion in the abusive version of the Rose Croix degree. Philemon then explains that Golgotha is death for the sake of the Gods and that the Gods want him to give his life to them and not to men. He says that doing this will ensure that he does not continue to procreate, that is, to create an even more fragmented psyche through vicarious trauma. Jung is unsure of what this means and asks Ka, who reinforces the idea of giving himself to the Gods. Ka states that Jung is of no use if he continues to procreate, and reminds him that he has drawn magic from the black rod. It seems that each of Jung's alters here – his soul, Philemon and Ka – are all urging him to give up his therapeutic practice and, in one way or another, are coercing him to join forces with the purpose put forward by the original abusers, that is, to become a leader in service of the cult, which will be discussed in Chapter Six. "I see the inevitable", Jung says, which may mean that he realises what he must do now (*BB 7*, p. 198).

Another five weeks pass and it is clear that Jung is becoming more and more distanced from the discussions with these inner characters. On April 30, 1919 (*BB 7*) he approaches his soul asking her to tell him what she knows, but says he will not ask again for a long while. She tells him of Philemon celebrating a triumph over men, but Jung cannot accept this. It is nearly three months before he approaches her again, on July 21, 1919, and wants to speak to her. He does not have any dreams at this time and she says that he does not need them, but that something is going on between Philemon and Ka, which she cannot see. She encourages Jung to keep going on his way, and seemingly to leave these internal matters alone for a while. Here, Jung is still feeling lost with all of this complexity, possibly exacerbated by the physical effects of the Spanish flu.

Despite nearly three years of attempting to understand this dark area of magic Jung has still not reached any real clarity and is just as puzzled by it as ever. This chapter has demonstrated that the reason for this is that his internal characters have been deliberately attempting to confuse him and lead him up "a thousand blind alleys" with a false atmosphere of profundity (*BB 7*, p. 191). It argues that the themes used by his initiators are taken directly from *Morals and Dogma*, but are distorted in order to mislead him. But even Pike, himself, was aware of the historical misuse of Masonic rituals in order to create bogus mysteries and a pseudo mysticism (1871, pp. 236–237). The bewildering form of complexity that Jung is being fed here appears to be aimed at keeping him perennially searching for answers that may never come.

Today, amongst reports by ritual abuse survivors, there are those who realise that to engage with the programming on its own terms is not useful. One survivor, C.A. Beck, talks about her attempts to unravel the complexity of her programming, which presented as an intricate system of mirrors and matrix programming. She writes:

> I had a diamond matrix ... It was composed of RA stuff like complicated belief systems such as the Kabbalah. I could have spent a lifetime confused and lost trying to figure it all out ... My complex programming initially frightened me. I thought it was so exotic, so otherworldly, that

I did not have a fighting chance against it ... Everything was geometrical patterns and mathematical codes ... I soon realized that I was thinking using the premises of the programming. It had been designed to block me, and as long as I thought in *its* terms, I was indeed blocked. I have come to believe that it does not work well to use the perpetrators' framework. By doing so you are buying into their belief system and reinforcing it (Cited in Miller, 2012, pp. 164–166).

By attempting to explore the magic practices discussed above Jung appears to have been doing exactly what this survivor describes, that is, trying to understand them only in terms of the perpetrators' framework. But there was no knowledge of these diabolically complex practices in Jung's time and he was also doing this work alone, with no outside help to provide a different perspective or to steer him through the minefield. Throughout 1919, though, the spaces between his entries are getting longer suggesting that he is beginning to pull away, at least from the frustrating and convoluted conversations between his inner parts. We shall see where this takes him in the next chapter.

Notes

1 In *Liber Novus* Atmavictu is spelled with a 'c', whereas in the *Black Books* it is spelled Atmaviktu.
2 The capitalisation here is Pike's.
3 Seven entries from September 1917 have been arranged in *Book 7* to follow the entry Jung's of October 7, 1917.
4 The underlining of this phrase is Jung's.

5

"What sort of dreams are these that rob me of sleep?" (*BB 7*, p. 206)

From August 1919 Jung begins to focus more on his dreams rather than investing so much energy in frustrating conversations with his soul. Six of them, from August 1919 to May 1920, are recorded in his dream book but the editor has included them in *Book 7*. The rest of this journal contains further dreams along with more examples of active imaginations and some final discussions with his soul; the last recorded mention of a dream is in 1932. Some of them are nightmarish, filled with overwhelming fear that robs him of sleep, while others appear to be directing him back to his original visions and fantasies, as if he must turn to these for answers rather than rely on the confusing, argumentative and sometimes nonsensical conversations between himself and his inner parts. This chapter will trace the themes of these dreams and examine the last conversations he then has with his soul, taking us to the final entries in the *Black Books*. It will demonstrate, again, that Albert Pike's *Morals and Dogma* and several Scottish Rite rituals will provide more answers to the obscure symbolism appearing in these dreams, visions and fantasies.

"Then I had a dream." (*BB 7*, p. 200, n. 138).

The first of these dreams in 1919 is recorded in a footnote to the entry of July 21 as it has no specific date other than the year when it took place, but Jung writes that he is not sure whether it was a dream or a vision. It comes during his struggle with the effects of having the Spanish flu which left him feeling that he was losing his grip on life. In this dream he finds himself in a small sailboat on a wild sea; a monstrous wave swamps the boat and he lands on a volcanic island, describing it as a dead country or lunar landscape. Here, he sees a sphere lying on the ground, although he wonders if it is hovering, while a beautiful scene of a wonderful evening sky vaulted over the island induces a sense of healing. The sphere floats between two trees and then is contained in a precious tent in the harbour of Sousse in Tunisia. This dream contains a prediction – that he would go to Sousse a few months later – and there, to his amazement, he will see the same type of boat in the harbour. Above all, it is a healing dream, guiding him through from a high fever and possible death through to a place of safety.

There is a wealth of symbolism contained in this dream or vision, and given that many of Jung's visions have been identified throughout the previous study as being related to memories of initiatory themes, it is possible that this is another example. Given the near-death threat of the dangerous flu, the experience of being in a small boat, overwhelmed by a giant wave and washed up on the shore is an apposite metaphor; but it is also a concept that has been used in fraternal side degree initiations, those initiatory practices not approved by the official Masonic lodges. These practices made use of use of equipment or devices in their initiatory theatrics aimed at tricking the initiates and creating states of fear or shock, which we saw in several of Jung's active imaginations in *Liber Novus* (Brunet, 2019). With the increase in membership of fraternal organisations during the late 19th century several companies arose that manufactured equipment for these side degrees. In America, for example, several enormous fraternal supply houses were established in the Midwest during the 1870s and 1880s (Moore, 2010, p. 26). One American company, DeMoulin Brothers, advertised a device in their 1908 catalogue known as the Ocean Wave Boat, which was used to manipulate the imagination of the candidate during an initiatory ordeal. The blindfolded candidate is conducted into a "boat" that is pushed around the lodge room by the members and then the candidate is "landed" onto a wet sponge or into a pan of water prior to further trials. The accompanying illustration to this device has a drawing labelled "As it appears to the Candidate" showing a figure in a boat in rough seas, demonstrating the role of the candidate's imagination during the ordeal (DeMoulin, 1908, p. 63). Given the evidence of multiple initiatory trials in Jung's *Black Books*, it is possible that the first part of Jung's vision could be connected with a memory of a similar type of initiatory ordeal undergone much earlier in his life.

At this point *Morals and Dogma* is again of use as one of the key themes running throughout the lectures is the belief amongst the ancient philosophers and celebrants of the Mysteries about the nature of the soul before birth and after death. This was the belief that the human soul returns to its source in the Infinite by ascending through the seven spheres of the seven planets, namely the Moon, Mercury, Venus, the Sun, Mars, Jupiter, and Saturn (Pike, 1871, p. 12). In Jung's vision, rather than passing through the spheres, the sphere becomes the symbol of his soul, which he first sees as grounded, but now floats. In other words, his soul is beginning to ascend and the fact that he is on a moonlike landscape suggests that he has reached the first stage. This would correlate with the feeling that he was losing his hold on life during his illness.

In Jung's vision the sphere then floats between two trees. In these ancient beliefs the soul's ascent through the spheres is associated with the signs of the Zodiac, based originally on Egyptian observations about the stars in relation to agriculture. In *Morals and Dogma* Pike discusses the signs of the Zodiac and mentions Mithraic monuments that contain a depiction of two trees, "one covered with young leaves, and at its foot a little bull and a torch burning; and the other loaded with fruit, and at its foot a Scorpion, and a torch reversed and extinguished" (1871, p. 344). Jung was well aware of the prominent role played by Mithraism in his own inner world and this metaphor of the two trees is an apt description of his life, beginning with the youthful one, full of bullish energy and enthusiasm, and the older tree that has produced much fruitful work throughout its life, but now must die.

However, the last dream picture shows the sphere in a new position: it is now kept in a precious tent near the Sousse harbour, where the traditional African boats are docked. The ancient city of Sousse was once part of the Carthaginian empire, which dominated the western Mediterranean until it was finally defeated by the Romans during the Third Punic War (149–146 BCE); during this war Sousse changed its allegiance from Carthage to Rome (Britannica, "Sousse", 2023). If we are to continue with the argument that Jung's visions relate to *Morals and Dogma* then the theme of ancient Carthage is another of

Pike's subjects. In his lecture for the First Degree he gives advice to the new apprentices about the attitude they must take towards their Masonic duty. He uses the example of a few Carthaginian soldiers who were taken prisoner during the Roman invasion and says these soldiers refused to bow to the Roman consul Flaminius: "Masons should possess an equal greatness of soul", he says (Pike, 1871, p. 19). Albert Pike was a Confederate general during the American Civil War so it is quite possible that his encouragement of apprentice Masons to behave like brave but conquered Carthaginian soldiers was a military analogy close to his own heart. It is possible that Jung's link between being washed up on shore and ancient Carthage was part of an initiatory narrative. In my own initiations conducted in my father's Masonic lodge during childhood I had a vision similar to Jung's, remembering it decades before the *Black Books* were published. This was where I was made to believe that I was a black man, an ancient soldier laying on the shore of the Mediterranean Sea in North Africa where I was to die. I felt that I was being encouraged to believe that it was an experience of a past death, but clearly it was another initiatory trick based on the Scottish Rite lectures and the moral tale of the Carthaginian soldiers. Like Jung, I must have been under some form of hypnosis.

The final resting place of Jung's sphere in his vision is in a "precious tent". This is an unmistakable biblical reference to the tabernacle of the Israelites during their journey through the wilderness. In Jung's vision it appears to represent his soul returning to the body, symbolised as a tabernacle, indicating that he is not going to die, and reflecting New Testament teachings of the body as a tabernacle (2 Peter 1:14; 2 Corinthians 5:1). The Old Testament tabernacle appears in two Scottish Rite degrees, the 23rd or Chief of the Tabernacle where the presiding officer represents the High Priest, Aaron, and in the 24th or Prince of the Tabernacle, where the Master represents Moses (Blanchard, 1905/2002, pp. 106, 122). The use of the term "precious" may have a further meaning in this context. In Pike's lectures he mentions the philosophical writings of Josephus or Titus Flavius Josephus (37/38–100 CE), a Jewish historian who descended from a family of high priests of Israel, who was also a military leader who opposed the Roman army (Poole, 2024); for this reason, he was possibly another of Pike's favourite authors. In his lecture for the 24th Degree Pike notes that Josephus argues that the Temple of Solomon contained many symbols of the universe, the constellations and the whole world; amongst them was the breast-plate of the High Priest, which contained twelve precious stones, symbolising the twelve months and the twelve signs of the Zodiac (1871, p. 294). Pike then adds that Hermes calls the Zodiac, the Great Tent or Tabernaculum. It is quite possible that, during the pandemic that killed up to fifty million people from 1918 to 1920, Jung's dream or vision was tapping into his earlier initiatory experiences to provide a series of potent symbols to pull him through from near-death back to life. It also suggests that his desire to go to Sousse in present-day Tunisia might have been prompted by the strength of this vision, and while it is a healing dream, it was also guiding him to undertake a physical journey to a place where he might learn more about his inner life.

In the same month in 1919 Jung records four more dreams, three of which include members of his family, namely his wife, his children and his mother, as well as two youths and two young men. It is possible that these references to children and youths are urging him to look back at his childhood memories and connect to them more closely. In the first dream he is in an anatomical museum, recently arranged by a great artist, and where there are four old anatomical books, "gloriously bound" (*BB 7*, p. 201). Jung disliked being called an artist, preferring to call his own image-making "an aestheticizing tendency" (1963, p. 181). But the dream may be saying that the recent arrangement of the museum refers to the work he has done on himself in the previous years and his emphasis on recording this process in his beautifully bound *Red Book*. If so, this would align with the advice Albert Pike offers in *Morals and Dogma*, which states:

> ... every man has a work to do in himself, greater and sublimer than any work of genius; and works upon a nobler material than wood or marble – upon his own soul and intellect ... [and] may so be the greatest of artists, and of authors [of] his life (1871, p. 253).

On the wall in this dream Jung sees a prepared heart with a piece of tendon and also individual "fingers". His five-year old daughter, Lili, wants to tear them down and play with them, but he stops her. The physical heart does contain tendons, the chordae tendineae, colloquially known as the heartstrings, and when the heart is illustrated anatomically the various arteries and veins, cut off from the rest of the anatomy, can appear like individual fingers. So, this image of a heart, totally separated from the body, and the reference to heartstrings might suggest some form of profound emotional disconnection. In the dream his little daughter wants to tear this object down and play with it, suggesting that the five-year old part of himself may provide more insight into his initiatory traumas if only he would allow her to have some input; but he prevents this from occurring.

In the next part of the dream Jung sees an old rotting ship's cannon that was discovered by two youths, who were using some form of magic wand, along with further references to military fortifications. Here we are reminded of an earlier entry from January 22, 1914 (*BB 4*) that was transferred to "The Three Prophesies" in *Liber Novus,* where old rusty weapons and traces of old magic talismans are brought to the surface. In the following entry the black rod of magic was offered to him and appears in "The Gift of Magic" in *Liber Novus*. In the previous study the author asked whether Jung was a youth undergoing these experiences and this dream may confirm such a conclusion (Brunet, 2019, p. 123).

Here, his wife Emma tells him that the cannon seems to be more relevant to his son Franz, who would have been nearly eleven years old at this time, so the dream may be suggesting that Jung should look back to this age in his own childhood. In the dream Franz is dressed in uniform, wears an American hat and carries a toy gun. In the previous dream, as we have seen, there is a military emphasis that reflects Albert Pike's role as an American general in the Confederate army, so it is possible that the American military garb worn by the boy might be alluding to Pike's military themes. Jung then describes the boy as "hollow-cheeked and bent like a medieval scholar", with his "mouth and eyes wide open, completely dumb and stupefied" (*BB 7*, p. 201), which could be read as a description of a child in a state of shock. The dream's image of the medieval scholar is clearly a reference to the adult Jung, buried deeply in his scholarly research into the ancient and medieval Mysteries in his attempt to discover the causes of his own psychological disturbance. But the dream indicates that it is the traumas of a military-grade initiatory process undergone during his youth that is the source, leaving an inner part, a boy of the approximate age of his son Franz, still frozen in a state of complete shock.

At this point Jung describes a vision that occurs on the same night, of a great angel praying in the corner of his bedroom. The angel is described as severe and is accompanied by a dark and dangerous ghostly mass. Then a deathly pale maiden with black hair around twenty-eight years old appears; her eyes are almost closed and she produces an uncomfortable sexual feeling in him. The atmosphere of this vision is oppressive with the angel a symbol of darkness, not light. The presence of the deathly young woman may be a dream reminder of his first meeting with Salome in "Mysterium Encounter" in *Liber Primus* where she enters as a beautiful blind maiden and asks him to love her; but he says he is horrified by her. In this vision in 1919 she is not fully blind, but her eyes are partially closed, signifying that Jung has partially uncovered her significance. As we have seen in Chapter Two, Jung related the character of Salome to his affair with Tony Wolff. Once again, this vision appears to be encouraging Jung to take another look at his earliest active imaginations, where the initiatory themes that he must address are perhaps in their clearest form.

Two more dreams in August 1919 may also be urging Jung to look back to his earlier visions. In the first, on the night of August 10/11, two young men are on a long adventurous journey that leads them through a vaulted tunnel where the stones threaten to fall. They come to the doorway of a palace, but it is owned by a small despot who wants to imprison them and leave them to starve; however, they know they will be able to escape using trickery. Entry into a sacred vault appears in a number of Masonic rituals, among them, the Sage of Mythras degree in the Ancient Primitive Rite of Memphis-Misraim and the 13th or Royal Arch Degree of the Scottish Rite (Brunet, 2019, pp. 16–17). In the latter, the sacred vault lies underneath King Solomon's Temple and in the ritual three candidates must descend into the vault and pass through nine arches, lifting each one as they go through, to arrive at the Dome where the Cubic Stone, containing the true name of the Great Architect of the Universe, is held (Blanchard, 1905/2002, Part 1, p. 265). The previous study suggests that this ritual is symbolic of the practice of Kundalini, studied in the higher degrees of the Scottish Rite, which aim at creating an explosion in consciousness or mystical experience involving the redirection of the sexual energies, an experience that can also be brought about through shock. It suggests that Jung was being trained as a young person to achieve this state after he underwent the shock of "The Sacrificial Murder" and that it entailed the construction of a prison arrangement to hold the precious energies as they rose up through the spinal chakras (Brunet, 2019, pp. 95–107). This dream seems to be reminding Jung to reflect on this experience, which appears to have occurred later in his youth or young adulthood. The dream suggests that he is aware, at some level, that the arrival at the palace is not a sacred mystical experience, but a trap from which he and his brother-self must escape.

The dream of August 11/12, 1919 (*BB 7*) involves Jung's two older daughters, their mother, Emma, and himself. They are guests of a rich peasant, an ostrich breeder, in either southern Siberia or South Africa; in other words, in a far distant place. It is very hot and he prepares iced lemonade, but Emma spills it and he reacts violently, throwing the glasses to the wall; although they bounce like rubber, suggesting no real harm was done. The iced drink implies a chilling of the emotions as something becomes too hot or intense for him. It could be a reaction to a private situation between Jung and his wife that suggests that Emma is not allowing him to react so coldly, or it could be an inability to face the emotional side of his active imaginations. In either case, he retreats into his old books, one of which is entitled Acta Thomasina and contains the archaic figure of a prophet and his words in hieroglyphics.

The reference to hieroglyphics here conveys an Egyptian element to the dream. The Judgement of Amenti, represented in the *Book of the Dead*, was a scene in which the heart of the deceased was weighed on the scales of justice against an ostrich feather, an emblem of truth, depicted in hieroglyphic form (Brown, 1882/2002, p. 102). So Jung's dream-self seems to be commenting on some truth in matters of the heart in relation to his wife and daughters which was troubling him. The dream also appears to be urging him to look back at the active imagination entitled "Nox Secunda" in *Liber Secundus*, first recorded in his journal on January 17, 1914 (*BB 4*). This narrative begins with a discussion of Thomas à Kempis's *The Imitation of Christ* with a fat female cook in a kitchen. The reference to Acta Thomasina suggests the trivialisation and feminisation of Thomas à Kempis's work via the banal remarks of the cook, while the archaic prophet in this narrative is the biblical Ezekiel who experienced a mystical vision. In his contemplation of this vision in *Liber Novus* Jung admits that his thinking is his dominant trait and his feeling side is least developed. It seems that this dream, five and a half years later, is saying something similar, reminding him that there may be more to this story that he needs to understand.

The next dream of significance appears on the night of May 4, 1920 (*BB 7*), nine months later. Here, he is on a journey with ten companions and he feels that there is a terrible cosmic event about to occur which will impact the present world. He is in an elevated state due to this impending miraculous event as it portends a complete spiritual shift. As they journey home, he and his companions fall into captivity in Italy but escape from the supernatural darkness that is building. He says they are protected because they are prepared and aware of the meaning of this event, described as the downfall of the world, and notes that the weather is warmer now. He is then on a volcanic island which is threatening to erupt and destroy the whole island, so he wants to leave.

Jung read this dream in terms of a geological disturbance north of Switzerland that creates a new mountain range and impacts Zurich, leading to a dangerous warmer climate; he associates this with a vision he had in 1913 of a terrible flood. It is possible that Jung could have been dreaming of an actual geological event in the future, but metaphor is the language of dreams and it is more likely to be commenting on a deep and potentially destructive disturbance in his own psyche. His ten companions may well be referring to his various inner parts who are traveling with him, and the fact that the weather is warmer suggests that he may be connecting more to his feelings. However, what is surfacing is so intense as to be both miraculous and catastrophic. As Alison Miller notes, in contemporary ritual abuse survivors can have programming for internal world disasters such as floods, fires, earthquakes or tornadoes, which can be experienced as a destruction of their inner world and can come into play when the survivor is showing signs of serious disloyalty to the cult (2012, p. 171).

Jung's captivity in Italy in this dream takes us back to an earlier vision recorded in his journals on January 5, 1914 and in *Liber Secundus* in "The Remains of Earlier Temples". This entry is humorous in tone and concerns another adventure where he meets two characters, the anchorite Ammonius and the Red One, who have been in Italy and have each undergone a complete personality change; Jung is being blamed for their degradation. But in the original journal entry Jung's vision begins much more seriously when he ponders the nature of the path that leads to this new in-between world and its unending darkness. "Where is this 'beyond'? Probably deep in ourselves", he says (*BB 3*, p. 116). In the fantasy Jung describes a feeling of becoming ice and darkness and then being reborn as a strange new character, a childish and superficial prankster. As the previous study noted, the title "The Remains of Earlier Temples" is a Masonic reference to the ruins of Solomon's Temple and in Jung's case symbolises the destructive nature of the initiatory process, especially if undergone by a child (Brunet, 2019, p. 73). Here, the child's previously socialised self can be broken down in a few short hours of calculated terror or imposed guilt and replaced by a new alter personality. The immature prankster in Jung's dream, six years later, seems to be reminding him of the process through which this alter and other alters were deliberately crafted. Nevertheless, his dream self tells him that he is prepared for what is to come and understands its meaning, confirming that the inner work that he has done to date is protecting him from being completely overwhelmed by this imminent internal cataclysm.

Nearly seven weeks later Jung is still feeling overwhelmed by these dreams and in February 1920 he records a very short entry. Here, he describes this process as "an unfathomable mystery" and asks, "who would understand the Godhead?" (*BB 7*, p. 201).[1] So, while the last dream states that he is aware, on one level, of the meaning of this impending volcanic eruption, he has not been able to consciously deal with it and does, in fact, leave these matters alone. Instead, he immerses himself in many external activities including giving seminars and having holidays while also making paintings and studying the *I Ching* and does not return to his journal for another 18 months.

"... the words that could describe the great pain do not want to cross my lips." (*BB 7*, p. 204).

On September 5, 1921 (*BB 7*) Jung records another entry that expresses more disconnection from a pain that he cannot describe, leaving him feeling cold and rigid. He berates himself for this and at the same time feels impotent, damned and empty, detached from his own heart. Only then does he mention his soul, wondering whether he should talk to her, but decides not to, preparing himself to face the possibility of silence and solitude until the end of his life. At the conclusion of this entry, he describes a heavy metallic feeling and names it "the wheel"; then he says he can no longer feel fear, only a feeling of rigidity and cold. He relates this feeling to his painting of an inexorable wheel crushing a naked figure that is lying on spikes in Image 127 in *Liber Novus,* one of four sacrifices depicted under the title "Amor triumphat".

As the previous study noted, this figure under the wheel is related to the ordeal in "Nox quarta" where Jung describes a repulsive enactment of the German version of the Grail legend, *Parsifal* (Brunet, 2019, p. 116). Here, he acknowledges that both the innocent youth Parsifal and the evil sorcerer Klingsor have his own features, suggesting that he feels simultaneously innocent and evil. This fantasy involves an image of a boy under the body of a prophet and Jung describes it in words that suggest it is a paedophilic scene; he then describes the boy as "the dead that cried the loudest, that stood right at the bottom and waited, that suffered the worst" (Jung, 2009a, p. 304; 2009b, p. 369). These comments were not included in the description of the *Parsifal* play when he recorded the original entry on January 19, 1914 (*BB 4*). In his entry in 1921, seven years and eight months later, he seems to be getting closer to facing a memory of abuse but he is still unable to fully define it, other than this wheel makes him feel as if he, himself, has become metal – soundless, heavy and tough.

The heavy metallic feeling that Jung names "the wheel" could be associated with another practice used in ritual abuse, which can involve strapping the child on a wheel-like device, aimed at producing almost complete amnesia following a traumatic ordeal. This practice was first noted by an American psychotherapist, John D. Lovern (1993), who named this practice "spin-programming" and noted that it is often combined with other traumatising experiences such as rape, in order to scramble the victim's memories even further. He notes that there are various forms of spinning, including a wheel of fortune type, which may be what Jung's comment suggests. This method of torture has since been confirmed by other researchers into ritual abuse and is referred to as the practice of spinning (Rutz et al, 2008, p. 74; Lacter, 2011, p. 62; Miller, 2012, pp. 103–104; Hoffman, 2016, p. 96). One survivor, Trish Fotheringham, describes being strapped to a device in her early teens and spun around with great force while being bombarded with flashing lights, with the aim of "[tying] all these colors into a knot – a highly effective control mechanism" (2008, p. 524). In my own case, at the age of eight, I was placed on a horizontal spinning device that looked like a barbeque spit in the basement of a perpetrator's house; the experience was accompanied by the sound of the men laughing at my plight. It was four decades before I remembered this experience (Brunet, 2007, p. 249). The aim of this and other tortures is to produce a tabula rasa or "blank slate" condition, described by one survivor as "an object waiting to be written upon" (Lacter, 2011, p. 78).

Jung's dream in September 1921 suggests that he is beginning to feel his way into the memories, even though what he feels is intensely painful and terrifying. The point at which it becomes too much is where he experiences a wheel-like heaviness and a frozen sense of complete emptiness, as if the soul has left the body: "Yes–empty–empty as hell", he says (*BB 7*, p. 204). Wendy Hoffman, a ritual abuse survivor and therapist, points out that the spinning always occurs as perpetrators end a traumatic sequence. Then, when a survivor tries to access the memories, the horrendous feelings of being spun are relived and can block passage to the memory (Personal correspondence, 24 October, 2023). If this is an example of spin-programming in Jung's case, then the use of the term "the inexorable wheel" and the title of the image "amor triumphat" have the darkest of meanings, implying a spinning that he was powerless to stop, accompanied by the abusive use of a sexual act to permanently traumatise him.

Two weeks later, on September 21, 1921, Jung is still grappling with an enormous tension and is yearning for it to be associated with the God who appeared to him, and the rapture and deep stillness of God's peace. But he realises that these are mere words. Instead, he stammers about an otherworldly fear that he associates with a meteorite "fallen behind the Milky Way", primordial longings and the mud of centuries, as well as "a mystery divined only by someone who has the animal behind him" (*BB 7*, p. 205). This collection of references is difficult to make out unless we turn again to *Morals and Dogma*. In his lecture for the 24th Degree or Prince of the Tabernacle Pike mentions the Eleusinian Mysteries, which were based on the classical myth of the rape of Persephone, and according to the Masonic author, J. N. Casavis (1955, p. 60), the Eleusinian Mysteries underpin the philosophy of

Freemasonry. As Bruce Lincoln notes, initiation through rape was a pattern found in numerous Greek myths and male-centred cultures (1981, p. 78). In Pike's lecture he describes the priestly officers at Eleusis who carried various symbolic objects: one pours milk from a golden vessel shaped like a woman's breast that symbolised the Milky Way, along which souls descend from and return to the Godhead; another carries a water-vase symbolising purification of souls by water; while another officer carries an image of a cow or ox, referring to the purification of souls by earth, represented by an animal that cultivates it (1871, p. 296).

It appears that Jung's concepts are drawn from the same imagery conveyed in Pike's lecture, suggesting that his abusers are again drawing on *Morals and Dogma*. The presence of a meteorite falling behind the Milky Way, however, is not in the lecture; it is Jung's addition, supposedly one that was devised by his abusers, that adds a disruptive element to this elegant ritual. It suggests the presence of Lucifer, traditionally associated with a comet or meteor, situated behind these beliefs. Pike was not enamoured by the concept of Lucifer: "Strange and mysterious name to give to the Spirit of Darkness!" he says (1871, p. 233). Jung concludes this entry castigating himself for his own stammering words but admits, "something trembles in me and this something wants to speak. For it was something somewhere smelt and touched and something that threatens to come to life" (*BB 7*, p. 206). By tuning in to his senses of smell and touch it is possible he may begin to remember.

"The divine youth ... he looks like a prince." (*BB 7*, p. 212).

It is over three months before we see Jung's next entry. On December 30, 1921 he is still disturbed by his dreams and the overwhelming fear that accompanies them. This time he decides to appeal to his soul for help and asks her what she can see, but her answers are cryptic. She describes a spirit of the East, a gloomy devil who is old, fat and oily, but Jung can make no sense of this and asks her for a clearer explanation. In answer, his soul imposes the condition that she should have some of his blood, or she will secretly drain him. Clearly, the attitude his soul displays here is irreligious and sarcastic. The description of the fat, gloomy devil implies a parody of the happy Buddha, and the lust for Jung's blood, a play on vampirism, so it is strange that Jung cannot see the farcical element in all of this. Nevertheless, he does agree.

Tasting his blood, and even asking for more, his soul then describes him as a cuckoo who must acquire the nests of others for his own purposes. She suggests that there are people in his circle who would willingly offer themselves to him in order to nurture his "egg" of knowledge and experience. He asks who these people would be, and in the entry next day she indicates that it is women. This leads to a month-long series of interactions with his soul over the problem of women in his life, discussed in Chapter Two, as well as his struggle over the plans for him to become a cult leader, to be discussed in Chapter Six. He is thus diverted away for most of the month of January 1922 from something terrifying and inexplicable that lies just below the surface of consciousness and wants to speak. On January 6, 1922 his soul sees something that introduces another element into the mix: she reminds him of a dream of an African scene, where he sees a citadel with an octagonal room and encounters a divine youth, whom his soul describes as a prince. Jung originally had this dream when he was in Tunis in 1920 and in the dream he wrestled with this youth and overcame him in the moat when he pushed the youth's head underwater.

This divine youth does not reappear again until Christmas Day, 1922 (*BB 7*) after Jung awakes in the night in a state of fear. The exchange with his soul is again argumentative and he even feels that she is not his soul and so should explain herself. Instead, she introduces the youth, decorated in green wreaths, almost naked and draped in silk, whom he relates to his African dream from 1920. The youth says that he now comes to be with Jung as the time is ripe and he has fulfilled the conditions, but Jung associates him with terror and death. Their conversation takes on a mysterious poetic quality, with the divine youth explaining himself as "the heart of the world, I am radiance, not light", "my robe is time" and so on (*BB 7*, p. 222). In turn, Jung explains how he has longed for this youth, his friend, ever since he first perceived his radiant beauty. However, the youth responds that it was Jung who was really the radiant one, who became so because he had overcome him and asks Jung whether he understands that. Jung admits that he does not understand and complains that the youth speaks in riddles, while the youth asks for Jung to teach him and "tell me who I am", (*BB 7*, p. 224). This scenario echoes earlier promptings by his soul to face his youthful self and probe into what has been disturbing his sleep. But given the many occasions on which his soul has led him astray, the question to ask is whether this re-introduction to the divine youth is a legitimate tactic aimed at helping him to face the truth, or yet another mystifying decoy diverting his attention from the memories.

Several entries appear in January 1923. The first on the night of January 2/3 involves a dream in which the divine youth again speaks. Jung's soul introduces the youth as "the master" and weaves more hyperbolic language around him: "Terrible is his beauty. Was death ever lovelier? Truly, he is more beautiful than death" and so on (*BB 7*, p. 224). This description has the air of insincerity, even deception about it, and Jung reacts to the youth with feelings of unspeakable dread and mistrust; the word "beautiful" to describe him gets stuck in his throat. The youth then describes having met with Jung's two dead dogs and his dead father, leaving Jung perplexed as to the reason for doing this. The conversation becomes more and more inane and circuitous as the youth claims to be everything and nothing at once: "I can sheathe myself in everything, be nothing and yet appear as everything", he says (*BB 7*, p. 225). At the same time, he wants Jung to define him and therefore overcome him again and reminds Jung of the castle where he stood at the gate waiting for someone to break in and capture him. So here we are possibly looking at an explanation of the divine youth as another internal alter personality or self-state who exists within the castle programming system created to symbolically house Jung's inner parts. This particular character is very fluid, like a chameleon, that can change itself at a whim to be anything or everything at once. But he sets Jung the difficult task of pinning him down and releasing him from his imprisonment, a task that Jung agrees to take on. At this point Jung admits that he is no nearer to the truth and asks his soul for help to do this.

On January 3 Jung asks his soul for her opinion about the divine youth, whom he calls "the dark one" (*BB 7*, p. 226). She describes him as very different to Philemon or Ka, and having left as if he had never been present, as beyond being and non-being. She also describes his deathly form in highly poetic terms: "inexpressibly beautiful, but of phosphorescent deathly pallor, the appearance of the full moon on snow, eyes shining like the great stars on a winter's night", she says (*BB 7*, p. 227). Jung, though, is concerned more with

144

the meaning of this being and recognises that his qualities are those of the Demiurge, connecting this with the myth of creation expounded in Plato's *Timaeus*. He recognises that he first understood this Platonic myth while in Africa where he saw the Greek letter Chi in the desert while gazing at the sky and had the dream that was one of the greatest experiences of his life. It seemed to express the "mystery of individuation" to him (*BB 7*, p. 227). At the time he understood the cross shape of this Greek letter to symbolise the world soul stretched out between heaven and earth but continued to contemplate this philosophy many years later. And yet Jung was unsure why he had this dream on his visit to Africa.

If we are to make sense of this whole scenario surrounding the divine youth, the African dream and Plato's *Timaeus* we need look no further than *Morals and Dogma* and the 26th Degree of the Scottish Rite known as the Prince of Mercy. This degree is regarded as highly philosophical (Blanchard, 1905/2002, Part 2, p. 165). The lodge for this degree is draped in green hangings, said to represent "the immortality of God, the soul and virtue" and the Master of this degree is called the Chief Prince and addressed as Most Excellent; he wears a tri-coloured tunic of green, white and red (Blanchard, 1905/2002, Part 2, pp. 163, 164, 178). As we have seen, Jung's soul has already described the divine youth as looking like a prince and addresses him as "the master", while surrounding him with superlatives. Furthermore, the green drapes he wears parallel the decorations in the lodge. There are many other elements which relate to this ritual: one of the explanations for the title of this degree, provided by J. M. Ragon, a foremost nineteenth century Masonic scholar, was that it referred to the "Fathers of Mercy, a religious society formerly engaged in the ransoming of Christian captives at Algiers" thus identifying an African connection in the ritual (cited in Blanchard, 1905/2002, Part 2, p. 163, n. 296). The first action undertaken by the candidate in this degree is to wash his hands as this rite is symbolic of the ancient practice of lustration, which represented the purification of the heart (Blanchard, 1905/2002, Part 2, p. 168, n. 301). The scene in Jung's dream where he pushes the youth's head underwater could then be read as a version of lustration or as a baptismal ritual; but subjecting the child to near-drowning is another of the terrifying practices used in ritual abuse (Rutz et al, 2008, p. 74; Lacter, 2011, p. 62; Hoffman, 2016, p. 88). It suggests the possibility that Jung, himself, may have been submerged underwater during a spurious version of the ritual, which would account for the terror he feels and the fear of death that accompanies the youth. This would align with the concept that the divine youth is another internal self-state that has been produced through the trauma of a near-death experience. The fact that his dream portrays Jung as the one who pushed him under the water suggests that he has been made to believe that he has done this to himself, rather than it being the action of his abusers.

But rather than connect to the traumatic aspects of this narrative Jung immediately gravitates to the philosophical themes of the degree, as he searches to find some intellectual meaning behind this scenario. Plato's *Timeaus* seems to resonate for him here and he understands the concept of being and non-being in terms of the Gnostic concept of the Pleroma. In his extensive lecture for the Prince of Mercy degree Pike discusses various Gnostic philosophies and their notions of the Deity, including the doctrine of the Trinity, as well as their explanations for the creation of the universe and how they accounted for the division between good and evil. Among them, he discusses Plato's *Timaeus* on the concept of the Demiurge, the lower God, to which was attributed the formation of the lower world. He states:

> This angel is a representative of the Supreme God, on the lower stage of existence; he does not act independently, but merely according to the ideas inspired in him by the Supreme God ... But these ideas transcend his limited essence; he cannot understand them; he is merely their unconscious organ, and therefore is unable himself to comprehend the whole scope and meaning of the work which he performs. As an organ under the guidance of a higher inspiration, he reveals higher truths than he himself can comprehend (Pike, 1871, p. 400).

In Jung's dreams and fantasies in January 1923 these characteristics are assigned to the divine youth, who admits he does not understand himself. We learn that Jung focused his attention on the *Timaeus* in some of his writings and in 1940 wrote an "Attempt at a Psychological Interpretation of the Dogma of the Trinity" (*BB 7*, p. 227, n. 210). It is possible that Jung might have been taught about Plato's *Timaeus* in the context of his initiatory training in his youth and that his urge to research this subject later could be attributed to the

146

repressed memory of the initiatory training partially coming back to him. However, despite his understanding of the philosophical aspects of this vision Jung is still concerned as to why these philosophical principles are being presented in the human-like form of the divine youth. "It completely exceeds my understanding for the moment. I can't make it out", he says (*BB 7*, p. 227). By not being able to remember the initiatory context of the 26th Degree Jung would be unable to make a connection between the teachings and those presenting them, such as the Master playing the role of the Chief Prince of Mercy and other members enacting the role of princes.

The fact that Jung's first and second introductions to the divine youth by his soul occur approximately a year apart may also be attributed to one of the conditions of the attainment of the Prince of Mercy degree. For this degree the candidate, who was initiated previously in the 25th Degree, must prove himself through a probationary period; in France and Germany the probation was one year (Blanchard, 1905/2002, Part 2, p. 168, n. 300). When the divine youth appears the second time, on Christmas Day 1922, he tells Jung that the time is ripe and the conditions have been fulfilled. So, the divine youth that Jung's soul calls "a prince" and "the master" appears to be an internalised alter or self-state based on the memory of his initiation into the Prince of Mercy degree. The fact that the youth describes Jung as the real radiant one would accord with the conclusion of the initiation process where the candidate, himself, becomes a Prince of Mercy and is "brought to light in Masonry" (Blanchard, 1905/2002, Part 2, p. 172).

"He is a mighty hunter, a hunter of men." (*BB 7*, p. 228).

On January 5, 1923 Jung hears the sound of another terrifying visitor in the middle of the night. His soul describes him as a mighty hunter, red-haired and bearded, his feet wrapped in animal skins. He carries a lightning hammer and fights with a sword, spears and arrows, while whistling to his bloodhounds who can carry "a whole man like a rabbit to their master's feet" (*BB 7*, p. 228). Jung's soul addresses him as the master and warns Jung not to speak to him unless spoken to, and describes him addressing the far-off dawn with an indifferent manner. His soul's description conveys this being as god-like and terrifying, but Jung is puzzled because he thought he was the friend of his previous entries, the divine youth. His appearance now, though, is frightful and unfamiliar.

This entry combines features from two Scottish Rite degrees, the 26th or Prince of Mercy and the 28th or Knights of the Sun. In the Prince of Mercy degree the Master of the lodge or the Most Excellent Chief Prince carries an arrow, with the spear white and the point gilded (Blanchard, 1905/2002, Part 2, p. 163). In the 28th Degree there is no actual mention of hunting, but Pike's lecture for this degree contains a discussion of Dionysos Zagreus, the Mighty Hunter of the Zodiac and god of the Orphic Mysteries (1871, p. 421). The Orphic Mysteries drew condemnation from early Christian writers, such as Clement of Alexandria (c. 150–c. 215 AD), who described them as savage rites (2nd C/1919, p. 37). In these rites Dionysus Zagreus was entrusted by his father Zeus with the thunderbolt and his mother was Persephone. Diodorus Siculus noted that the Greek god Dionysos had two forms, the ancient or rustic one, Zagreus the Great Hunter with a long beard, and the younger, youthful and effeminate one, much like Jung's divine youth (cited in Eckard, 2023, p. 7). So Jung's confusion here is understandable. In the 28th Degree the Master of the lodge symbolises the rising sun and the Candidate, when questioned by him does not answer for himself; instead, a member named Brother Truth speaks for him, approximating the warning given to Jung to not speak unless spoken to.

In the fantasy this red-bearded god then speaks to Jung, questioning him about how he could have overcome him, the Great Hunter. He then poses the same request as that posed by the divine youth: "Divine me and tell me who I am, you overcomer!" he says (*BB 7*, p. 228). Jung takes a suitably deferential attitude to this powerful god but decides that he must have overcome him without knowing it. He explains to this god the role of wisdom and knowing how to use right action and right thought, which, to a rustic god and one who normally responds with violence, is a new idea. The god leaves to return to the black clouds over the mountain, but thanks Jung for his good advice. This leaves Jung shocked and stunned by such a bizarre encounter, but pleased nevertheless, and credits this god from saving him from death during the Spanish flu.

This fantasy is not unlike the one involving Izdubar, recorded January 8, 1914 (*BB 3*), where Jung encountered a terrifying but fear-filled giant who believes he must reach the sun to achieve immortality. Here, Jung was able to convince the giant that science has proven the impossibility of his beliefs about the sun but explains that Izdubar represents an inner truth, not outward facts, which comforts the giant; they then sleep together next to the fire. From a psychological perspective, this new hunter god, encountered nine years later, is clearly another alter personality that has been stuck in the time of his original formation, in what would have been a terrifying experience for a child. This phenomenon, where traumatic events can feel frozen in time, is explained by van der Kolk to be associated with the deactivation of the pre-frontal cortex which results in the experience of being trapped in the moment, without a sense of past, present, or future (2014, pp. 68–70). But in the context of visiting the past in therapy, in a calm and grounded state, the once-traumatised individual can make sense of the memory. As Jung discovered in the processing of his fantasies in his self-therapy, these internal characters have remained as figments of the imagination, albeit installed in frightening initiatory circumstances in childhood, but the fear they hold can be dissolved by talking to them as if they are real and showing them that times have changed.

Two nights later, on January 7/8, 1923, this god returns, but this time as a pubescent boy who is ill, tormented by back pain and seeking help. Jung's soul tells him to speak to the boy as he is shy. Jung addresses him as a son (his own son, Franz, was fourteen at the time) and asks him to describe his suffering. The boy says he has a rash on his back that burns and says it began a few days previously, when he had a dream where he was hunting with hounds and had a mangy wolf fur hung over his shoulder; he was hastening to the mountains to find a bear cub to play with and wanted to put it on a leash, but then the mangy wolf fur produced the rash. He asks Jung to heal him and Jung answers, saying that it was a spirit wolf that made him ill and explains that the boy had been in the role of his red-bearded father, scaring animals and humans with his whistling and yelling, and therefore had become ill from this behaviour. The boy recovers and thanks Jung for his wisdom. "I have become wiser", the boy concludes (*BB 7*, p. 231).

In his lecture for the 28th Degree Pike explains more of Zagreus's story. As we have seen in Chapter Three, the boy Zagreus was pursued by the Titans and torn into pieces, but his beating heart was saved and returned to Zeus who then enabled him to be reincarnated. Zagreus was then regarded as an ancient subterranean version of Dionysos (Pike, 1871, p. 421). It could be argued that the Zagreus myth was describing the initiation of a boy and the theme of dismemberment, in symbolic terms, could be viewed as the accompanying fragmentation of the psyche. This time, in Jung's case, it involves the creation of an alter personality with two opposing natures, expressed in the two forms of Dionysos: the divine, poetic and beautiful youth and his counterpart, the repressed rage-filled savage. By talking to them both as if they are real people and explaining the situation to them Jung is able to dissolve the fear and rage associated with them, thus evaporating their negative impact on his psyche.

On January 9, 1923 Jung's mother dies and on the previous night he had dreamt of a Wild Huntsman and his gigantic wolfhound coming to carry away a human soul. He discussed this dream in *Memories, Dreams, Reflections* (1963, p. 290), but it appears to be the same encounter with the bearded hunter in the entry of January 7/8. He identifies the hunter as Wotan, otherwise known as Odin, and feels torn between the feelings of terror this figure elicits and a strange sense of joy, as if a wedding were being celebrated. He explains these mixed feelings as being related to the Christian misrepresentation of Wotan as a devil and the difference between the ego's response to death as a catastrophe and the psyche's pure joy of connecting with eternity, expressed as a mysterium coniunctionis. Pike discusses Odin on a number of occasions throughout *Morals and Dogma* and notes that the northerners worshipped a tri-une deity in the form of the great warrior Odin, his wife Frea and son Thor, not unlike the Egyptian trinity of Osiris, Isis and Horus (1871, pp. 14, 123, 266, 413). So, for Jung to respond to the hunter as Wotan, rather than Zagreus is understandable, given his Germanic roots. However, the myth of Zagreus seems to be more applicable to the appearance of the sick pubescent boy in his fantasy and to the simple character of Zagreus, as opposed the characterisation of Wotan as a great warrior and magician.

Just over a year later, on February 8/9, 1924, Jung has another dream, this time of an invisible horde of souls, people of the future, who are passing by his house and moving from East to West. They stumble over big stones and he asks them whether they are searching for the word. He offers them Philemon's temple and feels that something has come to pass but does not know what it is. He then offers them a meal in silence, and suggests something might speak to them from the fire, or that the stones may whisper to them. Jung, himself, feels that he cannot speak, but can only stutter. The gods and beggars then sit down for a meal and Jung feels transformed, though he is unable to explain what this transformation is.

This scenario has all the hallmarks of a ritual enactment and if we again turn to the Prince of Mercy degree and Pike's lecture for it, we can find many similar elements. After his lustration where he washes his hands in pure water the candidate is led by the Senior Deacon nine times around the Chapter while the Chief Prince or Most Excellent reads from the holy book, the Christian Bible (Blanchard, 1905/2002, Part 2, pp. 169–171). In the first three rounds the theme is the omnipotence of the one Supreme God and the role of Jesus of Nazareth, who is predicted to appear at the end of the world when a state of innocence will commence and all mankind will be unified. During the fourth round the Most Excellent describes the mountains melting in torrents of metal through which all souls pass so as to burn away their sins, to be "fitted for the bliss that awaits them. A new earth, more beautiful, more fertile, more delicious than the first, shall become the home of restored mankind". In the sixth round is a description of "a vast golden palace more brilliant than the sun" set to receive the just and in the seventh "the just return to the bosom of the Deity to enjoy eternal happiness in the realm of light and love". In the ninth round the Most Excellent quotes John 1:1: "In the beginning was the Word..." So here we have several elements from the ritual reflected in Jung's dream: the mountains melting and the souls passing through so as to be purified could be viewed in terms of an avalanche of big stones over which the souls stumble, while the vast golden palace is represented in terms of Philemon's temple. The final reference to John 1:1 in the ritual appears in Jung's dream as his sense that these souls are searching for the word, a theme that has appeared throughout many of the Masonic rituals that Jung's fantasies resemble.

In Pike's lecture for the Prince of Mercy degree he cites a long series of questions to be asked of the members and supplies the answers. For the final question: "What is to us the chief symbol of man's ultimate redemption and regeneration?" he provides a lengthy answer, beginning:

> The fraternal supper, of bread which nourishes, and of wine which refreshes and exhilarates, symbolical of the time which is to come, when all mankind shall be one great harmonious brotherhood ... and the bodies of the ancient dead, the patriarchs before and since the flood, the kings and common people of all ages, resolved into their constituent elements, are carried upon the wind over all continents, and continually enter into and form part of the habitations of new souls, creating new bonds of sympathy and brotherhood between each man that lives and all his race ... In the truest sense, we eat the bodies of the dead (Pike, 1871, p. 387).

Jung's reference to sharing a meal with these souls appears to be his dream's way of expressing this concept of the shared elements of all mankind, from the past and into the future, symbolised by the fraternal supper. But the fact that Jung feels that he is silent and can only stutter in this dream may be related to another part of the answer to this question of redemption and regeneration. This is where the members are reminded about the "infinite beneficence of God" which is bestowed in silence (Pike, 1871, p. 387).

Throughout his initiations Jung has been made to believe that he has had miraculous encounters with a series of gods and that he has rebirthed these gods, like Mithras or Phanes, into his own soul. At times he has even been encouraged to believe that he is god-like or even a god himself, from being told that he is Christ, the divine child, or the divine youth. The last in this series of gods that he must identify with are the two versions of Dionysos seen here. In this dream he is silent, like the description of the God in the teachings of the Prince of Mercy degree, but he falls short and is a stutterer. In other words, his dream is saying he is not godlike at all, but a fallible human being. Nevertheless, he feels that he has been transformed in some way and this may be due to the fact that this could have been the final initiation from his youth that he is recalling, where he is made to believe that he has undergone a complete and final transformation.

"The years go by." (*BB 7*, p. 235).

The years go by and we do not see another entry until November 16, 1926 (*BB 7*). It is a very short entry, recording the fact that he has been to Africa again, seeking the unknown god; but he fails to find him there. He realises that this god is not in the exterior world and wonders why his soul has become silent. She speaks briefly, suggesting he turn to his dreams. Looking back over his previous dreams, three weeks later, he realises that the death of his mother coincided with the death of the anima in himself, mentioned in Chapter Two. From this point onward many of his dreams are now concerned with the problems of his patients and illnesses and deaths of friends and only occasionally does he dream of his own internal state.

The first of these more personal dreams in *Book 7* that have not already been discussed occurs on the night of December 3/4, 1926. It is set in Stuttgart where he encounters enormous footsteps in the snow, which remind him of various animals, like a rhinoceros, hippopotamus or elephant. He feels that it refers to his African experiences in some way, but he concludes that the animal must have been afraid. Given the snow, he realises that a mammoth is more likely, suggesting an enormous prehistoric creature, and in his reflections he wonders if it refers to the way others see him, as "a strange animal" whom people have trouble understanding, but who nevertheless has a massive presence (*BB 7*, p. 237). This reminds him of a collection of Buddhist teachings, the Tripitaka, which records the impression of the Buddha's footprints in stone, a symbolic reference to this religious teacher's enduring legacy. Given Jung's extensive reputation at this stage of his life, it is quite possible that his dream is a comment on his powerful influence and the legacy he was already accumulating, but the fact that the animal is afraid is a telling sign that at the basis of his entire mission is a tremendous fear that this argument suggests was the result of a series of terrifying initiatory ordeals undergone in his early years.

The next dream that appears in *Book 7* is very brief. It is dated 2/3 December, 1926, but he has entered it after the dream of the following evening in his journal. In it he attempts to model a bust of a man from melted cow fat, but is anxious that he will not finish it on time. He understands the reference in terms of the novel *The Golem* (1915) by Gustav Meyrink, in which the narrator states

153

that he was reading the life of Buddha and describes a stone that looks like a lump of fat. So, it appears that the motif of the cow fat and the reminder of the Buddha's footprints in Jung's dream above was possibly influenced by Meyrink's novel. Jung is also reminded of ectoplasm, one of the accoutrements of the fin de siècle spiritualist movement. This dream produces an anxiety that his lifetime will not be enough for him to present himself.

Meyrink was the pseudonym of Gustav Meyer, born in Vienna January 19, 1868. He is held in great respect as an author of German-language supernatural fiction and was apparently a colourful, fascinating and controversial character with several starkly different sides to his personality. He was a dedicated student of the occult, which he pursued for most of his life, and this led to his involvement with many different secret societies and fraternities, including Masonic organisations (Mitchell, 2008, pp. 49–51). But he was also a sceptic and on one occasion proved that the ectoplasm supposedly emerging from a spirit medium was, in fact, a piece of cheesecloth dipped in chemicals. *The Golem*, his first novel, is set in Old Prague's Jewish Ghetto and focuses on its inhabitants as well as the legend of the Golem of Prague and other aspects of Jewish mysticism, although Meyrink himself was a Protestant. The novel also incorporates a spiritual puzzle, along with episodes of amnesia, hallucinatory terror, confusion and hypnosis not unlike those found in Jung's fantasies.

It seems that Meyrink's writing resonated with Jung, but his comment on this novel in the journal is very minimal, although there were other occasions where he mentioned Meyrink's work. In a discussion with Cary Bates in 1922, for example, he commented that another of Meyrink's novels, *The White Dominican*, had used exactly the same symbolism as in his own first vision (2009a, p. 212; 2009b, pp. 64–65). In 1925 he planned a seminar that was to discuss four literary examples that demonstrated aspects of his psychological theories and scholarly interests. Meyrink's *The Green Face* was to be one of the examples as it bore similarities to his confrontation with the unconscious recorded in his journals; but he decided to replace it with another novel (Fike, 2020, p. 2). Jung felt that Meyrink was able to use the novel format to convey this quite easily, whereas it was more difficult for him using the scientific and philosophical method. A preliminary investigation of *The Golem* reveals that Meyrink may have been struggling with the effects of the abusive use of

Masonic initiation rites in a similar way to Jung, although expressing it in the context of an entire novel, rather than in individual fantasies. A future study of this novel will probe whether he could have been another survivor of abusive occult practices or was simply making use of his occult knowledge to construct sensational stories.

At this stage Jung is unable to penetrate the cause of the fears that his dreams elicit or the meaning of the many riddles that have confronted him over the years and so by 1927 he is recording only occasional dreams and visionary experiences. These concern the death of a friend, Herman Sigg, the record of patients' problems and funerals, and a prophetic dream concerning his wife's inoperable cancer; the latter dream promoting a brief but angry interaction with his soul over his marital situation, as discussed in Chapter Two.

But his next entry on February 2, 1928 (*BB 7*) is an elaborate one. Here he engages in a now rare interaction with his soul, asking her if there is something he should know. She answers that he must make a detour and leads him to an abyss where he describes a rushing river and a long line of people in bright robes walking towards the end of the gorge where there is a long white house with colonnades. The group is led by an old man who knocks on the door with his stick and the people enter barefoot. Jung recognises him as Philemon. It is a type of religious service with the people passing through doors and passages into a circular portico with an octagonal basin full of blue water in the centre and a statue of a life-sized middle-aged man. The people sing praises to the water around this basin and drink from it like animals. They then eat bread silently, passing it along, while Philemon stands, leaning on his staff and conversing with the statue. He then waves his staff and the people separate, with the women on his left and the men on his right. The people then drop to their knees facing the pool while Philemon touches the water three times; he then kneels down, his brow on the edge of the pool, while a bell tolls, and then all rise. The people now stand around silently in groups and Jung recognises that the men all wear Gallic shorts and short Gallic mantles.

Questioning what this ritual enactment is about, Jung's soul tells him that the statue is of the Roman Caesar, Antoninus Pius, and to his question as to which country this is in, she answers: "Your land, your religion, water instead of wine, bread instead of flesh, silence instead of speech" (*BB 7*, p. 245). She tells him to keep looking: Philemon opens his arms and everyone surrounds the pool, holding each other by the shoulders while they sing about the "house of water" and the stars. The water becomes intermittently light and dark as dark clouds move across it and then Philemon ignites the fuel on a small altar while the people move back under the colonnades as it becomes dark again. He then douses the fire with wine and light returns, after which he throws raw flesh from a silver platter to the dogs outside. The old man then disappears, his rod falling to the ground, while the people leave the white building and wind their way through the valley. Jung admits that he does not understand this ritual and his soul says she cannot explain it either, apart from asking Jung what the Cult of Caesar meant to him, and stating that the wine was not an offering and that he was thinking of the fire and not of Caesar when he used it to quench the flames. She says she will wait to see whether anything further happens.

The key to the symbolism in this entry lies within Pike's lecture accompanying the 32nd Degree, or Sublime Prince of the Royal Secret, and with the figure of Antoninus Pius, who is mentioned in this lecture (Pike, 1871, p. 618). Pike attributes great significance to Antoninus Pius, along with his predecessor Hadrian, in terms of the Roman contribution to the development of Masonry. In his lesson for the First Degree or Apprentice he writes:

> Masonry is not the Coliseum [sic] in ruins. It is rather a Roman palace
> of the middle ages, disfigured by modern architectural improvements,
> yet built on a Cyclopæan foundation laid by the Etruscans, and with
> many a stone of the superstructure taken from dwellings and temples of
> the age of Hadrian and Antoninus (Pike, 1871, pp. 21–22).

Antoninus Pius (86–161 CE) was a Roman emperor from 138 CE until his death and was regarded as the fourth of "five good emperors" in a period of peace and prosperity (96–180 CE). His family originated in Gaul, thus explaining the men wearing Gallic shorts in Jung's fantasy (Britannica, "Antoninus Pius", 2023). As the editor notes (*BB 7*, p. 245, n. 274), Antoninus was renowned for his good government and amongst his enlightened policies he protected Christians rather than persecuting them. It is possible to view the ritual meeting in Jung's vision as a representation of the early Christians, as

Jung's soul tells him that it is his religion to which it refers. But it is also his land, suggesting that it might have something to do with Switzerland and therefore a modern-day Christian ritual of some kind. Antoninus was renowned as a builder of many public buildings and forms of infrastructure, including the construction of monumental aqueducts providing free access to drinking water throughout the empire, begun in the reign of his predecessor, Hadrian (Chiotis, 2018, p. 70), thus explaining the symbolism of the people praising the water in Jung's vision. The fact that they are kneeling down and drinking like animals, though, appears to be a reference to the part of Pike's 32nd Degree lecture where, just before mentioning Antoninus Caesar, he cites Bardesanes, the Syrian Christian who describes men's double nature. "In the things belonging to their bodies, they maintain their nature like animals, and in the things which belong to their minds, they do that which they wish, as being free and with power, and as the likeness of God", he says (Pike, 1871, p. 618).

In the second part of the vision the worshippers sing "the house of water" – "primordial home of the stars" (*BB 7*, p. 245). As Pike notes, the medals of Antoninus contain nearly all the signs of the Zodiac (Pike, 1871, p. 333). These were a series of bronze drachmas showing five planets and the Sun and Moon, set amongst the twelve signs of the Zodiac that were related to the ancient Egyptian calendar, based on 365 days per year (Vaneerdewegh, 2020, pp. 315–326). Astrology was very important in Roman society and coins frequently depicted astrological signs on them, but the significance of Antoninus in this regard was related to the fact that the gradual shift between the astrological signs and their calendar dates, from when they were first instigated in Egypt, took 1,461 years before they returned to their original position, known as the Sophic Cycle; the date of this return was 139 CE, the second year of Antoninus's reign. Antoninus also oversaw the minting of a coin in Egypt depicting Isis riding Sirius in the form of a dog. So, the symbols in this dream can be seen from an astrological perspective: Aquarius being the House of Water, the silver platter Philemon holds perhaps being related to the moon, and the dogs in the narrative to Sirius or the Dog Star, also known in Freemasonry as the Blazing Star. Sirius was the beautiful star that appeared just before the Nile flooded and was considered to mark the beginning of the Zodiac cycle when it was initially instigated in Egypt. The octagonal pool in Jung's vision could then be seen as representing the five planets plus the sun, moon and

Sirius. During the 2nd century, when Antoninus Pius was emperor (138–161 CE), the Mithras cult was gaining momentum, reaching its apogee in the reign of his successor, Emperor Aurelian in 274 CE, when Mithras was declared the Roman High God (Sol Invictus) and became the special protector of the emperor and the empire (Abruzzi, 2018, p. 13). The Cult of Caesar to which Philemon refers is thus likely to mean the Mithras cult. Given Jung's observation that "all this is Mithraic symbolism from beginning to end" (2009a, p. 252, n. 211/2009b, p. 197), it is probably relevant that throughout the whole of *Morals and Dogma* Pike cites Mithras no less than 72 times.

In the 32nd Degree ritual the layout of the lodge, known in this case as the Consistory, is similar to Jung's vision in that there is an altar near a polygon shape, only this time it is a nonagon, rather than an octagon, representing a military-style camp with fourteen biblical-sounding names. But the ritual even states: "These fourteen names must certainly appear arbitrary and without meaning. The rituals and other Masonic works say nothing of the meaning and reason why these names were selected" (Blanchard, 1905/2002, Part 2, p. 379). In the Masonic ritual the semiotic link between the symbolic signs and what they signify has been lost, but in Jung's vision they seem to be closely associated with the important role of astrology in the belief system behind his initiatory training. However, its symbolism is not being used to enlighten him but to add another layer to the impenetrable and frustrating nature of these so-called Mysteries.

But what is the significance of Philemon throwing raw flesh to the dogs in Jung's vision? According to Albert Mackey, the Masonic term "cowan" means an uninitiated intruder into Masonic secrets, an eavesdropper or pretender; he suggests it was derived from the Greek meaning "dog" and originated amongst the early Christians where the religion needed to be under the veil of secrecy and infidels were called dogs (1914, pp. 183–184). He cites two biblical verses: Matthew vii, 6, "give not that which is holy unto the dogs" and Philippians iii, 2, "beware of dogs, beware of evil workers". For Philemon to throw the raw flesh to the dogs could then be interpreted as an act of ritual betrayal and even a condemnation of him as collaborating with evil workers or, in Masonic terms, with a group regarded as spurious or fringe Masonry.

Jung had sometimes directed similar charges at Philemon himself, as well as to his soul, as they repeatedly subjected him to oscillations between gratitude for their support and despair at their psychological cruelty and betrayal. The intermittent darkness and light throughout the second part of the vision may be representing these oscillations, but it also points to what Pike describes as the Royal Secret of the 32nd Degree: "The Mystery of the Balance ... the Secret of Universal Equilibrium" (1871, p. 619). Here, Pike writes of all the positive values of divine wisdom, such as the principles of truth, justice, mercy and forgiveness, but he also notes the equilibrium between good and evil, and light and darkness in the world. He argues that the Royal Secret is to realise that:

> there is no rebellious demon of Evil, or Principle of Darkness co-existent and in eternal controversy with God, or the Principle of Light and Good ... [and] that the existence of Evil, Sin, and Sorrow in the world, is consistent with the Infinite Goodness as well as with the Infinite Wisdom of the Almighty (Pike, 1871, p. 619).

This principle of equilibrium, he says, operates on all levels of natural law and human activity. The question is whether this principle could be used to justify indulging in evil practices as long as they are balanced by good ones and, in the case of ritual abuse, to condone the deliberate exposure of children to criminal treatment as long as it is accompanied by experiences of the sublime.

It is five years and nine months before Jung records another interaction with his soul. He is now 57 years old and the last three entries in 1932 are the final ones in *Book 7*. He describes a dark dream on November 26, 1932 and has begun to consult the *I Ching* for answers, abandoning extensive discussions with his soul and telling her: "No more ancient pranks" (*BB 7*, p. 247). She complains that he has left her behind and also that he is only concentrating on the future, favouring ambition and desire over a contemplation of the past; the threatening dream, she says, was to urge him to look back and cease this endless rush towards the future. He vaguely agrees with her but then turns to the *I Ching* for its advice. It reveals a positive outcome, "Possession in Great Measure", an indicator that his life and career is bringing him all he desires (*BB 7*, p. 247). However, the following evening he is still in a state of unrest, having had further bad dreams, and in frustration appeals to his soul to tell him if it is related to her realms. But she becomes riddlesome again, alluding to vague ideas of being and non-being and says he lames himself, due to the fact that he is concentrating on the outside world and not on what is inside. In answer to his question about the meaning of this next dream, which he does not outline here, she tells him that the strange man wrapped in the colours of the dawn is himself. However, when he asks for further clarification she is evasive and will not explain further. He is left feeling that it is all too paradoxical and she concludes with, "pull yourself together. You must wane". Years later he associates this with "the experience of the self [meaning] a defeat of the I" (*BB 7*, p. 248, n. 281).

The final brief entry is on December 14/15, 1932. "The Quest begins", he writes, and records another hexagram from the *I Ching*. He then mentions a three-part dream that, due to its brevity, does not provide a lot of information: in the first part he is with a professor with whom he has travelled, then a farmer and his wife, completely drunk, are rolling naked in the mud, and finally, he dreams of his dog, Joggi, a favourite companion. This last part of the dream reiterates the theme of throwing meat to the dogs. In it, Jung's dream self was using a great piece of ham for fishing, but the dog had snapped at it and had taken a significant part of it. It implies that Jung's dedication to investigating this mystery for the previous nineteen years (fishing with the great piece of ham), has only been partially successful. A significant part of his effort has been taken by the dogs, that is, by his internalised perpetrators or cult members, who have been using their knowledge of the way the psyche functions under the duress of traumatic and life-threatening encounters, for the purpose of subjugating him to their will. It also recalls the classical conditioning techniques of Pavlov's dogs which has been likened to the methods used in cult programming and the creation of new alter personalities through the use of torture (Sargant, 1957 cited in Lacter, 2011, pp. 70–71).

In his comments on resolving trauma through dream interpretation Jung notes that the trauma will keep reproducing itself in the individual's dreams until such time as the traumatic stimulus has exhausted itself or the interpretation of the dream is correct (1974/2002, pp. 48–49). A similar observation is made by Bessel van der Kolk, a contemporary expert in the effects of trauma (2014, pp.

66–68, 260–261). He notes the timeless reliving of images, sounds, thoughts, emotions and physical sensations that, along with dissociation, take on a life of their own and keep replaying as long as the trauma is not resolved. Dreams play a role in this replaying as they recombine and reintegrate pieces of old memories, possibly for years, in an attempt to remind the dreamer to pay attention to this imbalance in the psyche. Furthermore, he states that dreams can help in forging new connections between seemingly unrelated memories.

So, despite Jung's success in his career and other aspects of his exterior life we see that by the end of *Book 7* his dreams are still bothering him. What *has* been exhausted is his method of dealing with them through extensive conversations with his imaginary female soul. These conversations have become fewer and farther between during these last years as he finally accepts that they are only leading him into further confusion with their riddles, paradoxes and circularity; and yet his soul also acts as a reminder to keep looking at the past. In fact, she encourages him to focus on his dreams and some of these, as we have seen, are urging him to look back at his own childhood memories and those of his youth. Other new dreams are urging him to revisit some of his earlier fantasies, described in a number of the chapters of *Liber Novus* such as "Nox Secunda", "The Sacrificial Murder" and "The Remains of Earlier Temples". There are also others that deal with new themes altogether, such as the African dream and the one involving the mighty hunter, that are impossible to decipher without an understanding of the Masonic rituals and, in particular, the themes in Albert Pike's *Morals and Dogma*. Despite Jung's amassed knowledge of ancient mythology and its symbolism, it is this Masonic element that is the absent key that would have enabled him to grasp the full meaning of his traumatic dreams. Consequently, by the end of this final journal he has still been unable to interpret the attendant traumas in their entirety.

The following chapter will now address another key issue that troubles Jung right throughout the *Black Books*: his struggle with ambition and the question of his calling.

Notes

1 Jung inserted this entry before he included the dreams of August 1919 and May 1920.

6

"But what is my calling?
The new religion and its proclamation."

(*BB 7*, p. 211)

A thread that runs through the *Black Books* that is only partially represented in *Liber Novus* is Jung's struggle with vanity, ambition and the question of whether he should become a sect leader. This struggle appears from the earliest entries in 1913 right though until those in *Book 7*. In a discussion with his soul on January 5, 1922, after a long period of disturbed sleep, he is told that the great work begins and that he must no longer hide the revelations he has received. Jung interprets this as being asked to publish what he has written, which he feels would be disastrous. He asks his soul: "But what is my calling?" She answers: "The new religion and its proclamation" (*BB 7*, p. 211). Jung promises to work with his soul on this, if only she will grant him some sleep; and like the taskmaster that she is, she says she expects him to begin this serious work with her the next morning.

The editor of the *Black Books*, Sonu Shamdasani, notes this struggle and that Jung balked at the idea that his calling lay in being a religious leader (*BB 1*, pp. 80–84). He points out that, instead, Jung turned to asking questions about the psychology of the religion-making process and did not intend that analytical psychology should become a creed. But as the *Black Books* reveal, this was not Jung's immediate response but the end of a lengthy and agonising battle with his soul's ongoing harassment on this front. Even in the first few entries he complains that he feels chained to this book, his pen driven furiously in order to follow his soul's orders (*BB 2*, p. 154). Then, despite repeatedly questioning where this activity is leading him, Jung continues to follow his soul's directive to keep working on *Liber Novus*, only putting it finally aside in 1930. Had he published it in his lifetime it would have amounted to a holy book for a new religion, but as Jung himself realised, the confusing and perplexing nature of his active imaginations may well have made it inaccessible: "And who would understand it?" he says (*BB 7*, p. 210).

This chapter will examine Jung's struggle with ambition and the pressure that his soul places on him in the context of cult indoctrination methods observed by key researchers since the mid-twentieth century, both in the political sphere and in domestic cult situations. It will demonstrate that Jung's accounts portray a pattern of indoctrination that has been explored by researchers into thought reform, cult programming, mind control and ritual abuse. Examining the type of coercive control that Jung's soul is seemingly applying to him, it will question whether he was being groomed towards becoming a cult leader. Whether Jung was secretly involved with a cult during adulthood is unknown, so it will treat Jung's discussions in this chapter as further examples of his internal dialogue with his soul, rather than conversations with an external cult member. As in the previous chapters it will treat Jung's soul as an introject, an internalised part of the psyche based on one or more characters from the initiatory ordeals undergone much earlier in his life, which has become automatised to express the aims of the cult. In the words of a current cult programming expert, Steven Hassan, this is "how the group gets inside a person's head and controls his internal dialogue" (2020, p. 27). But it will also demonstrate that by recording and analysing these memories Jung was critically examining their inculcated messages and struggling with them in order to try to understand what was happening to him.

The techniques used in these cult contexts involve a similar concept of death and rebirth as in the initiation process. The historian of religion, Mircea Eliade (1958/1995, pp. xii–xix, 9–35), describes the aim of the death and rebirth process as eliciting a tabula rasa state in the candidate that allows the rewriting of his personality. In Freemasonry we see many references to initiation as a death and rebirth process. Albert Pike describes initiation as a mystical death, "a descent into the infernal regions, where every pollution, and the stains and imperfections of a corrupt and evil life were purged away by fire and water" (1871, p. 269). He notes that this process was practiced in the ancient Mysteries as a means of perfecting the soul and reminding it of its noble origins, its immortality and its connection with the universe and the deity. Amongst some of the ancient cults this initiatory process could be very severe and one example of this was the military cult of Mithraism, whose symbolism Jung identified in his active imaginations. The extreme methods used in these cultic contexts amounted to a purging of the candidate's original personality and the installation of a new one, or multiple ones, in whatever form the group preferred.

During the Cold War there were a number of American researchers employed to investigate these themes in enemy contexts. Among them were the psychiatrist Robert Jay Lifton, who interviewed prisoners of Chinese thought reform programs, the psychologist Margaret Singer, whose research into cults emerged out of her investigations into the experiences of U.S. soldiers taken prisoner in Korea, and Edgar Schein, an Army research psychologist who also focused on brainwashing in Chinese Communist programs (Hassan, 2020, p. iii). As a result of this research, they each developed a model comprised of a list of criteria for identifying abusive indoctrination techniques: Lifton proposed eight criteria, Singer, six and Schein, three, and there was a degree of overlap between the different models. The Cold War example encapsulates one of Jung's observations concerning projection, on a national level: that it is easier to see the faults within others than to identify the same behaviour within oneself. But since that time these criteria have been developed to be used in both legal and psychological contexts to examine the practices of domestic cult groups. The more colloquial term of brainwashing has now been replaced by terms such as thought reform, mind control, undue influence or coercive persuasion.

In the 1990s the first clinical observations were made that Dissociative Identity Disorder (DID) patients with an alleged background in satanic ritual abuse (SRA) had all undergone some form of sophisticated mind control techniques using drugs, hypnosis, pain, terror, electric shocks, isolation, sensory deprivation or overstimulation (van der Hart et al, 1997, pp. 151–152). In the next decade the British psychiatrist Joan Coleman, who worked with a series of clients reporting extreme abuse in organised groups, made the observation that the techniques used on her clients were very similar to those of mind control and programming practiced during the Cold War (2008, p. 18). Since then, the coupling of the terms ritual abuse or extreme abuse with mind control and programming has now pervaded academic discussions of cruel forms of religious and non-religious based indoctrination and cult abuse in western cultures (Noblitt & Noblitt, 2008, 2014; Lacter, 2008, 2011; Epstein, Schwartz & Schwartz, 2011; Miller, 2012, 2016; Hoffman & Miller, 2017).

This chapter will apply Coleman's observation about the Cold War to Jung's case and focus on one example of research into the indoctrination techniques of that period, the work of Robert Jay Lifton (1961/1989). There is, however, a difference between Jung's situation and Lifton's subjects. Lifton's cases were each imprisoned as adults and, despite being highly affected by their experience, tended to revert to their previous identity, or at least a modified version of it, at some stage afterwards. Whereas in Jung's case, we appear to be looking at the use of similar thought reform processes on a young person, whose identity has been profoundly influenced, even moulded, by these practices. The reason for choosing Lifton's study is his observation that, at times, alongside the use of torturous techniques and relentless undermining of the personality, the Chinese re-education prison would take on a highly academic atmosphere where the inmates would be encouraged to have group discussions with fellow inmates, overseen by the prison guards who were regarded as their instructors. These discussions would be based around the Communist ideology, but the emphasis would be on correcting the prisoners' "wrong thoughts" which were preventing them from making progress (Lifton, 1961/1989, pp. 27–29). This aspect of intellectuality is particularly relevant to Jung's case as he was encouraged to discuss and debate a whole raft of philosophical concepts with the various characters who inhabit his fantasies. These characters, though primarily his soul, act as his instructors but he is continually bewildered by the obscure and illogical answers, the conflicting views and sometimes outright lies, that he often receives from them. This chapter will compare Lifton's findings with Jung's experiences, along with reports of similar practices in contemporary abusive ritual contexts.

Robert Jay Lifton's seminal study into brainwashing in China was based on a series of interviews with both western and Chinese prisoners who had been subjected to Chinese thought reform programs, shortly after their release. He observed that these programs resembled the practices of organised religion and various kinds of religious re-education and describes two former prisoners, Dr.

Vincent and Father Luca, as taking part in "an agonizing drama of death and rebirth" (Lifton, 1961/1989, p. 66). Another prisoner, an elderly Belgian Bishop, Hans Barker, who had lived in China for decades before his imprisonment, emerged from the horrors of the thought control program a resistor. But at the same time, he said he was struck by how similar the Communist conversion techniques were to those of the Catholic Church and "the identical methods, the identical terminology" of the two systems (Lifton, 1961/1989, pp. 133, 140). Looking back on his own study years later Lifton saw that it was less a record of Maoist China and more an exploration of a totalistic type of control that was emerging in the twentieth century more broadly in both the political arena and amongst fundamentalist religions (1961/1989, p. vi). As a result of this study Lifton devised a theory applicable to indoctrination processes in a range of contexts.

Lifton describes thought reform as being comprised of two basic elements: confession and a renunciation of past and present evil, plus re-education using intellectual, emotional and physical means (1961/1989, p. 5). The former prisoners he interviewed were repeatedly told to confess their crimes under the direction of the officials. This confessional component of cults, used to destabilise the individual's sense of self, is also observed by Singer and Schein (Hassan, 2020). Despite Jung's frequent protests, the confessional mode pervades his journal entries and at times borders on excess.

"You want to be a prophet and chase after your ambition."

(BB 2, p. 152).

On November 14, 1913, in the second entry in the *Book 2*, Jung identifies the struggle he has with an ambitious desire to become a prophet. He describes himself as egotistical, desiring glory, full of uncharitableness and zeal, and totally ignorant, and talks of his ambition as a wound that has not yet healed. He describes a speech "from the darkness" that is full of mockery and places it in inverted commas, as if he is quoting someone else: "You're starring in your own comedy, you're lying to yourself! You spoke so as to deceive others and make them believe in you. You want to be a prophet and chase after your ambition" *(BB 2*, pp. 151–152). He continues to describe being surrounded by mockery and scornful laughter "that the devils set up below the heart" *(BB 2*,

166

p. 153), suggesting that this self-deprecating attitude is being influenced by thoughts that are not necessarily his own.

He later transfers most of this material from November 1913 to "Soul and God" and "On the Service of the Soul" in *Liber Primus*. However, in the next entry, on November 15, there is a section that is not recorded in *The Red Book,* although it is mentioned in the editor's footnote (*BB 2*, p. 153, n. 25). Still engaging with his soul, Jung hears "someone whispering terrible things into my ear" (*BB 2*, p. 156), possibly the voice of conscience or the internalised words of others, that are berating him for writing this unusual material with the intention of creating a stir when it is printed and circulated. He likens his own creation to Nietzsche's *Zarathustra* and Saint Augustine's *Confessions*, though admits to the inferiority of his own attempts. This presents a conflict for Jung between an ambitious desire to become a prophet through the publication of this material and the fear that it is a falsely egotistical goal, a "nasty vanity" in him (*BB 2*, p. 157). He admits to the impertinence of wanting to trade on something that has not yet even been created, that is, the completed record of his fantasies. In fact, the recording of his fantasies has only just begun, so the idea that he should publish them is very premature as he is not yet aware of what they will be about. So, he asks his soul to decide for him, suggesting that the idea should be kept secret. But rather than include this conflict in *Liber Novus* Jung substitutes eleven additional paragraphs, written in larger text in the calligraphic volume and in italics in the translation. It is addressed to the reader as if he is offering it as a spiritual teaching, a series of exhortations or even a sermon, educating his followers in the first steps towards approaching the soul. At its core, though, it is a deeply confusing passage as it is based on his own profound sense of confusion as to what is actually happening to him.

Jung's reference to Saint Augustine's *Confessions* in this entry accords with one of the fundamental principles of Christian life, the confession of sin. But as we have seen previously that many of Jung's references relate to Albert Pike's *Morals and Dogma*, it may also be relevant that Pike refers to Saint Augustine five times in his lectures. On one occasion he refers to the saint's repeated references to initiation implying that he, along with other Christian saints, were describing initiatory knowledge based on the Mysteries that was to be kept secret from the uninitiated (Pike, 1871, pp. 392–393). So again,

Jung's references could be drawing on memories of lectures accompanying the Scottish Rite rituals. Facing one's own weaknesses and the admission of one's faults is one of the early stages in the initiation process in several Masonic rites. As the previous study argued, Jung's initial fantasies in *Liber Novus* closely parallel aspects of the 18th or Rose Croix Degree of the AASR (Brunet, 2019, pp. 24–26). In this ritual the candidate is required to meditate on the mockery and torment of Christ and to undertake a symbolic journey through the desert seeking for the Lost Word in darkness and humility, symbolising an internal process of self-examination. However, in abusive versions of this and other similar rituals the blindfolded candidate may undergo castigation through scorn, humiliation and mistreatment by his brothers, a process known in Freemasonry as "the Rugged Road" (Malcolmson, 1999, p. 55). It is possible that Jung's statement about starring in his own comedy might be the memory of a criticism applied by someone in an initiatory context, as Jung distinguishes it from his own words by framing it in quotation marks.

Lifton describes the establishment of guilt, where the inmates are told repeatedly that they are guilty and must learn to feel permanently guilty as an important component in the undermining of the identity of the inmates of the Chinese Communist prisons (1961/1989, p. 68). He notes that within this permeating atmosphere of guilt the inmates' subjective feelings of sinfulness became intertwined with the accusations of criminal behaviour by their guards, so that they eventually feel that their punishment is deserved. In the *Black Books*, at this early stage, Jung's self-deprecation only concerns the sinfulness of vanity and pride in his present-day adult life, and is not about criminal behaviour. On December 26, 1913 (*BB 2*) he is still castigating himself for his vanity when he prefaces his journal entry with two stanzas of Dante's *Purgatorio* but notes that, in contrast with the delicate sensitivity and profundity of Dante's words, his own words express his ignorance and incapacity. However, he replaces these stanzas in "The Images of the Erring" in *Liber Secundus* with two quotes from Jeremiah 23: 16, 25–28. These quotes are the words of the prophet Jeremiah concerning the false prophets of Baal and contain a warning not to listen to them as they encourage vanity and are filled with deceit. It seems that by the time he is creating *Liber Novus* Jung is questioning the vanity of his flirtation with the idea of becoming a prophet.

From the end of 1913 through to April 1914 Jung's concerns over the problem of vanity, his fear of being motivated by it and its relationship to the creation of his book appears frequently in his journal entries, suggesting that it is a real problem for him. Driven by conflicting thoughts he complains of an inner resistance towards this book of "my most difficult experiments" and ceaselessly devalues it (*BB 2*, pp. 163, 171). On December 11, 1913 his soul urges him to cease focusing on vanity and persuades him that he is not writing his book to satisfy his ego. This prompts Jung to consider that it is not hubris which drives him but that it is his soul who is pushing him. But in a paragraph not included in *Liber Novus* he says he is still feeling impatient and wondering what all this is about. It seems that he is still in doubt as to whether his soul's urging to keep writing is some form of manipulation to keep him on task and producing what will eventually become *The Red Book*. In an overall summary of his struggle with vanity recorded on December 29, 1913 Jung writes a paragraph that does not appear in *Liber Novus*:

> What a burden and danger is vanity! There is nothing about which one could not be vain. Nothing is more difficult than to define the limits of vanity. One who creates should be especially wary of success, though needs it (*BB 2*, p. 209).

However, this awareness does not dispel the problem and on February 23, 1914 he raises the issue of vanity and ambition again. He feels that something is holding him back from his work and his soul now answers abruptly: "Thirst for glory", to which he responds that he thought he had overcome this bad habit. It seems not, and he admits that he is "sick with ambition" but is unsure of where and how this has arisen (*BB 4*, p. 269). Jung's compulsive and ongoing need to confess everything to his soul and constant need to seek her approval, despite his occasional rebellion, bears a strong resemblance to the experience of Lifton's Communist prisoners who were forced to relentlessly criticise all their own thoughts, guided by the official. In Jung's case, the official here is his soul, discussed previously as the introjected voices of his original abusers. But the vanity that he berates himself for may have another purpose. In a fantasy recorded the previous day, in an entry not included in *Liber Novus,* his soul shows him a different way of viewing vanity and its possible usefulness in the task he has undertaken (*BB 4*, pp. 265–268).

This fantasy involves a rural setting where Jung sees shepherds in broad-brimmed hats and meets a German who has fled city life to become a shepherd. They have a discussion where they debate the relative values of city life and the development of civilised culture versus the primitive freedoms of a rural existence. The shepherd's view is that city life is deleterious and harmful, reflecting a reaction to industrialisation that arose in the 18th century, while Jung's position is that those who have the capacity to educate others have a responsibility towards the cultural and intellectual development of civilisation that rural life does not allow. In this context he states: "Cultural labor is not possible without egoism" (*BB 4*, p. 267), suggesting a positive role for the egotistical drive when accompanied by intellectual work. The shepherd then explains the reasons for his choice: he says that he once had a task that he realised was so immense as to prove insurmountable and overwhelming and that he was alone with it. Driven by stifling fear, he says he escaped into the desert and renounced civilisation, before gradually coming back to himself and living again. Jung responds with understanding for the shepherd's plight and recognises the need to remain silent for a long time in order to allow the human heart to heal. But he also believes that it is not possible to remain in the wilderness forever and urges the shepherd to return to the task.

This fantasy and the debate between Jung and the shepherd have a very similar, though ideologically opposite, atmosphere to the group discussions Lifton describes in the Communist prisons. In Jung's fantasy the problem of industrialisation highlights the need for egoism and an elite to produce cultural and intellectual work, whereas in the re-education program in the Chinese prison the concept of individual intellectual vanity was regarded as bourgeois, imperialist and exploitative and in opposition to "the people's standpoint" (Lifton, 1961/1989, p. 26). The question is, could Jung's fantasy be another memory of a type of mystery play aimed at some form of intellectual training in a cult context, undergone by Jung as a youth?

The debate between Jung and the German echoes themes that originated in the latter half of the eighteenth century and were expressed by philosophers and poets of the German Sturm und Drang movement, where pastoral settings were often represented as a means of escape from the complexities of city life (Pascal, 1953; Zosmer, 2021). In Goethe's first novel, *The Sorrows of Young*

Werther (1774/2018), for example, the protagonist is a young intellectual who is drawn to simple village life where he falls in love. But unable to marry his beloved he drifts into depression and takes the extreme course of ending his life. Goethe used this novel partly as a vehicle to contrast the simple beauty but monotonous reality of country life with the intellectual opportunities but elite and pretentious realms of court culture. It is possible that the German figure in Jung's fantasy may be a reference to this novel, as Jung was encouraged by his mother to read Goethe in his youth (1963, p. 68). J. W. von Goethe was a Freemason, initiated in Amalia Lodge in Weimer in 1780, although not all of his work is regarded as exemplifying the values of the Masonic Order (Hamill & Gilbert, 2004, p. 78).

In the fantasy, the German's description of his motives for escaping to the country might be viewed as a thinly veiled reference to Jung's reaction to the initiatory ordeals that he has been recording in his journals. These experiences have been so inexplicable and overwhelming that the task of trying to process them would have felt insurmountable, prompting him to look for an escape into a psychologically restful state away from the confusion they elicited. However, the German character states that his escape is into the desert rather than the countryside, which is a further reminder of several of Jung's initiatory ordeals that take place in the desert, and to the role of a symbolic journey into the desert used in the ritual of the Rose Croix degree (Brunet, 2019).

There may be other connections to this fantasy in *Morals and Dogma*. In a summary of the history and philosophies of Gnosticism Albert Pike discusses Philo's concept of the Word or Logos of the Supreme Being as being the world of ideas or the intellectual world, which he then describes as a city. He states: "The Intellectual City was but the *Thought* of the Architect, who meditated the creation, according to that plan of the Material City" (Pike, 1871, p. 184).[1] References to shepherds also appear throughout Pike's lectures, including the concept of Jesus as the Good Shepherd. So, it is possible that Jung's fantasy with the shepherd in the countryside in February 1914 could have also been drawing on Pike's Masonic teachings that focused on themes of nature and the intellectual world of ideas, expressed in terms of a city.

By April 19, 1914 (*BB 5*) Jung has been alone every night in a long series of frustrating inner conversations, only now he feels that they are no longer with his soul but with himself, his own "I". He admits that these conversations are becoming terribly boring and monotonous and that his constant self-criticism suggests a lack of self-esteem. Nevertheless, he believes that his soul has now fled to the eternal realms, abandoning him to the company of his "I" that he continues to denigrate fiercely:

> Yes, you are self-pitying and self-righteous, unruly, pessimistic, misanthropic, cowardly, dishonest with yourself, unamiable, venomous, and vengeful. One could write books about your childish pride and your sensitivities. Playacting becomes you badly and you abuse it to the best of your ability (*BB 5*, p. 217).

Similar self-castigation entirely fills the next day's entry, and to a lesser extent, the following one. It is extreme in nature and he again attacks his ambition and feelings of superiority, which he says he will stamp into the dirt. On May 23, 1914 his soul reappears and encourages him in his work, saying it will prosper and bear marvelous fruit, but Jung describes an incomprehensible fear in response. His soul then begins to pressure him, reminding him of his limited time and encouraging him to pursue solitude so as to get the work done. She becomes more and more demanding and on December 5, 1915 she makes her intentions very clear. "Listen", she says: "Build the Church. Write the holy books, the age-old new ones, that contain the echo of the eternal being, the mysterious ones – mocked wisdom – the lower and upper truth" (*BB 5*, p. 245).

So now we have it. Here the voice of Jung's soul appears to be embodying the intentions of the cult that he has been grappling with from the very first entries: that he is to write his holy books for the purpose of establishing a new religion and becoming a cult leader. These books are to contain the "mocked wisdom" that we have seen throughout his initiations where the Masonic rituals are themselves mocked and used abusively. But even while he is recording all of this faithfully in his journals Jung is still resisting the notion of producing such a book; it might be full of secrets and teachings but it also involves a great deal of trickery and farcical humour. By December 26, 1915, amid more urging from his soul he replies: "Shall I become a sect leader? What the devil! No, no, no!" (*BB 5*, pp. 254). But his soul reassures him that the church will be an internal one and the community involved will be an inner spiritual one and not an outer one, a community of the dead; so, at this point Jung offers a prayer to these dead. It is relevant to ask, though, whether these "dead" are in fact the dissociated parts of himself that have undergone the initiatory terrors.

In Jung's early entries we have seen this confessional attitude repeatedly, beginning with a submissive attitude towards his soul, whom he regards as a wise guide whose commands and schooling he must follow. But doubts gradually seep into this more obedient attitude where he questions who his soul is and whether he should really trust her and hand himself so completely over to her. These doubts continue and he oscillates between regarding his soul either as a friend or as a hostile and dangerous entity, right throughout the *Black Books*. But despite all his fears and misgivings it appears that Jung does decide to follow the directives of his soul to create an opus, which will result in the final version of *Liber Novus*, a decision recorded at the end of *Liber Secundus* (2009a, p. 330; 2009b, p. 457).

One of the attributes of indoctrination noted by cult expert Steven Hassan (2020), learned during his own experience in the Korean cult of Sun Myung Moon, is that he felt that he was making his own decisions but only later realised that it was an illusion of choice and he was actually being manipulated by others. Being programmed to perform particular roles is one of the mainstays of ritual abuse and this can include the preparation to becoming a cult leader (Lacter, 2011, p. 99). For the duration of his journal entries, it could be said that Jung was being manipulated by his soul, an introjected voice of the cult, to create a holy book. But it was only after he gradually distances himself from these conversations with his soul in later years that he is able to fully realise that this was not his own choice and he ultimately decides not to publish *Liber Novus*. But as we shall see, the process of grooming him towards this goal is one that involves much harsher methods than appealing to his vanity and pressuring him to keep writing.

"A feeling of guilt torments me – is it bad conscience?" (*BB 2*, p. 186)

Alongside the self-flagellation and subjective feelings of sinfulness, Lifton observes that in the Communist prisons the inmates were relentlessly made to believe that they were guilty of criminal behaviour (1961/1989). Referring to the experience of the prisoner Dr Vincent, he describes the application of guilt-producing scenarios in the following terms: "He found himself in a Kafka-like maze of vague and yet damning accusations: he could neither understand exactly what he was guilty of ('recognize his crimes') nor could he in any way establish his innocence" (Lifton, 1961/1989, p. 23). Jung is made to feel guilty on many occasions throughout his active imaginations. In the entry for December 18, 1913 (*BB 2*), he recounts a frightful dream where he feels that, accompanied by a youth, he has murdered the hero Siegfried. The guilt this experience produces is so great that he feels suicidal; he must solve the riddle of the dream otherwise he will shoot himself. Then he suddenly realises the absurdity of this situation and this releases enormous tension; a beautiful and magical image of a new world appears where there are forms clad in silk amid a coloured atmosphere and he falls asleep "like a convalescent" (*BB 2*, p. 176). Jung explains this shift as a rebirth process, of a new man reborn through painful guilt.

This dream was transferred to *Liber Primus* as a vision entitled "The Murder of the Hero". As the editor notes (*BB 2*, p. 175, n. 136), twelve years after the initial dream Jung revealed that he had never liked Siegfried and saw him as ridiculous, wondering why his unconscious had been so preoccupied with this hero figure as to create such intense emotions (Jung, 2009a, p. 242, n. 115; 2009b, p. 161). But he states that it felt as if *he* was the one who had been shot, that part of *him* was murdered, and that this part was his intellect. In a trauma reading this suggests the decommissioning of the forebrain or pre-frontal cortex due to intense emotional shock and the relegation of the memory of the initiation into the unconscious (van der Kolk, 2014, pp. 66–70). The comment that he fell asleep like a convalescent, a statement that was not included in *Liber Novus*, suggests that he may have been nursed after the shock while a deep hypnotic sleep rendered him amnesic towards the initiatory event. The ethereal vision of silk-clad figures might have also been a contrived theatrical scenario intended to calm him and help him recover from the psychological shock of the so-called murder. Nevertheless, inexplicable feelings of guilt could well have lingered just below the level of consciousness until his mid-life recollection of this initiatory scenario.

This is only one of many of Jung's active imaginations where an initiatory situation is contrived to make him experience extraordinary feelings of guilt; these episodes are covered in the previous study (Brunet, 2019). But his encounter on January 12, 1914 with a horrifying image of tortured bodies, cannibalism and being made to believe that he has eaten the liver of a dead child is arguably the worst of them. It makes him ponder the whole notion of evil and he rages at the fact that he has been forced to participate: "You make me a guilty party to this most hideous of all crimes ... I cannot participate in this horrible guilt" (*BB 3*, p. 135), he says; but then he does participate. In so-doing the child's soul then reveals herself to also be *his* soul. Fortunately, at the conclusion of the entry he realises that it is a trick and that it is some lesson that, as a man, he is capable of anything. Recalled by his adult self it is another means by which his manipulative soul, or introjected voice of the cult, has reminded him that he once desecrated himself in this manner and that he has already become "one of them".

The creation of guilt is used extensively in the ritual abuse of children. Alison Miller, a clinical psychologist who has worked with survivors of ritual abuse and mind control since 1991, describes the enormous guilt felt by survivors who feel they have participated in the abuse of others in rapes, murders or cannibalism, whether they were real or involved trickery, and that the survivors often feel too evil to be forgiven. The perpetrators, she says, often heap shame onto the children after they have committed one of these acts and claim that the children have now become evil, saying that it is proof that "you are one of us" (Miller, 2012, p. 242).

A deep hypnotic sleep can play an important role after such shocks and with each new shock more and more unknown parts of the self are formed, now hidden in different parts of the psyche. In January 1914, in a section not included in *Liber Novus*, Jung states as much when he says: "I have to crawl together out of many different corners in which I lost myself" (*BB 4*, p. 227). Wendy Hoffman, a survivor of an abusive mind control cult, makes a similar comment after a particularly abusive encounter with her programmers: "All my evoked parts went back to sleep in their internal nooks. In the morning I had tea and toast and remembered nothing", she says (Hoffman, 2020, "A Change of Tactics, a Near Fatal Visit", penultimate paragraph).

But if a deep sleep is used to settle the child and induce amnesia after an initiatory shock, sleep deprivation can be used to create destabilisation throughout the indoctrination process; in abusive cults more generally and in the ritual abuse of children it is one of the noted forms of mind control (Hassan, 2020; Rutz et al, 2008; Lacter & Lehman, 2008; Miller, 2012). In Lifton's study the former prisoners recalled that one of the methods persistently used to gain confessions was sleep deprivation, inducing fatigue, confusion, and helplessness. Father Luca, for instance, describes being kept constantly awake by being pinched, slapped and poked. Dr Vincent describes the results of this strategy: "You are annihilated ... exhausted ... you can't control yourself ... You do whatever they want ... You can't distinguish right from left" (Lifton, 1961/1989, p. 23).

In Jung's case we see references to being prevented from sleep in *Book 7*, where his soul is urging him to keep busy on the great work, the new religion. On January 5, 1922, he describes himself as weary, suffering from sleep disturbances and wondering why he is being kept awake. His soul's answer is that there is no time for sleep and points out that she has been disturbing his sleep for a long time. She also lures him with the concept that through a complete and utter dedication to this work that he will achieve a higher level of consciousness. While as an adult Jung is not being pinched and poked as the Communist prisoners were, his soul's push to work incessantly towards the "great work" with only minimal sleep bears similarities with the type of programming used in modern cults. As a youth, while a member of the Korean cult, Steven Hassan describes being similarly sleep-deprived and working fanatically for long hours with no pay, supporting the belief that Moon was the Messiah heralding a global theocracy and destroying all other religions and governments to establish "God's original ideal–the Garden of Eden" (2020, p. 2).

Another criterion for judging cult programming is what Lifton terms *mystical manipulation*, described as "the staging of seemingly spontaneous and supernatural events that are planned or contrived" (1961/1989, pp. 422–423; Hassan, 2020, p. 28). Amongst Margaret Singer's criteria she includes the use of hypnosis or altered states of consciousness in modern western cults (cited in Hassan, 2020, p. 44). Here, trance states are induced in the members using soothing, rhythmic story-telling, staring at spots on the wall, mantra meditations or chanting to induce hyperventilation or altered states of consciousness, interpreted by the cult leaders as "magic states" (Singer, 1994, points 16, 21). Edgar Schein also includes hypnosis and mystical manipulation as sub-categories of his three-stage model of coercive persuasion (cited in Hassan, 2020, pp. 36–37). As we have seen in previous chapters, hypnosis or crystal-gazing appears in a number of the fantasies from *Books 2* and *3* which Jung transfers to *Liber Primus* in the chapters "Descent into Hell in the Future", "Mysterium Encounter", "Instruction" and "Resolution". These practices are identified in relation to the historical use of magical séances and the association between Count Cagliostro and Anton Mesmer in the establishment of Egyptian Freemasonry in the 18th century.

The staging of seemingly mystical or magical events occurs right throughout Jung's fantasies as he is made to believe that he has been in deserts where he meets biblical figures, has been hung, Christ-like, on a cross and crushed by a serpent, carried the giant Izdubar, shrinking him to the size of an egg, and then seeing him emerge as a god from the cracked egg after feeling he was in a narrow coffin in a grave, and so on. These encounters produce ecstatic mystical feelings in Jung but on reflection he recognises that they are Mystery Plays. Mystical manipulation and hypnosis are staple practices in the realm of ritual abuse, for children can easily be fooled by staged events, particularly if accompanied by trance states or hallucinatory drugs. As Miller notes, simulations of religious figures and the afterlife are used throughout ritual abuse: in Christian versions hell can be simulated with paintings of flames on walls, dry ice is used to make smoke, people in devil and demon costumes frighten, hurt or rape the children, and children are put into graves or coffins to be "raised from the dead" (Miller, 2012, p. 66).

"I have ... prepared all the instruments of the torture chamber for you ..."

(BB 5, p. 223)

In addition to sleep deprivation and mystical manipulation Lifton notes that cruel forms of physical brutalisation accompanied the psychological methods of the Chinese thought reform program. This direct physical brutality is aimed at an assault upon identity and places the adult in the role of a helpless infant or sub-human animal, to be manipulated by his trainers (Lifton, 1961/1989, p. 67). Torture-based mind control is also a central feature of ritual abuse. Ellen Lacter, a psychologist who has been working with ritual abuse survivors for several decades, discusses the role of torture in ritual abuse in some depth. By firstly enumerating a list of painful bodily tortures that are systematically applied to the victims, such as the use of electric shocks, oxygen deprivation, spinning and so on, combined with various forms of conditioning, including hypnosis, spiritual threats and staged tricks, she notes that these practices are aimed at inducing a tabula rasa state and then the formation of new self-states. She writes:

> Mind control survivors report that their abusers understand well that torture induces a dissociate-prone psyche to form new programmable self-states, and calculatedly torture victims for this purpose ... sophisticated abusers recognize that a new self-state has arisen when the child no longer reacts with terror or pain to the torture. This new state is immediately named and given directives (Lacter, 2011, pp. 76–77).

During April 1914 Jung's severe castigation of his "I" becomes even more brutal, both in terms of the invective he uses and the series of extreme physical punishments that he describes. It seems that Jung has internalised the personalities, attitudes and agendas of the original abusers when he states:

> Do you believe that it is a pleasure to exist together with a fellow like you? ... I will tighten the vise around you and slowly peel off your skin ... I will stitch a cloth of new skin onto you, so that you can see feel its effect ... You find the pain unbearable ... I hold my rasp in the fire until it glows and then I will continue to abrade you with red-hot iron ... You think you cannot endure it any longer ... I will pull out your tongue, with which you have blasphemed, ridiculed and joked. I will pin all your

unjust and depraved words one by one to your body with needles so that you can feel how evil words stab ... I am screwing the vise tighter, and put the pilliwinks on you until the old desire for rebellion will have thoroughly left you. I will break all of your bones until there is no longer a trace of hardness in you ... Do you think I'd like an embuggerance such as you as a companion for ever? ... You call God for help? It's good that the loving God is far off and cannot help you ... The procedure is barbaric, but affective (*BB 5*, pp. 217–219).[2]

These tortures that Jung describes have also appeared in the reports of ritual abuse; some are real while others are threats or tricks. The stitching of a cloth of new skin has been reported by some survivors. Ellen Lacter (2021, Type 6, "Witch personalities") describes this as a ritual where the abusers appear to sew some of their skin onto the young victim's open wound in order to make the child believe that the abuser's spirit has entered the child. It is possible that hypnosis or trance states are involved or trick mirrors are used, but it is intended to make the child's personality-state believe that he has become the abuser as the skin cells multiply. Jung also describes a vise being tightened and putting the pilliwinks on. Pilliwinks are an old instrument of torture that squeeze the fingers. In my own case my father once put my thumb in a vise; I still have a mark on my left thumb from this experience. It was to teach me how to dissociate from pain and from that point onward he repeatedly told me to "think of your thumb" when I was going to the dentist, in order to undergo the procedures without anesthetic. I wondered why he always said this as I had completely forgotten the original ordeal. Decades later, the memory of it returned. Another ordeal I faced was having my tongue clamped to remind me never to speak about these experiences.

The use of pins or needles jabbed into the feet, along with other painful treatments, is used in ritual abuse to create psychological splits in very young children or infants (Katz, 2012, p. 101). In Jung's case, he is being threatened to be jabbed with needles, possibly as a reminder of similar treatment at some stage in childhood. The threat of being scorched with a red-hot iron is a trick used in fraternal initiation rites. Here the victim is generally held so he can see the hot iron glowing in the fire; but when it is taken towards his back it is quickly replaced with one that has been on ice. As the nerves in the back cannot differentiate between extreme heat and cold the victim feels as if he has been scorched with fire. In the 1908 catalogue of DeMoulin Bros & Co (p. 38), an American company which produced paraphernalia and costumes for fraternal side degrees, an electric branding iron is used for the same purpose and described as "only an innocent joke". It is interesting that Jung crosses out the word 'see' and replaces it with 'feel' when he describes these practices, as it is possible that he did not actually see what was happening at the time.

Two years later, in January 1916, the strategy used to create the atmosphere of this latter torture is revealed. Here, Jung is talking with his soul and smells "burdensome vapors" that indicate the presence of the devil. His soul tells him that he must not forget all the hardships that he suffered and that he has been confused by these narcotic vapours and caught in nets "by fidgeting little men in invisible snares, quiet mocking laughter in the distance, grinding teeth, captives trembling with fear" (*BB 5*, pp. 281–282). His soul describes a fiery glow and embers being poked and in the following entry his soul tells him that "everything happens behind your back" (*BB 5*, p. 282). So, it appears that Jung has been overcome by narcotic fumes and tricked by a group of men who are barely suppressing their laughter at his confusion and fear while poking the fire in readiness for this "innocent joke".

In the Communist thought reform context Lifton notes that the prisoners were pushed to mental and physical breakdown using a combination of psychological and physical torture leading to the loss of the ability to distinguish between what was real and what was imaginary (1961/1989, pp. 44). He likens the prisoners to a man taken from his ordinary routine and placed in a psychiatric hospital where he is supposed to confess to a vague crime and where the other inmates are reinforcing his guilt. On January 18, 1914 (*BB 4*) Jung describes a fantasy along these same lines which appears to be another staged event. This is where he finds himself in an old-fashioned kitchen where he discusses the writings of Thomas à Kempis with the cook until he is suddenly taken by the police to a madhouse. This fantasy was transferred to "Nox Secunda" in *Liber Novus* and discussed in the previous study, where it was related to the threat of madness often used in ritual abuse if the victim remembers the abuse or leaves the cult (Smith, 1993, p. 44; Miller, 2012, p. 127; Noblitt & Perskin Noblitt, 2014, p. 48; Brunet, 2019, p. 110).

Jung's fantasy scenario is very similar to Lifton's description, even though it appears to be another elaborate ruse. Here his soul is forcing him to accept his madness and even see it as "a special form of the intellect" (*BB 4*, p. 211). In the fantasy he meets a fat little professor who confirms that Jung is in the madhouse and diagnoses him as totally confused and incoherent. And yet, for a brief moment Jung asks if he has mistaken the professor for his own soul. He then describes being in internal disarray and wondering whether he really is going crazy; a feeling of chaos is approaching and then he feels the floor swaying, as if in a stormy sea. A character comments on how rough the sea is and offers him a cocktail.

Similar scenarios and trick devices to make the candidate feel he is going mad can be found in the DeMoulin catalogues. Here, various mechanical devices like swaying bridges, erratically moving footways or contraptions to produce seasickness are used in pranks to unnerve the blindfolded candidates (DeMoulin, 1908). A large array of theatrical costumes completes the ruse. In Jung's fantasy the fat little professor and a mad patient, "a man with a black beard, a tousled head of hair, and dark shining eyes" (*BB 4*, p. 213), produce unrestrained laughter from the onlooking members as they trick the youthful Jung into believing that he is truly in the madhouse. This farcical situation is now replaced by a mystical vision of the sun rising over the sea and an enormous palm tree or Tree of Life emerging, connecting Heaven with the interior of the earth. Potentially another theatrical construct aimed at signifying the birth of a new alter, this mystical vision leaves Jung feeling even more alone and disheartened, but he soon awakens in the kitchen where he realises that it was all a dream about a dreadful play.

As Hassan notes, "thought reform is intentionally and systematically practiced on people without their understanding of what is happening" (2020, p. 46). Applied in childhood this would undoubtedly be the case; as each of the ordeals are subsequently lost to amnesia, the confusion would be compounded. More chaos and confusion accompany Jung over the next months. On February 28, 1914 (*BB 4*), in an entry not included in *Liber Novus*, he reaches a point not unlike the sense of annihilation described by Lifton's Father Luca, where he will do anything his captors want when he says that he surrenders and asks what his soul wants. She replies that she wants nothing, but that they are both weary from these fierce struggles and now need to rest and put these things away. Lifton describes this as another technique incorporated into the thought reform process where fluctuations between assault and leniency create a bridge between the death and rebirth experience. At this point the prisoner begins to align himself with his captors becoming "their grateful partner in his own reform" (Lifton, 1961/1989, p. 73). In Jung's case the rest he is granted only provides a brief hiatus before the confusion and chaos reasserts itself and, despite his continued frustration with his soul, Jung concludes his next discussion with her with "but I shall obey" (*BB 4*, p. 276).

"My God, I want from myself what is right." (*BB 6*, p. 249)

In 1916, alternating between placing his trust in his soul and frequently enraged by her deception and manipulation, Jung is still struggling with the right way to proceed. Throughout this year he plies his soul with a series of questions in order to understand what his role is, but her answers are vague and elusive. On January 29, 1916, he asks her what her plan is; she says "I want to participate in your renown. You suit us" (*BB 5*, p. 281). The question of who is the "us" here is left unexplained. In August he states that he wants what is right for himself and asks his soul why she is not helping him. Her answer is: "I must preserve the right connection with the powerful of this world" (*BB 6*, p. 250). Who these powerful are, though, is not made clear. In October Jung's soul tells him that his work is like that of a worm, "that digs secret passages and brings down the mighty" (*BB 6*, p. 268). But, again, who the mighty are is not indicated. Then, when he asks for a glimpse forward to see the fruits of this work, his soul evades a direct answer, but instead offers a series of rhetorical questions:

> Temples in deserts? Secret societies? Ceremonies? Rituals? Colorful robes? Golden images of terrible aspect? None of them – those branded by the spirit of love, burnt by the fire recognize each other and speak the same language in hidden places. Small indications of the spirit placed here and there, hidden fire in hearts and minds (*BB 6*, p. 268).

Jung then questions if he is on the right way to this goal and his soul confirms that he is, but her answer is duplicitous and again aimed at sowing confusion. On the one hand her questions imply that his active imaginations *are* associated with the rituals of the secret societies, as the previous study clearly demonstrated, but then she denies this in the following sentence, saying it is none of them. In the internal world of Dissociative Identity Disorder (DID) sufferers there is often a complex relationship between those alter states that are able to face their suffering and those that deny that there is any problem at all. An article by Steven Frankel and Todd O'Hearn (1996) compared the internal dynamics of DID patients with the organisation of eastern European ghettos during World War II. They point out that DID develops in children who are both high in hypnotic capacity and are exposed to extreme and ongoing abuse, and the internal roles that emerge are not unlike those that develop within communities under siege, such as the Jewish populations under Nazi control. One type of alter that develops, they argue, is the denier, loyalist or self-blamer, that distorts or sows doubt about the emerging memories. These denier alters appear when important memories of abuse are emerging and act to prevent disclosure in order to protect the secrecy of the cult.

Jung's soul's evasive response, while not providing details, does suggest one thing: it seems that he has been selected by some powerful organisation to play a role in the promotion of a new religion. But what is this cult? On the surface Freemasonry appears to be involved but, as these two studies have illustrated, the narratives in Jung's fantasies might be based on Masonic rites and teachings, but they are not being used in a legitimate way. Instead, they fall into the category of Spurious Freemasonry or side degrees and on many occasions the Masonic rituals and its philosophies are even mocked. It could be said that the Masonic rites are only a tool in the indoctrination process. His soul's comment about those who have been burnt by the fire appears to be a euphemism for initiation and, if one inserts the word "brotherly" into the phrase "branded by the spirit of love" then the fraternal trick of mock torture with a red-hot iron and the Masonic motto of "Brotherly Love, Relief and Truth" comes to mind. It is all meant to be interpreted as harmless fun, creating a band of brothers who recognise each other and speak the same language.

In a discussion of fraternal side degree practices in the American context, William Moore (2010) notes this tendency towards the mockery of the Masonic rituals. He explains the development of side degrees in the late 19th century to be associated with increased industrialisation, an increase in wages and the availability of manufactured goods such as the paraphernalia required for these comical skits. Along with this was an accompanying shift in values from dignified behaviour to the high jinks, slapstick and amateur theatricals where men are encouraged to laugh at themselves and their troubles. Moore frames this shift in masculinity as "a shift from character to personality" where "American men found that the old artisanal and agricultural ideals of character based upon self-restraint and Victorian gentility were unsuited to the emergent industrial order" (Moore, 2010, pp. 29, 30). But if this powerful cult is initiating children in the way that Jung seems to have been then the ramifications are far more insidious and point to the darkest of plans. Clearly, Jung's experiences talk of a point well beyond these so-called innocent high junks among consenting adult males, and point to distorted versions of the ancient Mysteries in order to put a child or youth through highly traumatic ordeals. Here, the shift in values behind closed doors has crossed over from innocent fun, albeit abusive by today's standards, to a reckless disdain for childhood innocence and even punishment of the child in an evil transference of pain from the older generation to the youngest.

For now, Jung is still under the cult's spell and in 1916 he accedes to the demands of his soul to pass on the teachings by privately publishing *Septem Sermones ad Mortuos*; but by the end of the year Jung's doubts and suspicions have returned. When she demands that he serve her he strikes back angrily with the charge that she is the thief who has stolen from him and made him into a slave. He calls her "divine monster" and protests that he has given her enough and deserves his human freedom (*BB 6*, p. 272). As the previous study pointed out, another of the dissociated identities that can be produced in ritual abuse is that of the "spirit slave" (Noblitt & Perskin Noblitt, 2014; Brunet, 2019, p. 147). On January 7, 1917 (*BB 6*), Jung is still protesting that he will not be a servant, but his soul introduces him to another character, a man of the East who appears as a new sun rises and describes himself as an ancient brother who was burnt in the fire and lives in Jung's "below". In terms of the argument here, we seem to be looking at another alter, the spirit of gravity, possibly created in an abusive initiatory scenario, who is only now coming to the fore, seemingly to distract Jung from his protests. But by this stage Jung is getting bored by all these encounters and yawns at the man of the East's explanation. In the following entries he reveals more of his boredom with his soul's riddles and banal explanations and demands to know why she associates herself with this "shabby riff-raff" (*BB 6*, p. 276). But as we saw in the previous chapters, the re-introduction of the god Phanes, Atmaviktu and other mystical beings, along with his preoccupation with magic and with the women in his life, fills Jung's journals for several more years.

As the entries become fewer and farther between, Jung describes his soul continuing to drive him. On January 5, 1922 she begins to use the expression "the great work" to describe the proclamation of the new religion. Here, Pike's Scottish Rite lectures may again be relevant, as he uses the same term as Masonry's mission all through *Morals and Dogma*. In his earlier chapters it is written in lower case, but in the concluding chapters Pike uses the capitalised form, the Great Work, no less than 19 times when referring to the Gnostic tradition and the Hermetic science of alchemy. He ascribes various meanings to the term: firstly, he says it stands for the great secret that all religions as well as the Mysteries, Hermeticism and alchemy hold, which is only available to adepts and sages and deliberately kept from the unworthy (Pike, 1871, p. 77). He then talks of the great work of initiation as a means of purifying the soul and enabling it to recall its heavenly origins and restore its wings that had been stained by the earthly experience (Pike, 1871, pp. 373, 571). In order to do this the initiate is advised to follow the teachings and example of Jesus, expounding all of the Christ's virtues (Pike, 1871, p. 516). Pike then focusses on the Great Work as the understanding of the potential of the human will, the mind and the soul, but decries attempts to "subjugate the will of others and take the soul captive" (1871, pp. 56). He views the corrupt application of this knowledge as the most extreme form of the human thirst for power and associates it with proselytising and the early experiments of Anton Mesmer. Finally, Pike describes the Great Work of Hermes as a magical operation. It involves:

> the separation of the earth from the fire, the subtile [sic] from the gross, gently, with much industry [so that] it ascends from earth to Heaven, and again descends to earth, and receives the force of things above and

below. Thou shalt by this means possess the glory of the whole world, and therefore all obscurity shall flee away from thee (Pike, 1871, p. 556).

Pike's description of the Great Work of Hermes emphasises that it is a gentle approach of patient spiritual development. In Freemasonry this approach is embodied in the Second Degree which describes the building of Solomon's Temple. Interpreted metaphorically, it emphasises the rewards of steady spiritual progress, eventually leading to the experience of divine connection such as that pursued by mystics in their meditations. William James notes the positive effect these mystical experiences can have on the quality of life:

> They enrich it marvellously. A single one of them may be sufficient to abolish at a stroke certain imperfections of which the soul during its whole life had vainly tried to rid itself, and to leave it adorned with virtues and loaded with supernatural gifts. A single one of these intoxicating consolations may reward it for all the labours undergone in its life (James, 1985, p. 328).

In Jung's case we seem to be seeing the dark side of the Great Work, and the *Black Books* can be viewed as a record of how this is achieved; but his decision to call these journals *Black Books* may not be a random choice of terms. Wendy Hoffman (2016/2019, pp. 23, 44), a survivor of high-level ritual abuse, notes that this same term has been used in the realm of abusive cults, where all the mind-control procedures that the ritually abused individual has undergone, from conception to death, are recorded in a black book. In the 1990s, she adds, these black books went from paper to the computer (personal correspondence, September 25, 2024).

What we have seen in Jung's active imaginations is the creation of these divine states through repeated applications of shock and cruel treatment. This has produced multiple ecstatic experiences that Jung often regards with great suspicion as some part of him knows that there is something evil about them. John Horgan (2003), a scientist examining mystical experiences and the human nervous system, notes that there are two ways of attaining these elevated mystical states: on the one hand, through patient spiritual development as described above, and on the other, through intense activities or shock. These two approaches correlate with the two different functions of the autonomic nervous system. The first includes meditation, prayer and relaxation, which exploits the quiescent component of the autonomic nervous system, whereas the second such as dancing, hyperventilation, excitation and other processes, arouses the "fight or flight" response to exploit the arousal component of the autonomic system. "If either the arousal or the quiescent component is pushed far enough", he says, "the one activates the other through a 'spillover effect', producing a paradoxical state of ecstatic serenity" (Horgan, 2003, p. 74).

In Jung's case we seem to be looking at a thought reform process undergone during the malleable period of identity formation in a young person, and so there would be no reversion to a previously fully-formed identity, such as was seen in the case of the Communist prisoners. Furthermore, the thought reform prisoners Lifton studied did not forget their experiences, whereas Jung has dissociated and repressed the memories of the initiatory ordeals only to have them return in all their confusing intensity during his mid-life period. Lifton describes the overall process of Communist thought reform practices on an individual as "a relentless means of undermining the human personality" (1961/1989, p. 13). As the analysis of the *Black Books* demonstrate, it is this same quality of relentlessness that pervades Jung's active imaginations. By examining Jung's experiences alongside the techniques found in abusive cults it can be seen that he was being re-educated in extreme ways to reject the religion in which he was raised and to help promote a new creed. Moreover, it seems he was being groomed to become a cult leader of a new religion, one that seemingly supports the devastating abuse of children under the rubric of initiation. However, Jung's practice of accurately recording and intensely examining his active imaginations would help him to ultimately reject the role of cult leader that was being dangled, carrot-like before him.

Notes

1 The use of capital letters and italics in this quote is Pike's.
2 The crossed out see is Jung's.

7
Final thoughts

> Like a stray child you stand pitifully among the mighty, who hold the threads of your life. You cry for help and attach yourself to the first person that comes your way. Perhaps he can advise you, perhaps he knows the thought that you do not have, and which all things have sucked out of you (Jung, 2009a, p. 273; 2009b, p. 260).

Jung made the heartbreaking statement above while contemplating a fantasy from January 1, 1914 (*BB 3*) and recording it in poetic language in "Dies II" in *Liber Secundus*. He is approaching the fantasy from the perspective of a psychoanalyst trying to get into the mind of a child, of himself as a child, who has attached himself to something that he does not understand. In this fantasy Jung finds himself in Egypt again, in a strange hallucinatory world where he sees four horses carrying the sun and a thousand black serpents crawling into their holes, while stones line up like soldiers and move in ranks down the valley. This seems to be another memory of a hypnotised state, another example of crystal-gazing in the context of an Egyptian rite, undergone when he was "a stray child [standing] pitifully among the mighty". It is a child old enough to yearn for a morsel of rational thought after a whole series of terrifying and ridiculous ordeals and overwhelmingly confusing scenarios. In the previous study this fantasy was identified with themes from the Memphis-Misraim Rite and the Knights of the Sun Degree in the Scottish Rite (Brunet, 2019, pp. 64–65). Enter Ammonius, an anchorite of the desert, a calm, logical mind, who is prepared to have an intelligent discussion on religion and philosophy with him; a voice of sanity after the bizarre and confusing nonsense of the previous fantasies. It is easy for Jung to attach himself to such a character; as the son of a parson and with uncles also churchmen, he is at home with such discussions (Jung, 1963, p. 42).

The manipulation of attachment needs is a key strategy used in ritual abuse and, in extreme cases, can begin very early in a child's life. Here, it can involve the abusers systematically manipulating the normal attachment needs of a child, depriving them of their basic requirements, such as sustenance, warmth or touch, almost to the point of death, and then rescuing the children by telling them that only they or their gods can save them (Epstein, Schwartz & Schwartz, 2011; Lacter, 2023). In Jung's case, in this strange hallucinatory world, the anchorite's calm reasoning must have been just as vital as sustenance for him as milk to a starving infant. But without warning Ammonius lunges at him, calling him Satan, and Jung suddenly finds himself back in the 20th century, jolted back into the awareness that even his beloved philosophy is not safe in this bizarre underworld.

The confusing territory Jung finds himself in is not unlike the liminal realms of puberty rites observed by several key experts in the tradition of initiation, some of whom were of Jung's generation. The ethnographer Arnold van Gennep (1873–1957), for example, noted that these practices involved three stages; the first being the separation stage. Here, the boy is wrenched from the realm of the mother and exposed to a series of shocks, and, in some tribal contexts, undergoes some form of bodily mutilation. These mutilations, along with physical and mental weakening, are intended to make him "lose all recollection of his childhood existence" (van Gennep, 1908/1960, pp. vii, 75, 102). This is then followed by instruction in tribal lore, education in the tribal myths and religious ceremonies that can involve death and resurrection scenarios. The basic characteristics of these tribal practices, along with the memory loss they elicit, are not dissimilar to the lengthy process Jung describes and are not unlike those found in contemporary cases of ritual abuse. The American sociologist and anthropologist Hutton Webster (1875–1955) described similarly extreme effects on the youths undergoing initiation in indigenous American tribes. He cites the Tuscacora Indians, noting their process of confining the youths in total darkness for five or six weeks, along with other deprivations, until they were driven raving mad. Some even died, he said, "after this diabolical purgation" (Webster, 1908/1968, pp. 32–33). As Jung processed his own initiatory

189

experiences it was so overwhelming for him at times that he felt he was going mad; in the beginning he even contemplated suicide.

The anthropologist Marcel Mauss (1872–1950) noted that men's secret societies, which have preserved the tradition of initiation, have historically overlapped with the magical tradition (1902/2005, p. 54). As we have seen, magic plays a key role in Jung's active imaginations, in both the fantasies he transferred to *Liber Novus* and in his discussions with his inner parts in the later journals. The historian of religion Mircea Eliade (1907–1986) argued that the secret societies have traditionally envied women's capacity to give birth and that they have used birth symbolism in their initiations for this reason (1958/1995, pp. 80, 123). He also notes the retention of ordeals, special teaching and secrecy in contemporary secret societies and observes the pattern of initiatory torture, death and resurrection in ancient practices. Birth symbolism, including that of the egg, is illustrated in both the text and pictorial illustrations of Jung's fantasies (Brunet, 2019), and the initiatory torture he describes appears to follow the ancient model. Some of these tortures may have been literally used on him to induce altered states, but others were clearly tricks and seem to have been experienced under the influence of hypnosis.

Following on from these experts was Victor Turner (1920–1983), who observed that these traditional initiation rites portray a domain of chaos and disorder where the norms of social behaviour are turned upside-down and the laws of morality that hold good in everyday life are derided (1992, p. 152). These transgressions, he says, are enacted as demonstrations that include themes of human sacrifice, cannibalism, parricide and incest, as well as the use of crude gestures. They are carried out by trickster characters who deceive the initiates with simple magic into believing they are subject to powerful forces over which they have no control. Turner described the novices in these rites as "being taught that they did not know what they thought they knew. Beneath the surface structure of custom was a deep structure, whose rules they had to learn, through paradox and shock" (1982, p. 42). In Jung's active imaginations we see themes of human sacrifice and cannibalism enacted theatrically or created hypnotically, along with other transgressions of the moral order. Each one of these absurd scenarios sees Jung confused, angry or outraged, and in a state of torment or shock.

Jung was well aware of the role of initiation rites in tribal cultures, so do the *Black Books* tell us whether he was ever able to admit to himself the possibility that he might have been initiated in similar ways to those described by these experts? And was he ever able to connect more fully with his own deep inner knowledge about the source of his fantasies? This final chapter will explore these questions through a brief recapping of Jung's realisations that have already been noted throughout the previous chapters. It will then tie up some of the loose ends in an overall summary.

Jung's realisations

Jung began recording his active imaginations on November 12, 1913 and within the first month he was suspecting that they might be mystery plays. He describes a desert vision making him sick with its "comedy and drivel" and realises that it is theatre and involves trickery. "Ha, a work of art!" he says, but does not include this realisation in *Liber Novus* (*BB 2*, pp. 171–174). By December 20 of the same year, he has realised another important aspect of the fantasies: over two nights he describes a mystery play where he is told that he has been conceived in pain and describes being murderously grasped by lustful, ice-cold hands and being slobbered over in heat. On the second night he decides to further investigate this experience and sees a poster picture of an old man with a child that he finds disgusting; but he adds the word "survived" to his response. He clearly seems to be describing a debased sexual experience of some kind. But he vows to keep this knowledge an inviolable secret and chooses not to include the details in *Liber Novus*, recognising that this is his own personal experience that need not be shared with others. "This play that I witnessed is my play, not your play. It is my secret, not yours", he says (Jung, 2009a, p. 246; 2009b, p. 178). A further realisation in this same fantasy is where he describes being urged to look into a crystal and at the end of the vision finds himself back in front of the crystal; but he does not include this detail in *Liber Novus* either. So, within the first two months of journaling Jung seems to have become aware that crystal-gazing of some kind was involved, but he does not reveal to his public that these fantasies might have been experienced in a trance or under hypnosis. His observations in these first journal entries suggests that he has already begun to make connections that these fantasies are describing an initiatory path of some kind and twelve years later he comments on this fantasy saying he felt that he had been put through an initiation and that it was related to the ancient Mysteries in some way (*BB 2*, p. 195, n. 245).

From 1914 onward Jung continues recording his active imagination process to see where it takes him. He is led into experiences of abject horror, such as being made to believe that he has eaten the liver of a dead child. But his journal records the realisation that this is another theatrical trick: "The curtain drops. What dreadful game has been played here?" he writes (*BB 3*, p. 136). A fantasy recorded over three separate nights in January appears in *Liber Novus* as "Nox Secunda", "Nox Tertia" and "Nox Quarta". But by the time he transfers the journal entries to their final form the commentaries on them are filled with ambiguous and confusing language and an atmosphere of false profundity. He seems to be preaching to his followers as if he is some sort of religious leader. But within these passages are statements that confirm his awareness that some debased sexual experience was involved. When he describes the prophet laying on the boy, for example, he uses the terms "lusty repulsiveness, lecherous fear, sexual immaturity" (Jung, 2009a, p. 304; 2009b, p. 368). At another point, he wonders if what he has been dealing with are crimes of a religious nature and begins thinking in conspiratorial terms: "Have you heard of those dark ones who roamed incognito alongside those who ruled the day, conspiratorially causing unrest? Who devised cunning things and did not shrink from any crime to honor their God?" (Jung, 2009a, p. 296; 2009b, p. 341). Here, Jung is asking whether there is a corrupt system in place that involves these religious crimes, an understandable question that survivors of clergy or ritual abuse in our own time might also be asking.

Even from his earliest active imaginations Jung feels he has been driven to keep writing and feels chained to his journals and then to the creation of *The Red Book* under his soul's directive. He gradually becomes aware that he is being asked to become a sect leader, and on December 26, 1915 (*BB 5*) he emphatically declares that he will not do this. However, he continues to work on *The Red Book* until 1930, eventually choosing not to publish it in an ultimate rejection of this role (Jung, 2009a, p. 360; 2009b, p. 555). On October 9, 1916 (*BB 6*) he asks his soul for a glimpse into what lies behind all of these mysterious experiences and learns that it is the secret societies. He frames this information as if his soul is telling him this, but it appears to be something that he already knows at some level. As the argument here suggests, this knowledge may have been concealed in a dissociated part of his identity; that is, in an alter personality state that knows the whole story of his ordeals and their source, as well as the identity of his perpetrators.

Jung then inserts an undated note at the beginning of *Book 7* which mentions a dream that he interprets as being related to the papacy and the Catholic Church. He seems to think that it is telling him to play a role in bringing down Catholicism in some way, one of the goals of Continental Freemasonry since the 18th century. He also comments on the power structure behind this intention and mentions the Americans and the idea that there is a secret assembly of world delegates who belong to a "consistory" who play a role in this power structure (*BB 7*, p. 147, n. 1). It is not clear if he is referring to the Scottish Rite, who use this term for the highest level of their Order, but his statement that he came to it himself "through the rear door" and that the world already knows about it, suggests that he is now looking at his own initiatory experiences in the context of some overall political agenda. It is possible that, at least in some part of his psyche, he is now able to see that his childhood initiations were part of a strategy to indoctrinate him in a new belief system that overrides the old order of institutionalised Christianity and implants a new one based on a modern interpretation of the ancient Mysteries.

But even though he may have privately come to realise some of this, Jung admits that he still carries the deep pain of his experiences and cannot speak about it to others. On September 5, 1921 he writes of the isolation and coldness that this private knowledge imposes, describing it as "a bottomless abyss, a silence, a wordless solitude for the rest of one's life" (*BB 7*, p. 205). But then, in the more public context of his 1925 seminar, where he discusses the ancient Mysteries and the role of Salome in "Resolution", he tentatively states "one gets a peculiar feeling from being put through such an initiation" (Jung, 2009a, p. 252, n. 211; 2009b, p. 197). It seems that Jung has pieced together many parts of the puzzle that suggest he was making sense of his own inner states and the journey they involved in terms of initiatory ordeals that corresponded, in some way, with the ancient Mysteries.

But in Jung's day there was absolutely no mention of these practices and even though, today, there have been many reports of their existence, the broader society is still largely unaware of them and the same sense of isolation can still permeate the lives of survivors. Victor Turner was to comment on the invisibility of these practices in general society. He states:

> The subject of passage ritual is, in the liminal period, structurally, if not physically 'invisible'. As members of society, most of us see only what we expect to see, and what we expect to see is what we are conditioned to see when we have learned the definitions and classifications of our culture (1987, p. 6).

If our culture says that these things do not happen here, or that these practices are only performed in less civilised societies than our own, or in the distant past, then the child's or adult survivor's protests are not understood, and the mechanism that keeps the resistance to acknowledging these practices in place is very powerful. As we have seen, the *Black Books* reveal that Jung *was* aware, in some part of himself, that his active imaginations were related to the practices of the secret societies and he knew that there was a lot of trickery, hypnosis and excruciating treatment involved, including sexual abuse. But Jung was also a product of his time and was unable to speak openly about such realisations, or even fully admit them to himself. Even in his later years he was to say: "I have found no plain answer to myself. I am in doubt about myself as much as ever ..." (Cited in Dunne, 2000/2012, p. 205).

However, recently, there has been an interesting development in relation to the Masonic connection in Jung's work. In May 2023 a YouTube video appeared online entitled *Carl Jung: His Secret Masonic Lineage and Alchemical Studies* (Agrippa's Diary). It carries the logo of the Grand Lodge Alpina of Switzerland, so presumably it has been endorsed by this Grand Lodge. This video mentions Jung's grandfather and namesake C. G. Jung (1794–1864), who was a Grand Master from 1850 to1856, a fact already known since Jung mentions this in *Memories, Dreams, Reflections* (1963, p. 281); but it also identifies an uncle, Ernst Karl Jung (1841–1920), who was a Grand Master from 1884 to 1890. An earlier ancestor, it says, was a Rosicrucian. Noting that Jung's ancestry and milieu included such high-ranking Freemasons, the narrator concludes by saying that Masonic initiatory practices and teachings "without a single drop of doubt" influenced him and that he was "definitely aware" of the rites and symbols of Freemasonry. Furthermore, it says that he was not bound to an oath of secrecy that officially initiated Masons would observe. The narrator implies that he absorbed these aspects simply by being in the company of Masonic relatives. But as these studies reveal, Jung describes a great deal more about these secret Masonic rituals than he would have ever been permitted to know if he were not put through the initiations. Is this an acknowledgement by the Swiss Lodge that Jung *was* exposed to the rites, although in a way that did not bind him to such an oath or even allow him to clearly contextualise his initiatory experiences; in other words, in a spurious Masonic context and before he reached the legal age of initiation into the Order? Of course, the video fails to mention whether Jung's experience might have involved abuse.

Given the fact that one of Jung's uncles was a Grand Master, it might be relevant that Deirdre Bair conducted interviews with members of the Jung family about the possible identity of the man who Jung said had sexually abused him. He told Freud that it was a man he once worshipped (Freud, Jung, McGuire, 1974, p. 95). Some family members described the man as a distant uncle but could give no further details, while others talked of potential candidates such as a Catholic priest, who was a friend of his father (Bair, 2004, p. 71, n. 6). Given his Protestant background, how likely is it that the young Carl Jung would have worshipped a Catholic priest? But a Masonic Worshipful Master or Grand Master? Could he have been hinting to Freud, either deliberately or unconsciously, about the identity of his perpetrator?

Despite growing up in this milieu Jung had a very strong opinion about Freemasonry, which he carried into old age. Discussing the appeal of being in on a secret which others do not know and of secret societies more generally, he describes these collective identities as:

> crutches for the lame, shields for the timid, beds for the lazy, nurseries for the irresponsible; but they are equally shelters for the poor and weak, a home port for the shipwrecked, the bosom of a family for orphans, a land of promise for disillusioned vagrants and weary pilgrims, a herd

and a safe fold for lost sheep, and a mother providing nourishment and growth (Jung, 1963, p. 315).

It is very likely that Jung's antipathy towards these organisations was based on his memories of their role in his own experiences. But whether he ever attempted to confront Grand Lodge Alpina or any of his Masonic relatives with his realisations and reveal his memories of the early initiations is so far unknown.

A final word on *Morals and Dogma*

This study of the *Black Books* has shown that particular Masonic teachings, those of Albert Pike's *Morals and Dogma*, played a key role in Jung's indoctrination process, not only in regard to the choice of philosophical themes he described in the journals but also in serving to explain the strange magic symbolism found in *Black Books 6* and *7*. It demonstrates that Jung's abusers were simply taking Pike's wording and descriptions out of context and twisting them in order to create a thoroughly confusing and sinister atmosphere of pseudo-profundity. It seems that the intention was to overwhelm him and make him believe that he had encountered "a hellish sorcery" that he tried, in vain, to comprehend.

Albert Pike, himself, was extremely critical about the degradation of the Masonic Mysteries, which he intended to help repair with his own contribution towards the Ancient and Accepted Scottish Rite. In his lecture for the 20th Degree, or Grand Master of all Symbolic Lodges, he launches into a lengthy diatribe against Freemasonry's vulnerability to corruption, and its degradation from its earlier more simple and peaceful form. His language employs a similar tone to Jung's angry reactions to his own initiatory ordeals.

> Masonry long wandered in error. Instead of improving, it degenerated from its primitive simplicity, and retrograded toward a system, distorted by stupidity and ignorance, which, unable to construct a beautiful machine, made a complicated one … trifles and gewgaws and pretended mysteries, absurd or hideous, usurped the place of Masonic Truth

…Oaths out of all proportion with their object, shocked the candidate, and then became ridiculous, and were wholly disregarded. Acolytes were exposed to tests, and compelled to perform acts, which, if real, would have been abominable; but being mere chimeras, were preposterous, and excited contempt and laughter only … The rituals even of the respectable degrees, copied and mutilated by ignorant men, became nonsensical and trivial; and the words so corrupted that it has hitherto been found impossible to recover many of them at all. Candidates were made to degrade themselves, and to submit to insults not tolerable to a man of spirit and honor … the whole system was one grotesque commingling of incongruous things, of contrasts and contradictions, of shocking and fantastic extravagances, of parts repugnant to good taste, and fine conceptions overlaid and disfigured by absurdities engendered by ignorance, fanaticism, and a senseless mysticism (Pike, 1871, pp. 236–237).

Here, Pike was describing men degrading each other under the rubric of initiation, but his words could just as easily be representing the practice of Masonic ritual abuse when applied to children. As the evidence from Jung's journals suggest, Pike's lectures, themselves, have been similarly distorted and made deliberately complex in order to confuse and indoctrinate a child, and even a grown man who tries to untangle them decades later. The problem seems to lie with the blurred boundaries between symbolically marking a rite of passage and preparing the young for the vicissitudes of life through difficult tasks, and putting them through deliberately cruel and confusing ordeals in order to have a power over them that can effectively last their entire lives. What is clear from Jung's journals is how severe these indoctrination techniques can be, in terms of the physical, sexual, psychological and spiritual harm they enact on an individual.

The Collective Unconscious and the uses of theory

Jung finally chose to explain his own ordeals and those of his hospital patients and private clients through his concept of the Collective Unconscious, his most controversial and scientifically least provable idea. But what role did this concept play if he *was* aware of the source of his active imaginations? To answer this in any substantial way would require an extensive comparison with his writings beyond the parameters of the *Black Books* and *Liber Novus*, so here some brief comments will have to suffice.

Jung's theory proposed that the brain inherently contains knowledge of certain spiritual concepts or symbols that are not based on personal experience but are part of a phylogenetic layer of the unconscious that is related to the collective experience of humanity. He began to ponder this idea and the role of archetypes in his early encounters with his schizophrenic patients when he worked at the Burghölzli Hospital in Zurich. Some of these patients had hallucinatory visions and saw symbols that were similar to ancient concepts that they would not normally have known and Jung deduced from this that they could only have come from a deep layer of the unconscious that was common to mankind as a whole (cited in Ellenberger, 1970, p. 705). The key patient in this regard was Emil Schwyzer (1862–1931), who had resided at the Burghölzli since 1901 and stayed there until his death (Bair, 2004, p. 174). He suffered from depression, had attempted suicide and had delusions that he was God and the sun, regarding himself as "the Lord" who created everything from his own seed (Bair, 2004, p. 644). He became famously known as the Solar Phallus Man and Jung discussed his case throughout his career.

Jung had come across Mithraism in 1910 when he read the second edition of Albrecht Dieterich's 1903 book *Eine Mithrasliturgie*. The Mithras liturgy described the sun as having an unusual appendage "a so-called tube, the origin of the ministering wind ... hanging down from the disc of the sun" (cited in Bair, 2004, p. 177). This concept also appeared in Schwyzer's delusions. Jung's interpretation of this patient's symptoms, delusions and fantasies was that they demonstrated the concept of the Collective Unconscious, basing it on the similarities he observed between the patient's fixation on the sun having a gigantic phallus and aspects of the Mithraic liturgy, which Jung assumed the patient would not have known (Bair, 2014, pp. 176–177).

There has been considerable debate around the facts and circumstances of this case and Jung's interpretation of them, but recently, a meticulous examination of the details of the case by Ronald Huggins may have thrown up information that is relevant to the studies here. Schwyzer's childhood was in Zürich and his family shared a house with another family by the name of Scherer; the father of this family was the president of the local Masonic Lodge. Schwyzer regarded this family as having a "malevolent cosmic power", and that "the gods of the Freemasons" controlled everyone around them, using trickery (Huggins, 2021, p. 111). Huggins suggests that Jung's assistant, J. J. Honegger, who was appointed to work closely with Schwyzer, should have probed the significance of the patient's many references to the Freemasons more thoroughly.

These comments suggest the possibility that Schwyzer might have been describing Masonic teachings that included Mithraic themes, such as we have seen in Jung's case, from the perspective of a child. Honegger noted that the patient's ideas about the sun corresponded with "infantile notions of the sunbeam" and related these ideas to a particular children's book that was published in 1872 (Huggins, 2021, p. 135). Schwyzer also entertained himself with games where he would squint at the sun and move his head in order to "make the sun dance" as if he were able to control the real sun (Bair, 2004, p. 645). In the context of the trickery played on children in ritual abuse, it is easy to imagine a scenario where Schwyzer, as a child, might have been made to believe that he was a god and was now capable of making the sun move wherever he wanted, simply by manipulating his eyes. "Look how powerful you are, you can make the sun dance!" he might have been told.

A further aspect of this case, and one that has caused controversy, concerned Jung's assistant J. J. Honegger, not only because he was "intellectually brilliant" but also because he had a similar fascination as Jung with ancient myth and symbolism (Bair, 2004. P. 171–172). Honegger, himself, struggled with mental illness, but it seems that Jung resonated with him and they shared an excitement that there was some great meaning to be found in Schwyzer's delusions. However, after doing this work and presenting a paper on it at the International Psychoanalytic Congress in Nuremberg in March 1910, Honegger descended into mental disintegration and committed suicide a year later, at the age of 26 (Bair, 2004, pp. 185–186). This raises the question of whether Honegger might have also been a victim of some form of abuse where ancient mythologies and symbolism may have played a key role.

There is no doubt that archetypal themes appear across religions worldwide, but whether this can explain the presence of occult symbols in the context of psychological or spiritual disturbances such as Jung and his schizophrenic patients experienced is a far more complex issue. The material these studies have uncovered makes a direct challenge to the assumption that the brain stores these symbols phylogenetically and argues that Jung's series of disturbances that he called "doing a schizophrenia", appears to have been based on personal experience, albeit relegated to the unconscious due to the amnesic effects of trauma. It has argued that much of the symbolism and philosophical, mythical and magical themes in Jung's fantasies, while originally related to the ancient Mysteries, appear to have been *taught* and layered deeply into his psyche during traumatic initiations, demonstrations and lectures that he seems to have undergone and witnessed during his early years.

Jung's training in the above themes appears to have been particularly extensive due to the intent for him to become a cult leader, as not all who go through these initiations are taught this material in as much detail. However, his eventual choice to ignore this calling does not mean that his subsequent work was not useful to the cult: by establishing the concept of the Collective Unconscious he may have been unwittingly supporting the secrecy of these practices. For those individuals who experience extreme states of mental confusion or illness, coupled with obscure and inexplicable symbolism of an occult or mythical nature, the recourse to the explanation that it is due to the presence of the Collective Unconscious may conceal a more disturbing cause. Given the possibility that Jung might have been consciously aware that he had been put through actual initiations, it could be argued that this theory was a way to rationalise his active imagination experiences without touching on the sensitive topic of cults, secret societies and mind control that they entail.

There are parallels here with Freud's abandonment of his earlier seduction theory which he originally put forward in 1896 and his shift to the Oedipus complex in 1899, which researchers since have challenged as a cover-up (Rush, 1980; Masson, 1984). From an examination of Freud's previously unpublished letters, Jeffrey Masson concluded that, rather than dismissing his seduction theory altogether when he devised an alternative explanation, Freud was haunted for the rest of his life by his earlier realisation that some of his female patients had undergone violent sexual experiences as children. Just as Freud devised a theory which effectively camouflaged the problem of the sexual abuse of children by their relatives, Jung's theory of the Collective Unconscious could be seen as masking religious or spiritual crimes against children. Freud's Oedipus complex held sway in the psychology profession for a long period in the 20th century, concealing the plight of children who continued to be abused and framing it as something based on the child's erotic fantasies. Jung's theory did not gain the same sort of traction as Freud's in the realm of clinical psychology, but has been preserved by devotees of Jung's work and in popular psychology where the concept of the Collective Unconscious continues to play a role. In more recent times the work of Pierre Janet on trauma and dissociation has been re-evaluated as a more useful foundation, suited to the present-day awareness of crimes against children. Janet placed the responsibility for personality disturbances squarely in the social sphere, blaming human cruelty for the results. His original ideas have been developed further by present-day clinical psychologists, influencing trauma-informed practices across a range of contexts. In the case of ritual abuse, though, it could be argued that Freud, Jung and Janet all had something to contribute. Freud's original viewpoint, before he developed the Oedipus complex, was that sexual abuse was the most obvious cause of psychological disturbance; for Jung, it was the spiritual aspects that seemed to play a more important role, both in his own case and in that of some of his patients; while for Janet it was man's inhumanity to man that was the major underlying cause. Ritual abuse incorporates all three of these aspects.

In Jung's final entry in the *Black Books* on December 15, 1932, he writes: "The Quest begins" (*BB 7*, p. 248). It conveys a level of excitement and marks the beginning of a new venture for him: his research into alchemy. As Deirdre Bair notes, Jung thought that the study of the historical development of alchemy would give him insights into his own spiritual development (2004, p. 369). Alchemy is another favourite subject pursued by Albert Pike in *Morals and Dogma* and he makes extensive references to it in his long lecture for the 28th Degree or Knights of the Sun, a ritual that contains many elements that are relevant to Jung's fantasies (Brunet, 2019). Alchemy, Pike says, expresses "the end and perfection of the Great Work ... [which] is the purification of the Soul" (1871, pp. 569–571). In his prefatory note to the English edition of *Psychology and Alchemy* Jung states how amazed he was that European and American people were coming to him with symbolism in their dreams and fantasies that matched those in the mystery religions of antiquity, the mythology and folk tales from ancient cultures and the "apparently meaningless formulations of such esoteric cults as alchemy" (1968, p. v). He deduces from this that these clients are exhibiting evidence of the Collective Unconscious. However, given the emphasis in these studies it would be worth asking whether these clients might have undergone similar initiatory processes and perhaps had relatives who were members of initiatory groups.

Writing four decades before *The Red Book* was published Henri Ellenberger's extensive coverage of the discovery of the unconscious in the history of psychology and psychiatry included a dedicated section examining Jung's contribution alongside that of Janet, Freud and Adler. He asked whether the mystics and occultists could have influenced Jung's thinking, or whether they were merely objects of study for him. Ellenberger then states that he looks forward to a time when *The Red Book* and the *Black Books* would be published, predicting that this might reveal Jung in "yet another, unsuspected light" (1970, pp. 730, 737). The studies here have demonstrated the profound extent to which the occult knowledge found in Freemasonry, applied abusively, directly influenced Jung's thinking throughout his life, seemingly from a very young age. As such, they constitute an entirely unsuspected way of looking at his work. Based on the accumulated work of therapists and researchers and the mounting reports and memoirs of ritual abuse survivors since the 1980s, the study suggests that Jung's experiences are analogous to those described by these survivors. As these studies have argued, Jung's journals and *Liber Novus* reveal a great deal about a diabolical method of social control, particularly of the young, that parallels those of the Classical tradition of initiation and the initiatory practices of earlier and non-western societies. The mounting evidence suggests that this form of control is still very much in use in the West today.

As the editor of the *Black Books* and *Liber Novus* notes, Jung's process took him to places where the symbolism was so opaque that he regarded it as "un-openable and un-sayable" (*BB 1*, p. 45). However, what this study has demonstrated is that when one looks in the right place these mysterious symbols *can* open up. It shows that if we read these texts only in Jung's own terms then this can become a circular exercise, sealing them in an impenetrable casing that fails to answer many of the strange and disturbing elements within them. If we then enshrine them in an almost religious admiration and awe and regard them as mystical tomes from which to select passages for comfort or illumination, while ignoring the profound depths of pain in them, we only maintain their impenetrable status. But by applying present-day knowledge of cult abuse and asking some tough questions about the more disturbing elements within them we can move beyond the point that Jung himself reached to an understanding of the true nature of his ordeals.

Those who have undergone such practices and worked through them know that it is the child parts of themselves that hold the answers to the painful shocks they have endured, and so being able to listen to the internal child's point of view is a key part of the healing process. On the whole, Jung did not feel comfortable placing himself in the position of the child, but occasionally he did allow the child to come through, such as in the quotation at the beginning of this chapter. So, to bookend this discussion, the final word should go to another part of C. G. Jung's young self, a part that was clearly able to face the truth. Casting his mind back to his youth and the times when he would listen to the religious conversations, theological discussions and sermons of his father and uncles, he remembers thinking: "Yes, yes, that is all very well. But what about the secret?" (Jung, 1963, p. 52).

References

Abruzzi, W. S. (2018). Mithraism and Christianity. Academia.com
 https://www.academia.edu/38253240/Mithraism_and_Christianity_pdf

Agrippa's Diary (2023, May). Carl Jung: His secret Masonic lineage and alchemical
 studies.
 https://www.bing.com/videos/riverview/relatedvideo?&q=carl+jung+Fremason&
 &mid=3B8842C8C5A261B5AD3E3B8842C8C5A261B5AD3E&&FORM=VRD
 GAR

American Psychological Association. (2018). Ritual abuse. In *APA dictionary of
 psychology*. https://dictionary.apa.org/ritual-abuse

Anbar, R. D. (2021, November 2). Hypnosis techniques for young children.
 Psychology Today.
 https://www.psychologytoday.com/us/blog/understandinghypnosis/20211/hypnosi
 s-techniques-young-children

Antoninus Pius: Roman emperor. (2023). In The Editors of Encyclopedia Britannica,
 Encyclopedia Britannica. https://www.britannica.com/biography/Antoninus-Pius

Bair, D. (2004). *Jung: A biography*. Little, Brown & Co.

Becker, T. (2008). Re-searching for new perspectives: ritual abuse/ritual violence as
 ideologically motivated crime. In R. Noblitt & P. Perskin Noblitt (Eds.), *Ritual
 abuse in the twenty-first century* (pp. 237–260). Robert D. Reed.

Bernal, M. (2008). Egyptians in the Hellenistic woodpile: Were Hekataios of Abdera
 and Diodorus Sikeliotes right to see Egypt in the origins of Greece? In P. R.
 McKechnie & P. P. Guillaume, P. (Eds), *Ptolemy the second Philadelphus and his
 world* (pp. 142–160). Brill.

Blanchard, J. (2002). *Scotch Rite Masonry illustrated: The complete ritual of the
 ancient and accepted Scottish rite, parts 1 & 2*. Kessinger. (Original work
 published 1950)

Boechat, W. (2016). *The red book of C. G. Jung: A journey into unknown depths*.
 Karnac.

Bogdan, H. (2007). *Western esotericism and rituals of initiation*. State University of
 New York Press.Bogdan, H. (2010). The sociology of the construct of tradition
 and import of legitimacy in Freemasonry. In A.B. Kilcher (Ed.), *Constructing
 tradition: Means and myths of transmission in western esotericism* (pp. 217–238).
 Aries Book Series, Texts and Studies in Western Esotericism.

Brown, R. H. (2002). *Stellar theology and Masonic astronomy*. The Book Tree.
 (Original work published 1882)

Brunet, L. (2007). Terror, trauma and the eye in the triangle: the Masonic presence in
 contemporary art and culture. [Doctoral dissertation, University of Newcastle].
 NOVA: University of Newcastle. http://hdl.handle.net/1959.13/25875

Brunet, L. (2009). *A course of severe and arduous trials: Bacon, Beckett and spurious
 Freemasonry in early twentieth century Ireland*. Peter Lang.

Brunet, L. (2019). *Answer to Jung: Making sense of the red book*. Routledge.

Buck, J. D. (1967). *Symbolism of Freemasonry or mystic Masonry and the greater
 mysteries of antiquity*. Charles T. Powner. (Original work published 1911)

Budge, E. A. W. (1936). *Osiris and the Egyptian resurrection*. Philip Lee Warner.

Burkert, W. (1987). *Ancient mystery cults*. Harvard University Press.

California Freemason Online (April, 2002). Albert Pike and Freemasonry. https://web.archive.org/web/20061221064805/http://www.freemason.org/cfo/mar_apr_2002/pike.htm

Camphor. Safety Data Sheet. (2014). Carolina Biological Supply. https://www.durhamtech.edu/sites/default/files/safety_data_sheets/Chemistry-and-Biology/Camphor%20cas76-22-2%20SDS.pdf

Casavis, J. N. (1955). *The Greek origin of Freemasonry*. D. C. Drury.

Chiotis, E. D. (2018). The Hadrianic aqueduct of Athens and the underlying tradition of hydraulic engineering. In G. A. Aristodemou & T. P. Tassios (Eds.), *Great waterworks in Roman Greece: Aqueducts and monumental structures* (pp. 70–97). Archaeopress Roman Archaeology.

Chrysanthou, A. (2020). *Defining Orphism: The beliefs, the teletae and the writings*. DeGruyter.

Clay, C. (2016). *Labyrinths: Emma Jung, her marriage to Carl and the early years of psychoanalysis*. William Collins.

Clement of Alexandria. (1919). *Clement of Alexandria*. G. W. Butterworth (Trans.). William Heinemann & G. P. Putam Sons. (Original work 2nd Century) https://archive.org/details/L092ClementOfAlexandriaTheExhortationToTheGreeks/mode/1up

Coleman, J. (2008). Satanist ritual abuse and the problem of credibility. In A. Sachs & G. Galton (Eds.), *Forensic aspects of dissociative identity disorder* (pp. 9–22). Routledge.

Cory, I. P. (1832). *Ancient fragments of the Phoenician, Chaldean, Egyptian, Tyrian, Carthaginian, Indian, Persian, and other writers*. William Pickering. Ancient Fragments. https://sacred-texts.com/cla/af/index.htm

Davies, J. (2019). *Imagination: The science of your mind's greatest power*. Pegasus.

Davies, J. (2019, December 18). How do some authors 'lose control' of their characters? *Literary Hub*. https://lithub.com/how-do-some-authors-lose-control-of-their-characters/

DeMoulin Brothers & Co. (1908). Catalogue, p. 63. http://archive.org/stream/catalogue00demo#page/62/mode/2up/search/ocean+wave+boat

Duncan, M. C. (1866). *Duncan's Masonic ritual and monitor* (3rd ed.). Dick & Fitzgerald. https://archive.org/stream/DuncansMasonicRitualAndMonitorOfFreemasonryComplete18663rdEd/Duncan%27s%20Masonic%20Ritual%20and%20Monitor%20of%20Freemasonry%20complete%201866%203rd%20ed_djvu.txt

Dunne, C. (2012). *Carl Jung: Wounded healer of the soul*. Watkins. (Original work published 2000)

Eckard, J. (2023). Zagreus and the Hunt for Remembrance. https://www.academia.edu/29577332/Zagreus_and_the_Hunt_for_Remembrance

Eliade, M. (1995). *Rites and symbols of initiation: The mysteries of birth and rebirth*. Spring Publications. (Original work published 1958)

Ellenberger, H. F. (1970). *The discovery of the unconscious: The history and evolution of dynamic psychiatry*. Basic Books.

Epstein, O. B., Schwartz, J., & Schwartz, R. W. (Eds.). (2011). *Ritual abuse and mind control: The manipulation of attachment needs*. Karnac.

Evans, H. R. (1919). *Cagliostro and his Egyptian rite of Freemasonry* (H. P. McIntosh, Trans.). New Age Magazine. https://archive.org/details/CagliostroAndHisEgyptianRiteOfFreemasonry/mode/2up?view=theater

Fike, M. A. (2020). *Four novels in Jung's 1925 seminar: Literary discussion and analytical psychology.* Routledge.

Finkelhor, D., Williams, L. & Burns, N. (1988). *Nursery crimes: Sexual abuse in day care.* Sage Publications.

Fotheringham, T. (2008). Patterns in mind-control: A first-person account. In R. Noblitt & P. Perskin Noblitt (Eds.), *Ritual abuse in the twenty-first century: Psychological, forensic, social, and political considerations* (pp. 491–540). Robert D. Reed.

Frankel, A. S. & O'Hearn, T. C. (1996). Similarities in responses to extreme and unremitting stress: Cultures of communities under siege. *Psychotherapy: Theory, Research, Practice, Training 33*(3), 485–502. https://doi.org/10.1037/0033-3204.33.3.485

Fraser, G. A. (Ed.). (1997). *The dilemma of ritual abuse: Cautions and guides for therapists.* American Psychiatric Press.

Freud, S., Jung, C. G. (1974). *The Freud/Jung letters: The correspondence between Sigmund Freud and C. G. Jung.* (C. G. Jung & W. McGuire, Eds.). (R. Manheim & R. F. C. Hull, Trans.). Hogarth Press and Routledge & Kegan Paul.

Freyd, J. J. (1996). *Betrayal trauma: The logic of forgetting childhood abuse.* Harvard University Press.

Gaudissart, I. (2014). *Love and sacrifice: The life of Emma Jung* (K. Llanwarne, Trans.). Chiron. (Original work published 2010)

Grand Lodge of British Columbia and Yukon. (2023). Templar Cipher. *Grand Lodge of British Columbia and Yukon.* https://freemasonry.bcy.ca/texts/templars_cipher.html

Green, M. J. (1992). *Dictionary of Celtic myth and legend.* Thames & Hudson.

Gruber, H. (1913). Masonry/Freemasonry. *Catholic Encyclopedia, Vol. 9* (pp. 771–788). C. G. Herbermann, E. A. Pace, C. B. Pallen, T. J. Shannon & J. J. Wynne (Eds.). Knights of Columbus Special Edition. Encyclopedia Press. https://archive.org/details/V09CatholicEncyclopediaKOfC/page/778/mode/2up?view=theater

Guerra, M. H. M. (2014). *The love drama of C. G. Jung: As revealed in his life and his Red Book.* (A. Forma, Trans.). Inner City Books.

Guthrie Scottish Rite Masonic Centre (n.d.). Albert Pike. *Valley of Guthrie: Ancient and Accepted Scottish Rite.* https://www.guthriescottishrite.org/index.php/albert-pike

Hall, M. P. (2004). *The secret teachings of all ages: An encyclopedic outline of Masonic, Hermetic, Qabbalistic and Rosicrucian symbolical philosophy.* H. S. Crocker. (Original work published in 1928) https://sacred-texts.com/eso/sta/index.htm

Hamill, J. & Gilbert, R. (Eds.) (2004). *Freemasonry: A celebration of the craft.* Angus.

Harrison, D. (2019). The lost rites of the age of enlightenment. *The Transactions of the Leicester Lodge of Research, No. 2429* (2018–2019), 95–113. https://www.academia.edu/40661381/The_Lost_Rites_of_the_Age_of_Enlightenment_The_Transactions_of_the_Leicester_Lodge_of_Research_No_2429_2018_2019_pp_95_113

Harwood, J. (2006). *The Freemasons.* Hermes House.

Hassan, S. A. (2020). The bite model of authoritarian control: Undue influence, thought reform, brainwashing, mind control, trafficking and the law. [Doctoral Dissertation, Fielding Graduate University].
DOI: 10.13140/RG.2.2.12755.60965
http://www.researchgate.net/publication/348419785_THE_BITE_MODEL_OF_A
UTHORITARIAN_CONTROL_UNDUE_INFLUENCE_THOUGHT_REFORM
_BRAINWASHING_MIND_CONTROL_TRAFFICKING_AND_THE_LAW_A
_dissertation_submitted

Healey, D. (1993). *Images of trauma: From hysteria to Post-Traumatic Stress Disorder.* Faber & Faber

Henderson, R. (2010). The search for the lost soul: An 'enterview' with Murray Stein about C. G. Jung's the red book. *Jung Journal*, 4(4), pp. 92–101.

Hoffman, W. (2016). *White witch in a black robe: A true story about criminal mind control.* Karnac.

Hoffman, W. (2019). *White witch in a black robe: A true story about criminal mind control.* Aeon Books. (Original work published 2016)

Hoffman, W. (2020). *A brain of my own: A memoir about dissociation dissolved.* Aeon Books.

Hoffman, W. & Miller, A. (2017). *From the trenches: A victim and therapist talk about mind control and ritual abuse.* Routledge.

Horgan, J. (2003). *Rational mysticism: Dispatches from the border between science and spirituality.* Houghton Mifflin.

Huggins, R. (2021). C. G. Jung, J. J. Honegger, and the Case of Emil Schwyzer (the 'Solar Phallus Man'). *Phânes*, Vol. 4, pp. 82-151.
https://doi.org/10.32724/phanes.2021.Huggins

Hutton, R. (1999). *The triumph of the moon: A history of modern pagan witchcraft.* Oxford University Press.

Jackson, A. C. F. (1980). *Rose Croix. A History of the Ancient and Accepted Rite for England and Wales.* Lewis Masonic.

James, W. (1985). *The varieties of religious experience.* Harvard University Press. (Original work published 1902)

Jung, C. G. (1963). *Memories, dreams, reflections* (A. Jaffé, Ed.). (R. Winston & C. Winston, Trans.). Collins and Routledge & Kegan Paul.

Jung, C. G. (Ed.). (1964). *Man and his symbols.* Aldus Books.

Jung, C. G. (1968). *Psychology and alchemy.* (R. F. C. Hull, Trans.). Routledge & Kegan Paul.

Jung, C. G. (2001). *On the nature of the psyche* (R. F. C. Hull, Trans.). Routledge. (Original work published 1947)

Jung, C. G. (2002). *Dreams* (R. F. C. Hull, Trans.). Routledge. (Original work published 1974)

Jung, C. G. (2009a). *The red book: Liber novus* (S. Shamdasani, Ed.). (M. Kyburz, J. Peck & S. Shamdasani, Trans.). Philemon & W. W. Norton.

Jung, C. G. (2009b). *The red book: A reader's edition* (S. Shamdasani, Ed.). (M. Kyburz, J. Peck & S. Shamdasani, Trans.). Philemon & W. W. Norton.

Jung, C. G. (2020). *The black books 1913–1932: Notebooks of transformation* (S. Shamdasani, Ed.). (M. Liebscher, J. Peck & S. Shamdasani, Trans.). Philemon & W. W. Norton.

Karr, D. (2023). The Study of the Christian Cabala in English. Academia.com.
https://www.academia.edu/4881090/The_Study_of_Christian_Cabala_in_English

Katchen, M. (1992). The history of satanic religions. In D. K. Sakheim & S. E. Devine (Eds.), *Out of darkness: Exploring satanism and ritual abuse* (pp. 1–20). Lexington Books.

Katz, S. (2012). A reversed Kabbalah trainer speaks. In A. Miller, *Healing the unimaginable: Treating ritual abuse and mind control* (pp. 91–118). Karnac.

Kent, S. (1993). Deviant scripturalism and ritual satanic abuse part two: possible Masonic, Mormon, magick and pagan influences. *Religion*, 23(4), pp. 355–367.

King, C. W. (1887). *The Gnostics and their remains, ancient and medieval*. David Nutt. https://archive.org/stream/The_Gnostics_And_Their_Remains__C_W_King/The_Gnostics_And_Their_Remains_-_C_W_King_djvu.txt

Lacter, E. P. (2008). Mind control: Simple to complex. In A. Sachs & G. Galton (Eds.), *Forensic aspects of dissociative identity disorder* (pp. 185–195). Karnac.

Lacter, E. P. & Lehman, K. D. (2008). Guidelines to differential diagnosis between Schizophrenia and ritual abuse/mind control traumatic stress. In R. Noblitt & P. Perskin Noblitt (Eds.), *Ritual abuse in the twenty-first century: Psychological, forensic, social, and political considerations* (pp. 85–154). Robert D. Reed.

Lacter, E. P. (2011). Torture-based mind control: Psychological mechanisms and psychotherapeutic approaches to overcoming mind control. In O. B. Epstein, J. Schwartz & R. W. Schwartz (Eds.), *Ritual abuse and mind control. The manipulation of attachment needs* (pp. 57–141). Karnac.

Lacter, E. P. (2021, May 2). Work with "abuser personalities". *End Ritual Abuse: The Website of Ellen P. Lacter, Ph.D.* (Original work published October 6, 2006) https://endritualabuse.org/work-with-abuser-personalities/

Lacter, E. P. (2023). Systematic and organic psychological mechanisms that perpetuate the cycle of extreme abuse. *The Survivorship of Extreme or Ritualistic Abuse 2023 Online Conference* (May 19). https://survivorship.org/the-survivorship-ritual-abuse-and-mind-control-2023-conference-presentations/

Liagre, G. (2014). Protestantism and Freemasonry. In H. Bogdan & J. A. M. Snoek (Eds.), *Handbook of Freemasonry* (pp. 162–187). Brill.

Lifton, R. J. (1989). *Thought reform and the psychology of totalism: A study of 'brainwashing' in China*. University of Carolina Press. (Original work published 1961)

Lincoln, B. (1981). *Emerging from the chrysalis: Studies in rituals of women's initiation*. Harvard.

Lovern, J. D. (1993). Spin programming: A newly uncovered technique of systematic mind control. Paper presented at the Sixth Western Clinical Conference on Multiple Personality and Dissociation, Irvine CA. Revised 5 February 1993. https://kenniscentrumtgg.org/wp-content/uploads/spin-programming-1993.pdf

Mackey, A. G. (1882). *The symbolism of Freemasonry: Illustrating and explaining its science and philosophy, its legends, myths and symbols*. (N.P.). (Original work published 1869) https://archive.org/details/MackeyAGTheSymbolismOfFreemasonry1882/page/n207/mode/2up

Mackey, A. G. (1905). *The history of Freemasonry: Its legends and traditions, its chronological history*. The Masonic History Company. (Original work published 1898) http://www.billheidrick.com/Orpd/Masonry/HisFreMas-1.pdf

Mackey, A. G. (1914). *Encyclopedia of Freemasonry and its kindred sciences*, vols. 1 & 2. The Masonic History Company. Albert G Mackey - His Complete Works: Free Download, Borrow, and Streaming: Internet Archive

Mackey, A. G. (n.d.). *Encyclopedia of Freemasonry and its kindred sciences* (Original work published 1914–1916) http://www.themasonictrowel.com/ebooks/freemasonry/eb0091.pdf

Mackey, A. G. (n.d.). Guglielmus Tyrius. *Encyclopedia of Freemasonry and its kindred sciences*. The Masonic Trowel. www.themasonictrowel.com/ebooks/freemasonry/eb0091.pdf

Mackey, A. G. (n.d.). Morals and dogma. *Encyclopedia of Freemasonry and its kindred sciences*. Phoenixmasonry, inc. http://www.phoenixmasonry.org/mackeys_encyclopedia/m.htm

Mackey, A. G. (n.d.). Spurious Freemasonry. *Encyclopedia of Freemasonry and its kindred sciences*. Phoenixmasonry, inc. http://www.phoenixmasonry.org/mackeys_encyclopedia/s.htm

Malcolmson, W. P. (1999). *Behind closed doors: The hidden structure within the Orange camp [the Royal Arch Purple Order] examined from an evangelical perspective*. Evangelical Truth.

Masson, J. M. (1984). *The assault on truth: Freud's suppression of the seduction theory*. Farrah, Strauss and Giroux.

Mauss, M. (2005). *A general theory of magic*. R. Brain (Trans.). Taylor & Francis e-Library. (Original work published 1902)

Melville, H. (1864). *Initiation, passing, raising and exaltation, demonstrated by the median and Persian laws on the original tracing board*. H & C Best.

Menakem, R. (2017). *My grandmother's hands: Racialized trauma and the pathway to mending our hearts and bodies*. Central Recovery Press.

Miller, A. (2012). *Healing the unimaginable: Treating ritual abuse and mind control*. Karnac.

Miller, A. (2016). What's different about ritual abuse and mind control? In V. Sinason & A. Van der Merwe (Eds.), *Shattered but unbroken: Voices of triumph and testimony* (pp. 221-232). Karnac.

Miller, A. (2018). Dialogue with the higher ups. In R. Vogt (Ed.). *Perpetrator introjects: Psychotherapeutic diagnostics and treatment models* (pp. 111–132). Asanger.

Mitchell, M. (2008). *Vivo: The life of Gustav Meyrink*. Dedalus.

Meyrink, G. (2017). *The golem*. M. Mitchell (Trans.). Dedalus European Classics. (Original work published 1915)

Mollon, P. (2016). Dissociative identity disorder and its saturation with shame. In A. van der Merwe & V. Sinason (Eds.). *Shattered but unbroken: Voices of triumph and testimony* (pp. 211–220). Karnac.

Moore, W. D. (2010). Canned snakes, mechanical goats and spitting skeletons: Making sense of the 1930 DeMoulin Bros. & Co catalog. In *Burlesque paraphernalia and side degree specialties and costumes, catalogue no 439*. Fantagraphics Books. https://www.academia.edu/4097782/canned_snakes_mechanical_goats_and_spitting_skeletons_making_sense_of_the_1930_demoulin_bros_and_co_catalog

Morris, W. (1997). *Interview with Lynne Moss-Sharman* [Radio broadcast]. CKLN-FM Mind Control Series, Part 16. Interview with Lynne Moss-Sharman (tranquility.net)

Museum Haus C. G. Jung. C. G. and Emma Jung-Rauschenbach. cgjunghaus.ch

Noblitt, R. & Noblitt, P. P. (Eds.) (2008). *Ritual abuse in the twenty-first century: Psychological, forensic, social, and political implications*. Robert D. Reed.

Noblitt, J. R. & Perskin Noblitt, P. (Eds.) (2014). *Cult and ritual abuse: Narratives, evidence and healing approaches*. Praeger.

Noll, R. (1997). *The Aryan Christ: The secret life of Carl Jung*. Random House.

O'Donovan, E. (1994). *Ritual abuse: Information for health and welfare professionals*. NSW Sexual Assault Committee.

Pascal, R. (1953). *The German sturm und drang*. Manchester University Press.

Pick, F. L. & Norman, G. (1991). *The Pocket History of Freemasonry*. Muller. (Original work published 1955)

Pike, A. (1871). *Morals and dogma of the Ancient and Accepted Scottish Rite of Freemasonry*. Supreme Council of the Thirty-Third Degree for the Southern Jurisdiction of the United States. http://www.sacred-texts.com/mas/md/index.htm

Poole, G. W. (2024). *Flavius Josephus*. In The Editors of Encyclopaedia Britannica, *Encyclopaedia Britannica*. https://www.britannica.com/biography/Flavius-Josephus

Regardie, I. (1945). *The middle pillar: A co-relation of the principles of analytical psychology and the elementary techniques of magic*. The Aries Press. (Original work published 1938)

Rush, F. (1980). *The best-kept secret: Sexual abuse of children*. McGraw-Hill.

Rutz, C., Becker, T, Overkamp, B. & Karriker, K. (2008). Exploring commonalities reported by adult survivors of extreme abuse: Preliminary findings. In R. Noblitt & P. P. Noblitt (Eds.), *Ritual abuse in the twenty-first century: Psychological, forensic, social, and political considerations* (pp. 31–84). Robert D. Reed.

Sakheim, D. K. & Devine, S.E. (Eds.) (1992). *Out of darkness: Exploring satanism and ritual abuse*. Lexington Books.

Salter, M. (2023). The antiepistemology of organized abuse: Ignorance, exploitation, inaction. *The British Journal of Criminology, vol 63* (1), pp. 221-237. https://doi.org/10.1093/bjc/azac007

Sargant, W. (1957). *Battle for the mind: A physiology of conversion and brain-washing*. Heinemann.

Schacter, D. L., Addis, D. R., Hassabis, D., Martin, V. C., Spreng, N.R. & Szpunar, K. K. (2012). The future of memory: Remembering, imagining, and the brain. *Neuron 76* (4), pp. 677–694. http://dx.doi.org/10.1016/j.neuron.2012.11.001

Schuchard, M. K. (1995). William Blake and the promiscuous baboons: A Cagliostroan séance gone awry. *Journal for Eighteenth-Century Studies, 18*(2), 185–200. https://doi.org/10.1111/j.1754-0208.1995.tb00188.x

Scott, S. (2001). *The politics and experience of ritual abuse: Beyond disbelief*. Open University Press.

Serrano, M. (1997). *C. G. Jung and Herman Hesse: A record of two friendships*. Daimon Verlag. (Original work published 1966)

Sherry, J. (2008). Carl Gustav Jung, avant-garde conservative. [Doctoral dissertation, Freie Universität Berlin]. https://refubium.fu.berlin.de/botstream/handle/fub188/4439/jay_sherry_complete.pdf;sequence=1

Singer, M. T. (1994). What is a Cult and How Does It Work? *International Cultic Studies Association*. Lexon Inc Video Production. https://www.youtube.com/watch?v=8bRBFhMEQFk

Smith, A. D. (2020, July 30). Confederate monuments: General Albert Pike joined an effort to expel free Blacks from Arkansas. *The Times Record*.

https://www.commercialappeal.com/story/news/2020/07/30/confederate-monument-albert-pike-arkansas/5448301002/

Smith, M. (1993). *Ritual abuse: What it is, why it happens and how to help.* HarperCollins.

Somer, E. (2016). Cross temporal and cross-cultural perspectives on dissociative disorders of identity. In A. van der Merwe & V. Sinason (Eds.), *Shattered but unbroken: Voices of triumph and testimony* (pp. 89–110). Karnac.

Sousse. (2023). In The Editors of Encyclopaedia Britannica, *Encyclopaedia Britannica*. https://www.britannica.com/place/Sousse

Truscott, R. (2012). Introjection. In T. Theo (Ed.). *Encyclopedia of critical psychology* (pp. 1013–1016). Springer. https://link.springer.com/referenceworkentry/10.1007/978-1-4614-5583-7_535

Turner, V. W. (1982). *From ritual to theatre: The human seriousness of play.* PAJ Publications.

Turner, V. W. (1987). Betwixt and between: The liminal period in rites of passage. In Mahdi, L. C., Foster, S. & Little, M. (Eds.), *Betwixt and between: Patterns of masculine and feminine initiation.* Open Court.

Turner, V. W. (1992). *Blazing the trail: Way marks in the exploration of symbols.* E. Turner (Ed.). The University of Arizona Press.

van der Hart, O., Boon, S. & Heitjtmajer Jansen, O. (1997). Ritual abuse in European countries: A clinician's perspective. In G. A. Fraser (Ed.), *The dilemma of ritual abuse: Cautions and guides for therapists* (pp. 137–166). American Psychiatric Press.

van der Hart, O. (2016). History of trauma-related dissociation, with a focus on dissociative identity disorder. In A. van der Merwe & V. Sinason (Eds.). *Shattered but unbroken: Voices of triumph and testimony* (pp. 61–89). Karnac.

van der Kolk, B. (2014). *The body keeps the score: Brain, mind, and body in the healing of trauma.* Viking.

van der Kolk, B., McFarlane, A. C. & Weisaeth, L. (Eds.) (1996). *Traumatic stress: The effects of overwhelming experiences on mind, body and society.* Guilford Press.

van der Merwe, A. & Sinason, V. (Eds.). (2016). *Shattered but unbroken: Voices of triumph and testimony.* Karnac.

Vaneerdewegh, N. (2020). The Egyptian "Zodiac Coins" of Antoninus Pius and the Sothic Cycle. In F. Stroobants & C. Lauwers (Eds.), *Detur dignissimo: Studies in honour of Johan van Heesch* (pp. 315-326). Cercle d'Etude numismatiques. https://www.academia.edu/44445229/The_Egyptian_Zodiac_Coins_of_Antoninus_Pius_and_the_Sothic_Cycle

van Gennep, A. (1960). *The rites of passage.* (M. B. Vizedo & G. L. Caffee, Trans.). (S. T. Kimball, Intro.). University of Chicago Press. (Original work published 1908) https://archive.org/details/theritesofpassage/mode/2up?view=theater&q=boy

Vogt, R. (Ed.). (2018). *Perpetrator introjects: Psychotherapeutic diagnostics and treatment models.* Asanger.

von Goethe, J. W. (2018). *The sorrows of young Werther.* R. D. Boylan (Trans.). Amazon Classics. (Original work published 1774)

Waite, A. E. (1913). *The book of ceremonial magic: The secret tradition in Goëtia, including the rites and mysteries of Goëtic theurgy, sorcery and infernal necromancy* (2nd ed.). N.P. (Original work published 1898) https://sacred-texts.com/grim/bcm/bcm00.htm

Waite, A. E. (1925). *Emblematic Freemasonry and the evolution of its deeper issues.* William Rider & Son

Walden, H. (1938). Gottfried Keller's 'Apotheker von Chamounix'. *The German Quarterly, 11*(1), 21–28. https://www.jstor.org/stable/399906

Webster, H. (1968). *Primitive secret societies: A study in early politics and religion.* Octagon Books. (Original work published 1908)

Wehr, G. (1987). *Jung: A biography.* (D. M. Weeks, Trans.). Shambhala.

Wells, R. A. (1978). *Some Royal Arch terms explained.* A. Lewis.

Wilkinson, R. H. (2003). *The complete gods and goddesses of ancient Egypt.* Thames & Hudson.

Wilmshurst, W. L. (2008). *The ceremony of initiation.* Cornerstone. (Original work published 1932)

Wudka, E. & Leopold, I. H. (1954). The Action of Curare Alkaloids on the Pupil. *American Journal of Opthalmology*, 37(1), pp. 41–44.

Yarker, J. (1911). *The secret high degree rituals of the Masonic Rite of Memphis.* Kessinger. http://www.themasonictrowel.com/ebooks/freemasonry/eb0336.pdf

Yarker, J. (Trans.). (2005). *Lectures of the antient and primitive rite of Freemasonry: Masonic charges and lectures, lectures of a chapter, senate and council.* Unspeakable Press. (Original work published 1880–1882) https://www.scribd.com/document/3045777/Yarker-Lectures-of-the-Antient-and-Primitive-Rite

Zosmer, D. (2021). The sorrows of young Werther: That which must not be read – psychiatry in literature. *The British Journal of Psychiatry, 218*(6), 351–351. Doi:10.1192/bjp.2021.24

Index

Ha, the sorcerer, 4; an internal part that cannot feel, 118; describes complex programming, 119-120; represents satanic evil, 113; says he's just a remnant, 116
Hassan, S., 163, 173
Hermeticism: and alchemy, 108, 185; Emerald Tablet, 108; symbolism in Egyptian Rite, 28
hieroglyphics, 48 52; 119; The Judgement of Amenti, 137
Hoffman, W., parts going back to sleep, 175; pseudo-integration, 83; spinning, 141
Honegger, J. J.: Jung's assistant, 199
Horgan, J.: mystical states, 186
Huggins, R., 199
hypnosis, 7-8; crystal vision, 28, 50; crystal-gazing, 35, 66, 177, 188, 191; deep hypnotic sleep after initiatory shocks, 174; may account for strange unreality of fantasies, 62; temple sleep, 29; trance states in young children, 107; trance states of mediums, 24

I Ching, 139, 159-160
imagination: and experiences of the gods, 24
individuation, 16, 145
initiation: as mystical death, 62, 163; DeMoulin Bros, 131, 180, 181; fraternal side degrees, 180; Jung felt he was put through an initiation, 66, 92, 192
introjection, 19, 37; abuser personalities, 95; amongst fiction writers, 38; brain research, 38; Jung's term, the shadow, 37; Lacter's description, 37; Miller's definition of perpetrator introjects, 37; Vogt's definition of perpetrator introjects, 37
Izdubar, 24, 41, 84, 89-90, 149, 177

Jackson, A.C.F., 90
James, W., 186
Janet, P., 5, 34, 126, 201-202
Jeremiah, 168

Jung (née Rauschenbach), E., 26; complaint to Freud, 42; paper 'On Guilt', 45
Jung, C. G.: as fearful schoolboy, 32; betrayal of marriage vows, 27; childhood experiences, 6; childhood fascination with stones, 109; death of his mother, 5, 53, 71, 153; decision regarding Toni Wolff, 27; deepest depression, 84; doing a schizophrenia, 12, 34, 200; exposed to vicarious trauma, 127; feels chained to this book, 162; felt he was practising a rite, 3; four psychological types, 3; read Goethe in his youth, 171; love triangle, 42; marriage date, 26; opinion about Freemasonry, 195; otherworldly fear, 141; outrage, 18, 54, 58, 61, 69, 190; polygamy, 42, 44, 54; publishes Septem Sermones ad Mortuos, 184; realises he was the shaman, 118; sexual assault in boyhood, 2, 64, 195; sexual guilt, 44; Spanish flu, 128, 130, 148; suicidal ideation, 19, 58, 174; triumvirate with Emma and Toni, 50, 52; urged to give up his practice, 127; what is my calling? 21, 162; wife's cancer, 5, 54, 155; words not his own, 62; Pierre Janet, 34
Jung, C. G. (senior): Beneficent Knights of the Holy City, 28; Grand Master of Grand Lodge Alpina of Switzerland, 6, 68, 194
Jung, E. K.: Grand Master of Grand Lodge Alpina of Switzerland, 194
Jung's soul: a drinker of blood, 34; as a girl child, 25; as an introject, 95, 163; bitter disputes with her, 36; compared with 'brother I', 33; comprised of multiple parts, 55; confusing discourse on God as the seed, 123; contains daimonic characteristics, 94; contradictory advice on women, 46; false ritual souls, 35; felt as multiple, 6, 82; his criticism towards her, 23, 36; internalised abuser, 97; maternal soul, 45; prevents him from sleeping, 176; Salome is my soul, 32; calls his

soul "dirty animal!", 83; talks of
rocks that salvage him, 99; says to
let Toni Wolff go, 49; wedding of
souls, 99

Ka: arguments between Ka and
Philemon, 121; decries Philemon's
crimes against the innocent, 121;
depicted in Image 120; says Jung has
become "psychically feminized",
126; the brother of Buddha, 122; the
other side of Ha, 120
Kabbalah, 10, 15, 104; four words in,
125; Reversed Kabbalah, 10, 106,
120
Katz, S., 106, 110, 120
King, C. W.: Mithraism and
Freemasonry, 72
Knights Templar, 74, 87
Kundalini, 112, 119, 136

Lacter, E., 37, 95, 178, 179
Lévi, E., 15, 29, 94
Liagre, G., 67
Lifton, R. J., 21; Chinese thought reform,
164, 165, 178; confession and re-
education, 166; difference between
Jung's situation and Lifton's
subjects, 165; fluctuations between
assault and leniency, 182;
Communist conversion techniques
and those of the Catholic Church,
166
Lincoln, B., 142
Lovern, J. D.: spin-programming, 140-
141
Lucifer, 142
Lulle, R.: medieval alchemist, 115
lustration, 145, 151

Mackey, A., 15, 74
magic, 1; absurd words, 53; black magic,
8, 11, 20, 41, 47, 94, 113, 120;
Ceremonial Magic, 11, 108, 119;
Dogme et Rituel de la Haute Magie,
15, 94; Ha's magic chant, 115; Jung
draws magic symbols, 96; Middle
Pillar exercise, 11, 108; *The Lesser
Key of Solomon,* 119
mandala paintings, 87

Marconis, J. E., 28
Masonic degrees, 9; 10th or Illustrious
Elect of Fifteen, 122; 13th or Royal
Arch, 73, 89, 136; 17th or Knight of
the East and West, 72, 77, 98; 18th
or Sovereign Prince of Rose Croix,
8, 45, 99, 102, 110, 125, 168; 19th
or Grand Pontiff, 104; 1st or Entered
Apprentice, 29, 60, 71, 123, 133,
156; 22nd or Knight of the Royal
Axe, 90; 23rd or Chief of the
Tabernacle, 105, 133; 24th or Prince
of the Tabernacle, 73, 115, 133, 141;
25th or Knight of the Brazen
Serpent, 117, 119, 147; 26th or
Prince of Mercy, 72, 145,147, 148;
28th or Knights of the Sun, 85, 94,
110, 111-115, 122, 148, 150, 201; 2nd
or Fellow Craft, 101, 125, 186; 30th
or Knight Kadosh, 28; 31st or Grand
Inspector Inquisitor Commander, 90;
32nd or Sublime Prince of the Royal
Secret, 44, 78, 90, 100, 124, 156-
158; 3rd or Master Mason, 76, 96-99,
101-103, 108, 113-116, 125; Sage of
Mythras, 9, 136; Scottish Master of
St. Andrew, 31; Templar degrees, 74
Masonic rites, 5, 7, 8; Ancient and
Accepted Scottish Rite, 7, 8, 9, 13,
24, 60, 112, 196; Ancient and
Primitive Rite, 77; Memphis Rite, 7,
9; Memphis-Misraim Rite, 136, 188;
Rectified Scottish Rite, 7, 9, 28, 31,
77; Royal Arch, 73, 89, 136; true
and false versions of the Scottish
Rite, 90
Masonic symbols: and impact of trauma
on brain and psyche, 101; Blazing
Star, 111, 119; Freemasons as stone
cutters, 87; Jung family's coat-of-
arms, 6, 112; pelican, 45; point
within a circle, 80; rough and perfect
ashlar, 117; skull and cross bones,
102; Templar cipher, 87; the number
four, 51, 87, 125; the six lights, 81;
three pillars, 11, 105
Mauss, M.: confusion central to magic,
93; secret societies and magic, 190
Melville, H.: an Egyptian mummy, 73

217

www.ingramcontent.com/pod-product-compliance
Lightning Source LLC
Chambersburg PA
CBHW060020100426
42740CB00010B/1545